# GREAT WALKS
## OF THE
# NATIONAL PARKS

# GREAT WALKS
## OF THE
# NATIONAL PARKS

General Editor

FRANK DUERDEN

**BROCKHAMPTON PRESS**
**LONDON**

**A WARD LOCK BOOK**
First published in the UK 1994 by Ward Lock
Wellington House, 125 Strand,
London, WC2R 0BB
An imprint of the Cassell Group

Reprinted 1995
First paperback edition 1995

Material in this book was originally published in the Great Walks series.

**This edition published 1998 by Brockhampton Press.**
**a member of Hodder Headline PLC Group**

A British Library Cataloguing in Publication Data block for this book may be obtained from
the British Library

**ISBN 1 86019 8775**

Walks in the Brecon Beacons National Park and Pembrokeshire Coast National Park
© Roger Thomas 1989, 1994
Walks in the Dartmoor National Park and Exmoor National Park © John Weir and Brian Le Messurier
1988, 1990, 1994
Walks in the Lake District National Park © Colin Shelbourn 1987, 1989, 1994
Walks in the Northumberland National Park © Ward Lock 1994
Walks in the North York Moors National Park © Malcolm Boyes and Hazel Chester 1988, 1990, 1994
Walks in the Peak District National Park © John and Anne Nuttall 1987, 1990, 1994
Walks in the Snowdonia National Park © Frank Duerden 1986, 1989, 1994
Walks in the Yorkshire Dales National Park © Frank Duerden 1986, 1990, 1994

© Photographs Ward Lock 1986, 1987, 1988, 1990, 1994

Photographs by David Ward (pages 17–44, 93–130, 149–176, 215–240, 277–308), John Heseltine (pages
45–92, 177–214, 241–276), Jeffrey Beazely (pages 9, 131, 134, 135, 148), Philip Clegg (pages 121, 139,
141) and Tony Hopkins (page 146).

Typeset by Litho Link Ltd, Welshpool, Powys, Wales
Printed at Oriental Press, Dubai, U.A.E.

*Frontispiece* Sweetworthy Combe, Exmoor

# Contents

# THE NATIONAL PARKS

The first practical steps on a national level—as distinct from a local or private level—to protect areas of outstanding beauty or of great ecological importance were taken in the United States late in the nineteenth century. In response to increasing public concern over indiscriminate land use, the Yellowstone National Park in north-west Wyoming was designated in 1872, followed by several others over the next forty years or so, although adequate provision for their protection had to wait until 1916 when the National Park Service was established (Nowadays the Service has more than 18,000 full-time staff with an annual budget of more than a billion dollars). Over the border, a Park was set up at Banff in Canada in 1885.

In Europe the first Parks were created in Sweden, in the wild and largely uninhabited northern region of Lapland near or within the Arctic Circle; Abisko and Peljekaise in 1909 and Sarek in 1910. From then the movement gained momentum. The Swiss National Park was established near Zernez, towards the far eastern border with Italy, in 1914; Covadonga and Ordesa in Spain in 1918; and the Gran Paradiso and Abruzzo in Italy in 1922-3. The designation of areas as National Parks— both in Europe and elsewhere—has continued up to the present day.

Ten National Parks were created in Britain between 1950 and 1957, almost exactly in the middle of European developments in this field. Finland, Greece, Iceland, Eire, Italy, Spain, Sweden and Switzerland established Parks before we did, while Austria, France, the former West Germany, Norway, Portugal and the former Yugoslavia were all later in designating their first.

As far as is known the earliest proposal that National Parks should be established in Britain was made by William Wordsworth, who lived at Grasmere in the Lake District from 1813 to 1850, but from time to time suggestions along similar lines were made by others. In 1931 a National Parks Committee, set up by Ramsay MacDonald the first Labour Prime Minister, considered the establishment of National Parks, but the real preparatory work was done during the Second World War and immediately afterwards. It says much about the foresight and confidence of those involved that matters such as these could be considered at so difficult a time. The Scott Committee of 1942 (the relevant committees are invariably referred to nowadays by the names of their chairpersons); the Dower Committee of 1945; and the Hobhouse Committee of 1947 were the milestones on the road which led to the National Parks and Access to the Countryside Act of 1949 under which the Parks were established.

Although many people, in government, the civil service and in outdoor organizations, were involved in the creation of the Parks, no one played a more important part than John Dower, the chairperson of the second and the most influential of the three main committees, who so tragically died in 1947 at the age of forty six. It was he who gave what is still regarded as the most appropriate definition of a National Park as we know it in this country:

> A National Park may be defined, in application to Great Britain, as an extensive area of beautiful and relatively wild country in which, for the nation's benefit and by appropriate national decision and action:
> (a)     the characteristic landscape beauty is strictly preserved
> (b)     access and facilities for public open-air enjoyment are amply provided
> (c)     wildlife and buildings and places of architectural and historic interest are suitably protected, while
> (d)     established farming use is effectively maintained.

Twelve areas were recommended as fulfilling this definition, of which ten were designated in the 1950s. (The two excluded were the South Downs and the Norfolk Broads.) The first to be designated (in 1950) was the Peak District; appropriately, because it was here that some of the fiercest access battles had been fought and where pressure for access due to the proximity of great conurbations was at its greatest. The list on the page opposite shows the present eleven National Parks with some relevant data:

All the National Parks which have been designated to date lie in the north and west of England and Wales. This has been seen by many as an anomaly; for if the Park structure does give some measure of protection to the countryside then it is strange that the areas most under attack from agriculture and development, i.e. the Midland, eastern and southern areas of England, are those without the benefit of this protection.

Many also find it surprising that Scotland, with its large proportion of wild beautiful country and low population density, does not have any National Parks. (It does, however,

| Name | Designation | Area (sq miles/sq km) | | Popularity |
|------|-------------|------|------|------------|
| Brecon Beacons | 1957 | 522 | 1351 | 7 |
| The Broads | 1989 | 117 | 303 | 1* |
| Dartmoor | 1951 | 368 | 954 | 10.17 |
| Exmoor | 1954 | 268 | 693 | 2.8 |
| Lake District | 1951 | 885 | 2292 | 20 |
| North York Moors | 1952 | 555 | 1436 | 11 |
| Northumberland | 1956 | 405 | 1049 | 1 |
| Peak District | 1950 | 555 | 1438 | 20 |
| Pembrokeshire Coast | 1952 | 212 | 548 | 1.5 |
| Snowdonia | 1952 | 867 | 2142 | 9 |
| Yorkshire Dales | 1954 | 683 | 1769 | 7.5 |

* The Broads, under the Broads Authority, received special protection under legislation introduced in the late 1980s and it may be regarded as a National Park in all but name. Some walking opportunities exist in the area, but it is as an inland waterway that the area is famed and thus it is beyond the scope of this book.

The popularity of the Parks is given in million visitor-days/year.

have regional and local parks.) This is despite considerable debate, which is still continuing today with undiminished intensity. The need for a Park structure to give protection or access has not been seen by the public as a whole to be necessary. With increasing pressure from tourism, leisure activities, afforestation, hydro-electric schemes, and such like, it is doubtful, however, if this will continue to be the position for much longer.

Ireland has several National Parks—all within the Republic —although these are comparatively small compared to those in

*View north from Windy Gyle, Northumberland*

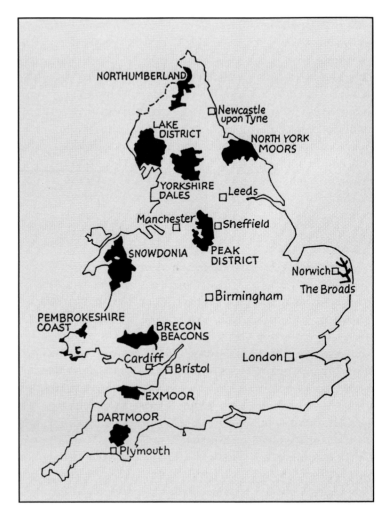

*FIGURE 1 The National Parks of Great Britain*

Britain. Killarney National Park, founded in 1932, is in the south in County Kerry and comprises the Lakes of Killarney and the area around; Connemara National Park is in the far west of County Galway and includes some of the summits of the Twelve Bens mountains; and Glenveagh National Park is in the north in a wild area of mountain and moorland in County Donegal.

Since 1957 a number of other areas in Britain have been proposed for National Park status, for example, the Cambrian Mountains and the North Pennines. In no case has a proposal been successful. However, the Broads Authority was established in 1989 and the New Forest was designated an Area of National Significance in the early 1990s when provision was made for the same protection as is accorded to a National Park.

Each Park is the responsibility of a separate Authority which is charged with its administration. These Authorities have two main aims. The first is to preserve and enhance the natural beauty of the areas designated as National Parks, and the second is to encourge the provision or improvement of facilities for the enjoyment of open-air recreation and the study of nature within the National Parks. They must in addition have due regard for the social and economic needs of the people living there. At present, only two of the Parks are run by independent autonomous committees; the other Authorities are special committees of the county councils in which the Parks lie. Imminent legislation will mean that these Parks are also run by independent authorities. The actual work on the ground is done by a team of full, part-time and voluntary staff under the control of a National Park Officer. Approximately three-quarters of the finance for their work comes from the government, the remainder from the local county councils, and a little from self-generated income.

An important function for each Authority is to consider planning applications for development within its area. In addition it may promote schemes for the enjoyment or convenience of visitors, and provide facilities such as training centres, information centres, car-parks, toilets, etc. The negotiation of permissive paths and Access Agreements, the waymarking of public rights of way, the leading of guided walks in the countryside or around local places of interest, and the preparation and publication of guide books and pamphlets, are some of the tasks of the Authority staff.

It is a matter of debate whether or not the present National Park structure is sufficiently strong and whether additional powers should not be made available to the Authorities. From the walkers' point of view much has certainly been achieved. De facto access exists over large areas of, for example, the Lake District and Snowdonia; Access Agreements have greatly improved the situation in others, particularly in the Peak District; and the enlightened attitude of organizations such as the National Trust has widened or safeguarded access in important cases. Unrestricted access over areas of uncultivated land—which many walkers regard as their moral right and ultimate aim—has not, however, been achieved. It is a sad fact that walkers are still prevented from walking over large areas of uncultivated mountain and moorland within our National Parks.

In a broader context also there have undoubtedly been successes. The purchase and renovation of quarries on Hadrian's Wall in Northumberland; the Upland Management Scheme in the Lake District; control of power boats in the same area; the management of the public rights of way network in the Yorkshire Dales; the Snowdon Management Scheme which has improved the paths on Snowdon and restored summit facilities; and many more. But there have also been the failures:

afforestation within the Northumberland National Park has increased from 10 to 20 per cent since designation and about one-fifth remains under the control of the Ministry of Defence who deny public access to most of it; quarrying continues in the Yorkshire Dales as it does in the Peak District; a bypass was pushed through the Dartmoor National Park instead of outside it; thousands of acres of heather in the North York Moors were ploughed up to increase the amount of cultivatable land; and an Early Warning Station was built at Fylingdales on the North York Moors as was a nuclear power station at Trawsfynydd in Snowdonia. To mention the failures is not to decry the success, but to warn against complacency and to urge the need for more resources and still greater efforts. The words of the National Parks Committee written in 1931 are still appropriate: 'We desire to record our conviction that such measures as we have advocated are necessary if the present generation is to escape the charge that in a short-sighted pursuit of its immediate ends it had squandered a noble heritage'.

The walks in this book have been carefully chosen to show the best of that heritage. They are intended to lead the walker through some of the most beautiful areas of our National Parks and to some of their most interesting features. To cater for all levels of ability and inclination, they vary considerably both in length and in difficulty, offering a wide range from short strolls in easy terrain to very tough walks in rough and wild country. To cater for all interests they vary in nature: some follow coastal paths; some rivers, streams and burns; a high proportion take to the mountains and moorlands; a few keep to lowland fields. In spite of their differences they all have one thing in common. They are walks of quality. They are meant to be enjoyed.

*Chirdon Burn, Northumberland*

# INTRODUCTION TO THE ROUTE DESCRIPTIONS

As far as is known, the walks described in this book: (a) follow public rights of way (i.e. footpaths, bridleways or carriageways), (b) use permissive paths, (c) cross private land over which access is allowed on payment of a small fee, (d) cross land over which there is a current access agreement, (e) cross commons over which there is legal public access, or (f) use paths or cross open country which have been walked for a long time without objection. It is not expected, therefore, that any difficulties will be encountered. Nevertheless, responsibility must rest with the walker to ensure that he or she has any necessary permission before commencing the walk. (See also page 309.)

Any local byelaws and regulations which apply to commons or access areas (and which are usually displayed on boards at access points) must be respected; for example, access may be withdrawn on certain days each year. In particular, 'short cuts', which may lead to proliferation of paths or to the annoyance of local people, should not be taken. Paths are sometimes, however, deliberately diverted by a National Park Authority, for example to allow a badly-eroded section to recover; such diversions should always be followed.

As Ministry of Defence Firing Ranges on Dartmoor are entered on Route No. 9, firing times must be checked before starting as entry is then forbidden (see pages 311–12).

The amount of climbing involved in each route has been estimated from 1:25 000 maps (Outdoor Leisure or Pathfinder) or 1:50 000 maps (Landranger) as appropriate and should be regarded as approximate only. In some route descriptions information is given on the length and height of individual climbs. In all cases the data has been given in both feet and metres as both are now in common use.

In most cases the walks start from a car-park or from a town or village where parking is available. For others the nearest car-park or suitable parking area is suggested. There will be many places where cars may be parked by the wayside, but this must always be done with care to ensure that they do not cause any

ACCESS

ASCENT

CAR-PARKS

obstruction for local people; in particular, gateways should never be blocked.

Unfortunately car break-ins are a common occurrence, even in the National Parks. It is advisable to take valuables with you or leave them at home.

INTERESTING FEATURES ON THE ROUTES

The best position for seeing these is indicated both in the route descriptions and on the maps by *(1)*, *(2)*, etc.

LENGTH

These are strictly 'map miles' estimated from Outdoor Leisure, Pathfinder or Landranger maps; no attempt has been made to take into account any ascent or descent involved. The data has been given in both miles and kilometres. Shorter distances within the route descriptions have been given in both yards and metres.

MAPS

The maps are drawn to a scale of approximately 1:25 000 with the exception of the maps for Exmoor where a scale of approximately 1:50 000 is used. Usually the scale for small features, e.g. farm areas, has been exaggerated for clarity.

In the main the maps have been drawn so that the route goes from the bottom to the top of a page; this will enable the reader to 'line up' the map in the direction walked while still holding the book in the normal reading position. In the case of relatively small circular walks, however, the full route has been given on the same map for greater convenience.

Where field boundaries are given these should be regarded as a 'best description' as often a boundary changes several times within a short distance (many are also a mixture of fence, hedge and wall). The arrow on each map points to grid north. Finally, for cross-reference, corresponding Ordnance Survey Landranger, Pathfinder or Outdoor Leisure sheets are shown on each map.

ROUTE DESCRIPTIONS

The letters 'L' and 'R' stand for left and right respectively. Where these are used for changes of direction then they imply a turn of about 90° when facing in the direction of the walk. 'Half L' and 'half R' indicate a half turn, i.e. approximately 45°, and 'back half L' or 'back half R' indicate three-quarter turns, i.e. about 135°. PFS stands for 'Public Footpath Sign', PBS for 'Public Bridleway Sign', OS for Ordnance Survey' and PW for 'Pennine Way'.

To avoid constant repetition, it should be assumed that all stiles and gates mentioned in the route description are to be crossed (unless there is a specific mention otherwise).

STANDARD OF THE ROUTES

The routes described cover an enormous range of both length and difficulty; the easiest can probably be undertaken by a family party at almost any time of the year, while the hardest are only really suitable for experienced fell walkers who are both fit and well-equipped. Any walker therefore who is contemplating following a route should make sure before starting that it is

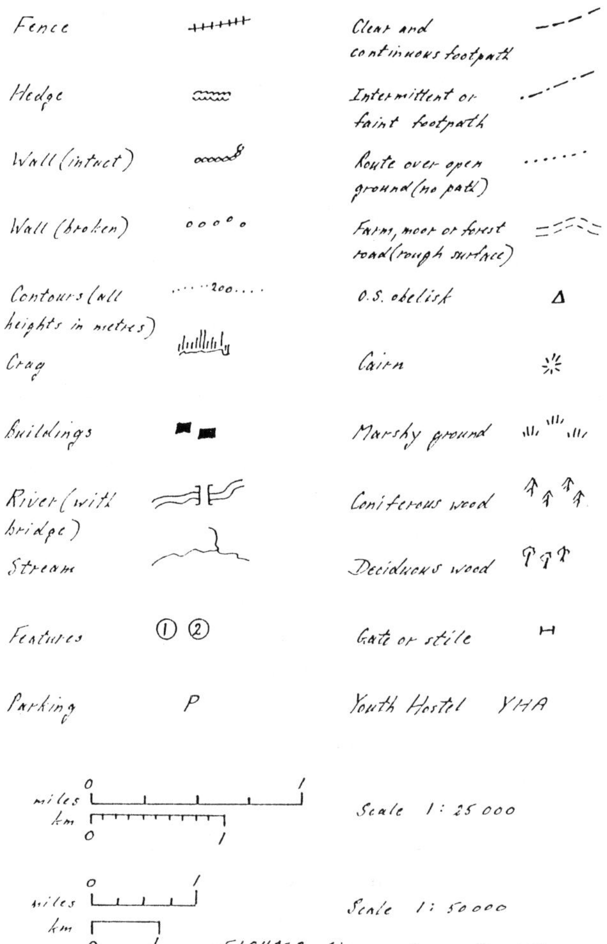

| | | | |
|---|---|---|---|
| Fence | +++++++ | Clear and continuous footpath | --- |
| Hedge | ⌒⌒⌒ | Intermittent or faint footpath | .-.- |
| Wall (intact) | ∞∞8 | Route over open ground (no path) | ....... |
| Wall (broken) | o o o° o | Farm, moor or forest road (rough surface) | =≡≡≡ |
| Contours (all heights in metres) | ....200.... | O.S. obelisk | △ |
| Crag | ⊔⊔⊔⊔⊔ | Cairn | ☀ |
| Buildings | ◄ ▄ | Marshy ground | ⍸⍸ ⍸⍸ |
| River (with bridge) | ⟊⟍ | Coniferous wood | ⋔ ⋔ ⋔ |
| Stream | ⌒⌒⌒ | Deciduous wood | ♀ ♀ ♀ |
| Features | ① ② | Gate or stile | ⊢ |
| Parking | P | Youth Hostel | YHA |

miles 0 —————— 1
km 0 —————— 1   Scale 1:25 000

miles 0 ——— 1
km 0 ——— 1   Scale 1:50 000

FIGURE 2  Signs used on route maps

within his or her capability (see Safety, page 311).

In practice, however, it is not easy to give an accurate picture of the difficulty of any route, which is dependent upon a number of factors, some of which are subjective. It is probably best to attempt an overall assessment of difficulty based upon the length, amount of climbing, problems of route-finding and finally, upon the roughness of the terrain.

Each of the routes has therefore been given a grading based upon a consideration of these factors and represented by the numeral which precedes each walk number and title. Thus, 1.15 Cat Bells (page 100) is Route No. 15 in the book and is of Grade 1, i.e. Easy grade; 3.46 Carnedd Llewelyn from Ogwen (page 267) is Route No. 46 and is of More Strenuous grade, and so on.

A general description of each grade is given overleaf. (Note that these are rough guidelines only and a walk may be given a higher grading than the distance indicates if the terrain is particularly difficult.)

*Easy (1)* Generally short walks (up to 5 miles, 8 km) over well-defined paths, with no problems of route-finding. Some climbing may be involved, but mostly over fairly gradual slopes with only short sections of more difficult ground. The paths may, however, sometimes run alongside cliffs, streams, steep slopes, etc. where care should be taken, particularly of children.

*Moderate (2)* Rather longer walks (up to about 10 miles, 16 km), mostly over paths, but with sections where route-finding will be more difficult. Mountain summits may be reached with climbing over steeper and rougher ground.

*More strenuous (3)* Perhaps longer walks (10–20 miles, 16–32 km) with prolonged spells of climbing. Some rough ground, calling for good route-finding ability, perhaps with stretches of scrambling.

*Very strenuous (4)* Only for the few, involving long distances (over 20 miles, 32 km), with a considerable amount of climbing over difficult ground.

For each National Park the routes are given in order of increasing difficulty, so that the first given is the easiest and the last given is the hardest. In addition, a summary of each walk is given at the head of each section with information on length, amount of climbing and any special difficulties.

Finally, it must be appreciated that weather conditions can make an enormous difference to the difficulty of a walk and must be taken into consideration at all stages (see page 311).

STARTING AND FINISHING POINTS

The majority of the routes are circular, returning to their starting point, as this avoids any problems with transport when the walk is completed. The location of each starting point (and finishing point where this is different) is given by a six-figure grid reference prefixed by the number of an appropriate Ordnance Survey Landranger map; thus (98–900627) indicates that the starting point is at grid reference 900627 on Landranger Sheet No. 98.

TIME FOR COMPLETION

As the time for completing a walk depends considerably upon the individual ability of each walker, no times are given here. However, the usual method for estimating time is by Naismith's Rule: 'For ordinary walking allow one hour for every 3 miles (5 km) and add one hour for every 2000 feet (600 m) of ascent; for backpacking with a heavy load allow one hour for every 2½ miles (4 km) and one hour for every 1500 feet (450 m) of ascent'. For many walkers this tends to be over-optimistic, however, and it is better for each walker to form an assessment of his or her own performance over one or two walks. Naismith's Rule also makes no allowance for rest or food stops or for the influence of weather conditions and a suitable amount of extra time must be allowed for these.

# WALKS IN
# THE BRECON BEACONS
# NATIONAL PARK

*Black Mountain from Mynydd y Llan*

# 1.1

# Sgwd Gwladus
# Waterfall Walk

## STARTING AND FINISHING POINT

Parking area near Angel Inn at the village of Pontneddfechan (Outdoor Leisure Sheet 11/901076)

## LENGTH

2½ miles (4 km)

This delightful walk, along the beautiful wooded valley to the waterfall of Sgwd Gwladus, is suitable for all the family (though little children should be kept under control at all times, as the path runs beside a fast-flowing river). It serves as a perfect introduction to the limestone scenery—with its attendant wooded gorges, tumbling rivers and falls—that can be found along the southern rim of the National Park. The walk is full of interest, both in terms of its industrial archaeology and its natural beauty. Take something to eat with you and take advantage of the plentiful picnic sites along the way.

## ROUTE DESCRIPTION (Map 1)

There are many places to park the car in the general area around the Angel Inn. The entrance to the walk is just behind the inn, beside the old stone bridge over the River Neath (Afon Nedd). Go past the barrier marked 'Sgwd Gwladus Lady Waterfalls' and follow the path along the western bank. The pathway here, elevated high above the river, soon skirts a massive, overhanging rocky outcrop known as the Farewell Rock *(1)*. The path *(2)*, well engineered and wide, is much better than the usual riverside walk—a legacy, no doubt, of the fact that it follows an old tramway for about the first ⅔ mile (1 km).

Within ¼ mile (400 m) or so of the start, you will come to the ruins of a corn mill *(3)*, after which the riverside opens out a little into a grassy field. The valley sides soon close in again to reveal evidence of old mine workings *(4)*. Just north of the mines, where the stream running down from Cwm Gored joins the Neath, there is a most attractive picnic site set in a leafy riverside glade.

From here, the path becomes much narrower as it climbs a short series of steps up into the steep hillside above the river. Within about ¼ mile (400 m) of the picnic site you will come to a large pool at the confluence of the Neath and Pyrddin rivers.

*The ruined mill beside the Afon Nedd*

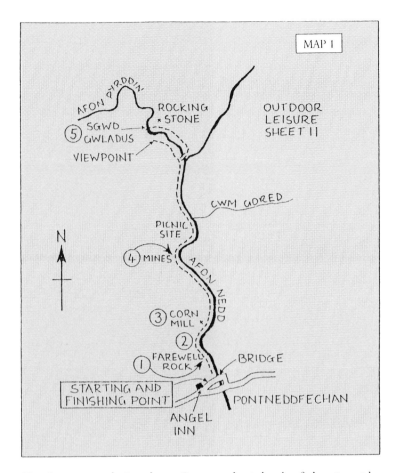

You have two choices here. Stay on the L bank of the river (do not go over the footbridge) signposted 'Sgwd Gwladus Viewing Platform' and follow the Pyrddin as it flows down a rocky staircase of small falls to the picnic site and view-point which looks across to the major fall of Sgwd Gwladus *(5)*.

If you prefer, you can get even nearer to the waterfall by crossing the footbridge and turning half L along the opposite bank of the Pyrddin. This muddy path initially climbs the hillside, then drops down to a pretty clearing beside the riverbank just below the fall. You can climb up past the little log cabin and picnic site to the top of the fall, but do not go near the edge of the overhanging ledge.

From here, retrace your steps back to Pontneddfechan.

*1 Farewell Rock*

This dark, concave rock face is so called after the colloquial name for hard, close-grained sandstone. This sandstone forms the upper levels of the millstone grits found along the southern rim of the National Park. Its local name is most expressive; in geological sequence, the rock lies below the coal measures, so when miners struck this sandstone with their pick axes, they knew they had bid farewell to their coal seams.

2  *The pathway*

The route beside the River Neath in this first section of the walk follows the course of an old tramway. Horse-drawn trams would haul silica from the mines, sunk into the sides of the valley, to Pont Walby over ¼ mile (1.2 km) south-east of Pontneddfechan. From here, cargoes were carried 14 miles (22 km) by barge along the Neath Canal to Briton Ferry and the sea.

3  *The Old Mill*

These are the overgrown and quite extensive ruins of a double-race mill that was used by local farmers to grind corn.

4  *Silica mines*

Both banks of the river were mined for silica. Mining activity here was extensive—and quite prosperous—from the early 1820s up until the turn of the century. The valley sides bear plentiful evidence of mining, an enterprise based on the fact that fire-bricks of exceptional quality and value could be made from this local 'Dinas Silica'. Silica bricks were made at Pont Walby until 1920. In its heyday, Dinas fire-brick was known all over Europe and America, its exceptional properties making it ideal for lining iron- and steel-making furnaces and lime kilns as well as domestic fireplaces.

5  *Sgwd Gwladus*

This waterfall is on the Pyrddin, a tributary of the River Neath. It has an almost primeval quality to it, a product of its gloomy, mossy and atmospheric setting beneath tall, dark cliffs. At the top of the fall there is a flat platform of rock, which overhangs the pool below a little. Keep away from this dangerous ledge—there is a fine view of the fall from the poolside. When the river is low, you may be able to scramble to a point behind the waterfall, but this is never as accessible as the path that runs behind the famous fall of Sgwd yr Eira on the Afon Hepste.

Sgwd Gwladus is reputedly named after Gwladus, one of the twenty-five daughters of Brychan, a fifth-century chieftain who ruled Brycheiniog (which became, in time, Brecknock or Breconshire). The waterfall is also known as the Lady's Fall. On the eastern side of the fall there is a huge boulder. This was a carefully balanced rocking stone (it is claimed you could crack nuts beneath it) until a gang of workmen dislodged it in the nineteenth century.

*Sgwd Gwladus, set in a shady, wooded natural amphitheatre*

# CARREG CENNEN AND RIVER LOUGHOR

**STARTING AND FINISHING POINT**
Carreg Cennen Castle car-park beside Castell Farm (Outdoor Leisure Sheet 12/666194)
**LENGTH**
4½ miles (7 km)
**ASCENT**
400 ft (120 m)

This attractive circular walk along agricultural lanes and footpaths is suitable for all ages and makes a great half-day out for all the family. The walk descends into the Cennen Valley along a waymarked route through field and meadow to the source of the River Loughor, then returns to Carreg Cennen along an old farm road to the foot of the castle cliff. The final mile (1.6 km) of the walk is mostly uphill through castle woodland, to reach the high limestone crag above. There are several natural and historical features along the way, the most outstanding of which is Carreg Cennen, a spectacular castle complete with dungeon and ancient cave.

## ROUTE DESCRIPTION (Map 2)

From the car-park go back along the minor road, then turn L at the first junction and walk downhill into the Cennen Valley for ½ mile (800 m). Cross over a stile in the hedgerow on the R just before Pantyffynnont Cottage, then go straight down across the fields, crossing two further stiles to reach the river. Take care where the path is slippery and steep, just above the water-meadow. Cross over the river by the narrow footbridge (note the novel sheep barrier), walk on to an iron-rail gate, then go uphill along the public path to reach Llwyn-bedw farm. Turn R and follow the stony farm track for ½ mile (800 m) through fields and rough grazing land to ford a stream, then carry on uphill to a junction just beyond a small cattle-grid. Turn L through the open gateway and follow the approximate track to reach a stream and a stone-flag bridge. Look back along the stream's course for a view across fields and woodland to the castle cliff. A solitary heron can often be seen flapping along the Cennen Valley, seeking fishing grounds in the marshy land below.

Walk on, crossing two stiles, then on beside a stream for ¼ mile (400 m) to reach a small enclosure of trees and a stile on

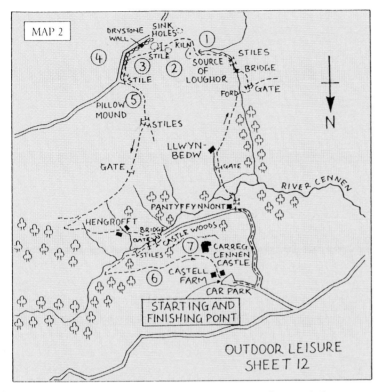

the right. This is the source of the River Loughor and the river-cave and pool can be seen from the high bank above. There is a short limestone cave system here, reaching into the depths of the hillside and only accessible to the experienced caver *(1)*. Continue along the track, bearing R past an old lime kiln with a limestone quarry behind *(2)*. The kiln was last worked around the turn of the century, producing burnt lime for local industry.

Just beyond the kiln the track disappears into open grazing land. Follow the line of the old stone wall to a stile between two large craters. These are shake holes caused by the ground collapsing into limestone caverns beneath *(3)*. Several mature trees growing in these holes indicate that they were formed some time ago.

Walk straight on to reach a drystone wall at the edge of a narrow tarmac road. Turn L and go along the line of the wall to a stile. The open land to your right is the western edge of the Black Mountain *(4)*, a vast area of wild upland stretching for many miles to the south and east.

Cross the stile, walk L along the road for 100 yards (90 m) then turn L again onto a grass track past the ancient Pillow Mounds *(5)* to a row of trees, where you can glimpse Carreg Cennen Castle in the distance. Go straight on, crossing a stile, a stream and another stile on your R into a field. Walk the length of this open pasture to a gate, a trackway and a National Park

sign at the further end. To your L is a magnificent view of the castle and tree-clad slopes of the high limestone cliff.

Follow the directed path on along the hillside, descending by the muddy track toward Hengrofft Farm in the valley below. Walk through the farmyard, then onto the minor road at a bridge across the Cennen. Turn sharp R through a gate and go on beside the river across several small meadows and stiles to join a waymarked path that climbs back half L up through the castle woodland *(6)* to the cliff-top above. On reaching the summit turn L to visit the castle *(7)* or R down the tarmac path, through Castell Farm to the car-park and your starting-point below.

1 *Limestone caves*
   The limestone areas of the National Park are riddled with water-worn cave systems created by natural underground rivers and streams that descend from mountain and moorland heights above. Whole rivers are often swallowed up, disappearing into a cave or pothole, to re-emerge some distance lower down.

2 *Old lime kilns*
   Limestone quarrying was once a major industry in the area and there are a number of disused kilns and quarries hidden away amid the farmland. Limestone had various uses in the local economy, among them providing stone for barns and houses, limestone dust for making cement and render, and, when burnt in kilns, agricultural quick-lime. The nearby quarries on top of the Black Mountain once employed hundreds of local people, making limestone products for both farming and industry.

3 *Shake holes*
   Pits, craters and holes in the ground appear everywhere in limestone country and are caused by a collapse of the millstone-grit layer into the water-eroded caves of the carboniferous limestone below. Shake holes can be enormous, and it is not unknown for whole buildings to disappear swallowed up by the earth.

4 *The Black Mountain*
   Designated as a Remote Area and a Site of Special Scientific Interest, the Black Mountain is one of the last truly wild areas of countryside left in Britain and has several fascinating geographical and geological features. These include extensive limestone pavements on the summit, crevasses which contain alpine plants and the great knife-edged Fan Hir ridge which has been sculpted by glaciation.

*Dramatic Carreg Cennen Castle, perched on its limestone crag*

5 *Pillow Mounds*

The area of hummocky land known as the Pillow Mounds is thought to be a Bronze Age burial site, dating from about 3000 BC. However, a less romantic explanation suggests that the long low mounds are Victorian rabbit warrens, created in the late nineteenth century as part of the local industry of breeding rabbits for meat.

6 *Castle Woodland*

The steep hillside of Carreg Cennen is clad with self-seeded oak woodland. Over the years many good trees have fallen owing to the steep, unstable ground and others have died of disease and old age. Because of constant grazing by sheep, there are no saplings to replace the declining tree stock and it seems that the woodland of Carreg Cennen is doomed to disappear unless a management scheme can be agreed.

7 *Carreg Cennen Castle*

Built on a natural 300-ft (90 m) limestone crag above the Cennen Valley, the main structure and defences of the castle were erected during the great thirteenth-century building boom, under the victorious English king, Edward I. Many castles were built all over Wales to consolidate English rule and Carreg Cennen was a key stronghold in the local area of South Wales. The Earl of Hereford and John Gifford constructed most of the major fortifications, adding various towers and employing defensive ideas borrowed from the great castles of Europe.

The castle has passed through several sieges and periods of destruction, having been attacked and taken by various Welsh and English armies over the centuries. Its captors include Llywelyn the Prince of Wales and the last great Welsh national leader, Owain Glyndŵr. The castle was partly demolished in 1462 to render it unusable by local bandits, who plagued the countryside at that time.

Carreg Cennen is one of the great historic spectacles of Wales. Its location—it teeters on a sheer cliff in the foothills of the Black Mountain—is unforgettable. There is even spectacle beneath the ground here. A narrow passageway cut into the cliff leads to a cave-like dungeon and a natural tunnel, where the bones of four Stone Age skeletons (two adults and two children) were discovered. A torch and guide-book are available from Castell Farm tea-shop.

*Castell Farm, in the shadow of Carreg Cennen*

# 2.3

# HAY BLUFF AND GOSPEL PASS

STARTING AND FINISHING
POINT
Small car-park next to a standing
stone on Hay common (Outdoor
Leisure Sheet 13/239374)
LENGTH
8 miles (13 km)
ASCENT
825 ft (250 m)

This circular walk around the Hay Bluff escarpment makes an excellent afternoon and evening stroll suitable for most walkers of average ability. The first mile (1.6 km) of the walk, straight up to the Bluff summit, is extremely steep but, once achieved, the remainder and majority of the route is easy going, with one steep descent down on to Rhiw Wen common.

## ROUTE DESCRIPTION (Map 3)

Cross over the road from the car-park and walk straight ahead, across the gorse-covered common, toward the summit of Hay Bluff. You will soon be labouring uphill, climbing the steep foothill in front of the main summit. Frequent short halts may be advisable to catch breath and admire the panorama of woods and fields below. Head towards the left edge of the bluff to find a narrow sheep-path, then go straight up for the final assault. On cresting the ridge, go on across the bilberry moor to the white OS obelisk, then bear R to follow a well-worn path along the top of the escarpment. Leave this main track after 100 yards (90 m) bearing R to find a narrow path close to the edge, then on along the length of Ffynnon y Parc for 1 mile (1.6 km) to reach the tarmac road at Gospel Pass.

Look north-west across the Wye Valley for a fine view into mid-Wales, while down below, close to your feet, are the rolling woodland and fields of Wenallt and Tregoyd common. The flat-topped highlands around the Hay Bluff escarpment have suffered severe erosion in places, largely due to pony-trekking *(1)* and the continuous passage of sheep.

The narrow Gospel Pass is part of an ancient high-level route *(2)* for travellers between Abergavenny and Hay-on-Wye. The view south from the top of the pass looks down a rugged, steep-sided valley toward Capel-y-ffin and Llanthony. This is the head of the Vale of Ewyas, a remote area of border country steeped in history and legend.

Cross the single-track road at Gospel Pass and go on along the worn path ahead, climbing uphill for 1 mile (1.6 km) towards the Twmpa. You will reach two walkers' cairns, one on either side, and a third cairn at the summit, marked with paint. Go on past this last cairn, following the track toward Rhiw Wen, a deep gash in the escarpment visible ½ mile (800 m) ahead. The moorland landscape in front and to your L reveals the remote nature of this high borderland *(3)*, a formidable mountain barrier between Wales and England.

Turn back half R at Rhiw Wen and go down the steep track toward the farmland. The bare cliff-face on your left is a good example of local geology *(4)*, revealing strata lines of the old red sandstone. Walk on downhill, following the worn path across two streams, to reach a small group of mature larch trees visible ahead, then straight on to the edge of the farmland below. A watercourse crosses the valley bottom and a very wide track follows the boundary fence. Turn R along this established trekking route.

Look back across the wild common land for a fine view of the hills. The northern heads of the Black Mountains form an impressive range, stretching away to the west into the heartland of Wales. The common in front is an area of upland grazing, dotted with may and oak trees, and viewed at its best during early June when the hawthorn blossom is in full bloom.

Follow the very worn track to where the fence ends, then on across the open land, walking toward Hay Bluff now visible ahead. To enjoy a walk across the common choose a route 50 yards (45 m) to one side of the heavily eroded path and go on for 1 mile (1.6 km), following the trekking route to the narrow tarmac road at Caemarchog. The mixed woodland here provides a delightful contrast with the bare windswept hills and includes a surprising mixture of oak, chestnut, ash and hazel. Turn R along the road, cross over two fords and continue along the tarmac for 1¼ miles (2 km) to reach once again your starting-point. The small meadows and woodland to the L of the road are fine examples of the traditional farming landscape now fast disappearing in other parts of Britain.

*1 Pony-trekking*

Located on the border of Wales with easy access from England, the Black Mountains are under considerable pressure from recreation and tourism. Much of this activity, such as walking and touring, is relatively benign, with little or no impact on the environment. However, the development of pony-trekking as an additional source of income for farmers and landowners has led to severe erosion of the countryside,

*Ruined farmhouse below Twmpa*

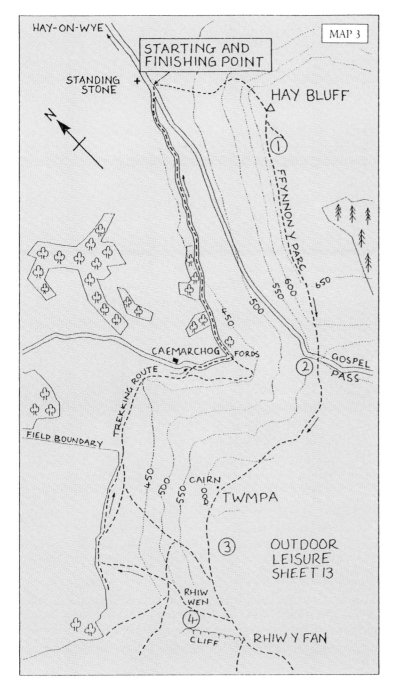

turning public rights-of-way through the farmland into muddy swamps, while tracks across the open hill become badly scarred.

2 *Gospel Pass*

This narrow gap in the hills is one of several ancient roads across the uplands and is contemporary with nearby Offa's Dyke Path. The Gospel road is much the easier route and has

remained in use throughout the centuries. The thirteenth-century canons of Llanthony Priory were regular travellers over this pass to visit their properties and fellow clerics in mid-Wales.

3  *The moorland landscape*

These mountain heights have served as a natural barrier for hundreds of years. When under attack from invading Saxons in the fifth century, the Romano-British retreated to the Black Mountains and, together with the native Welsh, defended wild Wales, the last outpost of the empire, from invasion by the Germanic tribes. The remote moorland in the centre of the mountains is largely unchanged and retains the same bleak, forbidding aspect of Roman times. This remoteness is part of the moorland's beauty and is highly valued by experienced walkers and lovers of wild country-side. To your left is the Nant Bwch Valley leading down to Capel-y-ffin and, looking south, the peak of Mynydd Llysiau can be seen on the horizon.

4  *Local geology*

Horizontal bands of hard brownstones are the very bones of the mountains, and good examples can be seen at Rhiw Wen. The steep cliff-face here has lost its grass cover, revealing the crumbling layers of rock beneath. The brownstones, solid blocks of old red sandstone, often drop out as a result of the weathering of the softer layers in between.

*Looking towards the central Beacons from the ridge below Twmpa*

# BRECON BEACONS LINEAR RIDGE WALK

STARTING POINT
Small parking space at Blaen
taf-fechan (035173) or Forestry
Commission car-park a little farther
south (037170)
Both locations on Outdoor Leisure
Sheet 11
FINISHING POINT
Pont ar Daf car-park on the A470
(Outdoor Leisure Sheet
11/988198)
LENGTH
6½ miles (10 km)
ASCENT
1500 ft (460 m)

This demanding walk along the central mountain spine of the Brecon Beacons takes in the best-known features of the area, and offers panoramic views of the rugged mountain landscape along all of the route. Starting from the great green and golden bowl known as the Neuadd, the walk climbs up the straight road (probably Roman in origin) to the historic gap in the hills between Cribyn and Fan y Big. It then turns westward, going steeply up to Cribyn, and on along the high escarpment ridge towards Pen y Fan and Corn Du beyond.

This route is very exposed in bad weather to high winds, rain and poor visibility. A compass, map and adequate clothing are essential. Also, remember that the Beacons are infamous for fatalities as well as famous for their magnificent upland landscapes.

## ROUTE DESCRIPTION (Maps 4, 5)

From the parking space (or the spacious Forestry Commission car-park a little way south) turn L up the road. Turn R off the tarmac road onto a rough boulder-strewn trackway, leading along the edge of the conifers. This is the celebrated 'gap' road, thought to be a Roman track leading north across the hills toward Brecon and the ancient Roman fortress of Y Gaer just west of the town. Go on, climbing gradually uphill above the enclosed pasture land. After ½ mile (800 m) you will reach a steep gorge. This is the course of the Nant y Gloesydd, which cuts deeply across the track. The best way of crossing is to go down the easier L-hand path, jumping over the stream by the flat rocks below. Go on along the road walking steadily up into the Neuadd *(1),* a huge amphitheatre in the centre of the hills.

The gap road skirts along the slopes of Tor Glas, passing above the Upper and Lower Neuadd Reservoirs, and climbs the long gradual slope up to the dip in the escarpment visible ahead. Pen y Fan and Corn Du are the main summits to your L, easily

*Opposite: On the summit of Pen y Fan, the highest point in South Wales*

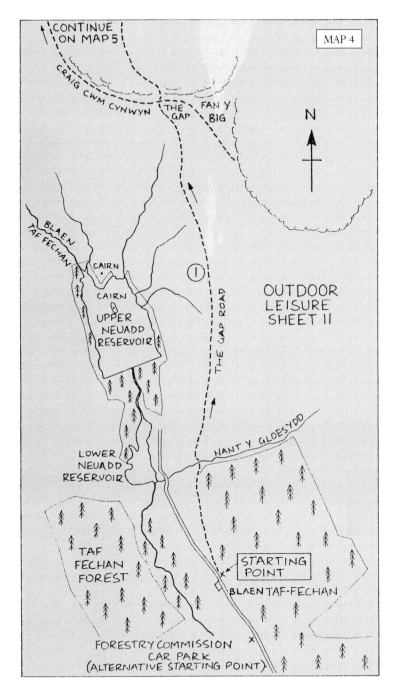

identified by their characteristic flat tops.

The gap itself is a distinctive worn gully at the highest point of the road and the stunning view northward into Cwm Cynwyn is a great reward for the long but gradual 2-mile (3 km) haul. This is a good place for a tea break and a look around at the hills. The sheer face of Cribyn looms above you to the L and Fan y Big is the summit with a long northward spur on your R.

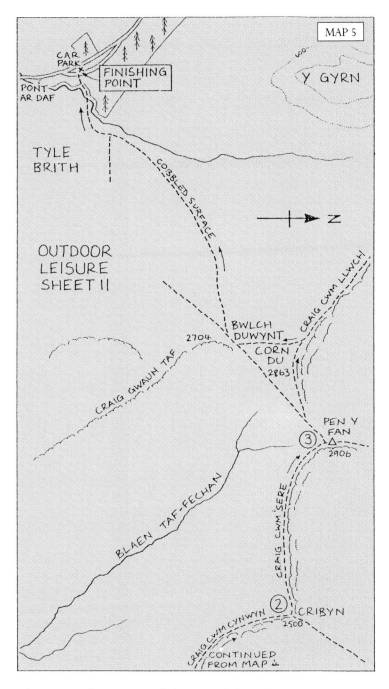

MAP 5

CAR PARK
FINISHING POINT
PONT AR DAF
TYLE BRITH
COBBLED SURFACE
OUTDOOR LEISURE SHEET 11
Y GYRN
N
BWLCH DUWYNT
2704
CRAIG GWAUN TAF
CORN DU
2863
CRAIG CWM LLWCH
PEN Y FAN
③
△
2906
BLAEN TAF-FECHAN
CRAIG CWM SERE
②CRIBYN
CRAIG CWM CYNWYN
2500
CONTINUED FROM MAP 4

*Craig Cwm Llwch and its glacial lake
from Corn Du*

The gap road goes on and downward from here, hugging the L
side of the *cwm*. Brecon town can be glimpsed on the horizon.

From the gap go west straight up the steep path toward
Cribyn, walking the long ridge of Craig Cwm Cynwyn for 1 mile
(1.6 km) to reach Cribyn's summit. This part of the walk is
deceptive, because when you think you have reached the top
there always seems to be another long slope ahead. The view

west *(2)* from Cribyn is one of the main features of the walk and takes in the central massif of the Beacon range.

The route ahead to Pen y Fan is laid out before you along the escarpment track of Craig Cwm Sere, leading first downhill then up again for 1 mile (1.6 km) to reach the final, very steep slope up to the obelisk and flat-topped summit. The last 200 yards (180 m) can be a little treacherous, particularly during wet weather, when the stones and muddy slope are very slippery. The view *(3)* from Pen y Fan never fails to impress, despite the over-popularity—and consequent serious erosion—of the summit and its approaches. On a Bank Holiday it can be difficult to find standing room here, at 2906 ft (886 m) the highest point in South Wales. It is always very windy on this exposed spot, and not very comfortable for any length of time.

Go on west from Pen y Fan across the saddle to neighbouring Corn Du. Then turn L, walking south-west along Bwlch Duwynt by the very worn path, to descend the steep slope of Tyle Brith for 1½ miles (2.5 km) toward the conifer plantation and car-park at Pont ar Daf on the A470 below. The eroded path cannot be missed, and lower down the National Trust is cobbling the surface in an attempt to stop the wear and tear.

Cross over the stream at the ford, walk through the gate at the forest corner and go on 500 yards (450 m) to your finishing-point at Pont ar Daf car-park.

*1 The Neuadd*

'The hall' is the literal translation of *neuadd.* Whether this refers to an ancient building that once stood here or merely to the steep walls of the surrounding hills is unclear. There was certainly an early settlement in the valley bottom and remains of this can be seen today. The small island in the upper reservoir has a Bronze Age cairn on top. The island itself may well be man-made, perhaps an ancient crannog (a raised area of dry land) built as a refuge in the middle of a swampy area.

The lake was created at the turn of the century, the great age of reservoir building, to catch the fresh springs and streams of the hills to provide drinking water for the industrial valleys of the south. The building style is Victorian Gothic, and this can be seen to good effect in the romantic tower jutting up above the surrounding pines. The tower is the outlet for the reservoir, where water pours down into a culvert below.

*2 View from Cribyn*

This view west from Cribyn is the showpiece landscape of the Beacons. The full height of the northern rampart of Pen y Fan is revealed—a drop of almost 1000 ft (300 m) from the summit to the slopes of Cwm Sere below. When there is snow on the ground is the best time of year to see this view, for then the strata lines of the great old red sandstone cliff-face are picked out in dramatic black and white. Corn Du, the second summit, is a little to the left, behind Pen y Fan.

*3 View from Pen y Fan*

Looking north from Pen y Fan across the Usk valley there are fine views into the heartland of Wales, with the Cambrian uplands clearly visible on the horizon. The view westward looks past Corn Du across the wastes of Fforest Fawr to the Black Mountain and Fan Hir escarpment, while to the south the high ridge of Craig Gwaun Taf snakes its way along the west side of the Neuadd, down to the Taf Fechan Valley. The Pontsticill Reservoir chain can be seen among the conifers of Taf Fechan Forest beyond. Closer to hand is the line of the gap road, going down past the Neuadd Reservoirs to the walk's starting-point at the forest edge.

The little lake, high up on the northern slope just beyond Corn Du, is Llyn Cwm Llwch, the glacial lake of the deep *cwm* that stretches north towards the town of Brecon.

*Above the clouds on the summit of Corn Du*

# 3.5

# FOOTHILLS OF THE BLACK MOUNTAIN

STARTING AND FINISHING
POINT
Llanddeusant Youth Hostel car-park
(Outdoor Leisure Sheet
12/776245)
LENGTH
10½ miles (17 km)
ASCENT
600 ft (190 m)

This is a fairly demanding walk into the wilderness area of the remote Black Mountain. The walk starts from the Youth Hostel at Llanddeusant, following old farm lanes to reach the open hill above. It then changes to mountain track, to find and follow the River Usk, which flows down to Pont 'ar Wysg and the Glasfynydd Forest. The return journey across the beautiful hills of Fedw Fawr passes Arhosfa'r Roman Camp and descends into the intricate old footpaths of the Afon Llechach Valley. You will be exposed to the full force of wind and rain during bad weather and a compass is essential for navigation on the open mountain.

## ROUTE DESCRIPTION (Maps 6–8)

From the Youth Hostel car-park walk past the village's fourteenth-century church to the junction. Follow the road signposted Llyn y Fan for 250 yards (225 m) to a stile and farm track on the L. Walk up this old lane for ¼ mile (400 m), turn R at the waymarker post and continue uphill to reach the mountain gate at Pen Tyle. The rough mountain track ahead is one of the old Coffin Routes *(1)* and leads right over the mountain to the industrial valleys of South Wales. Climb up the steep hill ahead, following the rutted path due east above the magnificent Afon Sawdde Valley *(2)* for 1½ miles (2.5 km), crossing several stream courses to reach a gap in the hills below Bryn Mawr. The path divides here, near the valley bottom. Take the L fork and continue on a bearing of 60° magnetic for ½ mile (800 m) to find the glacial cutting of the River Usk flowing down from Fan Foel above. This appears as a broad, shallow valley with the river following a zig-zag course across the flat, stony floor. Look for a narrow sheep-path on the high L-hand bank and follow the Usk Valley for 1½ miles (2.5 km) on a bearing of 20°, to reach the bridge and tarmac road at Pont 'ar Wysg beside Glasfynydd Forest.

Cross the road, continuing along the L bank of the river to

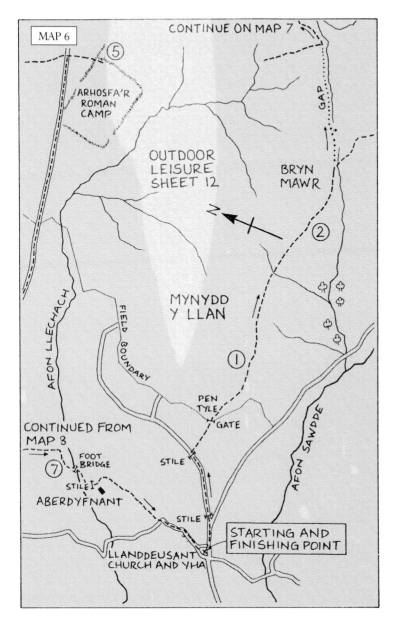

find a stile into the forestry land. Go across the water-meadow, following the river, to reach a hard forest track and ford. Do not cross the ford but go on over the meadowland to climb the high bank on the far side. The river enters the Usk Reservoir by a deep-cut channel below. For a sight of the reservoir and channel continue along the line of trees for 500 yards (450 m). Return by the same route. On returning to the forest road turn R.

Follow the forest road around the reservoir for 1 mile (1.6 km) to reach the far western end, where the open moorland of Fedw Fawr stretches south-west for ½ mile (800 m) to the deep gorge *(3)* of the Afon Clydach. Climb over the stile onto

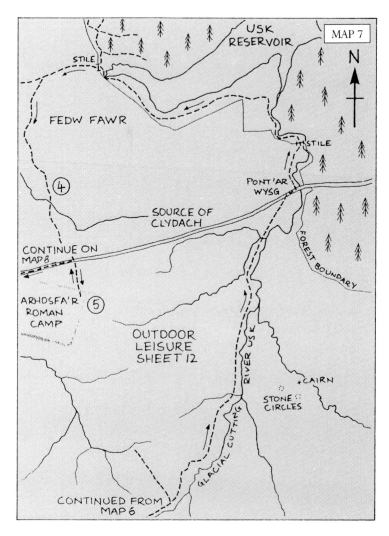

the moorland and walk along the valley bottom on a bearing of 250° magnetic, avoiding the lower marshy ground to find a well-defined path above the gorge. Turn L and go south along the rough moorland track for 1 mile (1.6 km) to reach the tarmac mountain road. This is the best part of the walk for mountain scenery, with the whole length of the Carmarthen Fans *(4)* visible ahead.

The faint outline of Arhosfa'r Roman marching camp *(5)* can be found on the hill above the road. Walk straight uphill, looking for a line of very low earthworks at the sharp north-east corner of the camp. Return by the same route. Follow the tarmac road westward (i.e., to the L after returning), cross the cattle grid and walk on for 1 mile (1.6 km) to the attractive Blue Chapel *(6)* at Talsarn. Just beyond the chapel on the same side of the road is a gate and entrance to an old public road. Walk down this narrow sunken path into the valley, keeping R at the

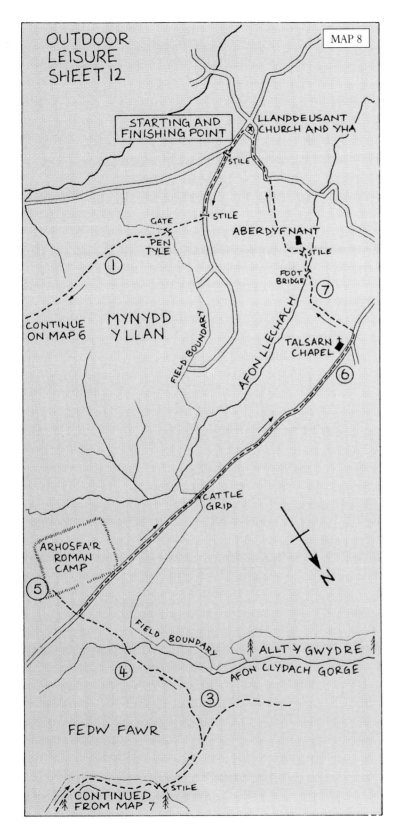

OUTDOOR
LEISURE
SHEET 12

MAP 8

STARTING AND
FINISHING POINT

LLANDDEUSANT
CHURCH AND YHA

STILE

GATE

STILE

ABERDYFNANT

PEN
TYLE

STILE

FOOT
BRIDGE

①

⑦

CONTINUE
ON MAP 6

MYNYDD
Y LLAN

FIELD BOUNDARY

AFON LLECHACH

TALSARN
CHAPEL

⑥

CATTLE
GRID

N

ARHOSFA'R
ROMAN
CAMP

⑤

FIELD BOUNDARY

ALLT Y GWYDRE

④

AFON CLYDACH GORGE

③

FEDW FAWR

STILE

CONTINUED
FROM MAP 7

Overleaf: *The bulky, bare Black
Mountain from Mynydd y Llan*

first junction, to reach a field and track just beyond a makeshift gate. Turn R, follow the overgrown lane downhill to a stile and a bridge over the beautiful wooded gorge of the Afon Llechach *(7)*. Cross the river, walk on to the working farm of Aberdyfnant, bearing L at the farmhouse, to follow the hard lane steeply up, then carry on for ½ mile (800 km) to the tarmac minor road. Turn L and continue for a further ½ mile (800 m) along the road to the Llanddeusant Church and Youth Hostel.

1  *Coffin Routes*

The Industrial Revolution of the nineteenth century brought about a migration of labour from the rural areas to the new mines and quarries in South Wales. Dangerous working conditions caused many deaths among the workforce, which made necessary the regular conveyance of the dead back over the mountain for burial in Llanddeusant or Gwynfe. The rough tracks known as 'coffin routes' came into use, and the gambo-cart, a two wheeled vehicle pulled by a horse and the dead man's workmates, transported the coffin. There is a flat area at the half-way point, just below the summit of Fan Brycheiniog, where a short religious service was held before the coffin was handed over to mourning relatives.

2  *Afon Sawdde Valley*

This deep-cloven valley winds up into the hills to the source of the Afon Sawdde at Llyn y Fan Fach, a small glacial lake at the foot of Bannau Sir Gaer. The great cliffs of the old red sandstone escarpment dominate the skyline, towering above the lake and valley. This landscape is truly primeval and has changed little since rivers of ice shaped the hills and valley during the last Ice Age. The fields and small farms in the valley bottom date from the Middle Ages, and the field pattern remains largely unaltered since the Victorian period.

3  *Afon Clydach gorge*

Of all the streams and rivers that descend from the Black Mountain, the Afon Clydach is the most dramatic. The stream rises on the moorland of Fedw Fawr and plunges down into the deep, winding gorge, heading north-west through the wooded hills to join the Afon Bran near Myddfai.

4  *Carmarthen Fans*

Walking south above the Clydach Gorge reveals a whole panorama. In front looms the high wilderness of the Black Mountain, stretching up to the Carmarthen Fans. This mountain range is the western end of the great old red sandstone escarpment and marks the historical boundary of the ancient Kingdom of Brecknock founded by Brychan Brycheiniog, the eighth-century Irish king.

5 *Roman marching camp*

This square earthwork was made nearly 2000 years ago by a Roman legion while on the long march west to Carmarthenshire. The low walls, sunk to almost nothing over the centuries, were dug by the troopers in one evening before they settled down for the night. The camp would probably have been used by other marching columns and may have been a regular stopping point on this lonely stretch of Roman road.

6 *Talsarn Chapel*

The tiny Blue Capel (chapel) at Talsarn is one of many independent Methodist meeting houses built during the nineteenth-century revival of the movement. Methodism was quite a political force in its heyday, attracting a majority of the local population away from the Anglican Church. Many chapel members refused to pay the hated Church Tithe, levied on every family in the parish as the dues and living of the incumbent vicar. This popular dissent was later ratified in Parliament by the disestablishment of the Anglican Church in Wales and the subsequent abolition of the vicar's tithe. The present congregation at Talsarn is reduced to a handful of local farmers supporting the chapel out of their own resources.

7 *The old lanes*

These old agricultural lanes and paths are the remains of the nineteenth-century road system connecting farm dwellings. Parts of this Victorian infrastructure are still in regular use today for the passage of sheep and cattle.

*The empty moors near Pont'ar Wysg*

# Walks in
# the Dartmoor
# National Park

*The medieval Windy Cross Post*

# 1.6

# BENCH TOR

STARTING AND FINISHING
POINT
Venford Reservoir on the Holne to
Hexworthy road. Car-park to the east
of the dam (191/202-689709). 5 miles
(8 km) west of Ashburton.
LENGTH
2¼ miles (4 km)
ASCENT
Mostly level walking

Bench Tor is a rugged climax to the River Dart's departure from the Dartmoor granite and from it are breath-taking views of the river some 500 feet (152 m) below. This easy walk follows the rock ridges of the tor, it penetrates the woods below and then follows a pipe-line track running above the Venford Brook back towards Venford Reservoir.

## ROUTE DESCRIPTION (Map 9)

Follow a path uphill from the back of the car-park which offers good views over Venford Reservoir and Holne Moor. On reaching a banked-up leat (on R), which supplies water to the settlements at Stoke, continue straight on keeping the leat on the R. After a short distance go straight on along a wide path running beside the field boundaries on the R, and follow to the rock-crowned summit of Bench Tor *(1)*. In summer keep close to the wall on approaching the tor to avoid a large area of bracken on the L. Walk along the rock ridge to the northern pile—a distance of 500 yards (457 m).

From the tor go back half L and then R downslope to enter the wood below *(2)*. Continuing in the same direction go down amongst the trees to reach a waterworks pipe track. Turn L onto the track, edged by granite kerbs, and follow the Venford Brook (down on R) upstream to almost the perimeter fence of the treatment works. Here cut half L up the slope and, keeping the fence on the R, continue straight on to return to the road and car-park *(3)*.

A very pleasant round-reservoir walk, about 1 mile (1.6 km) in length, can be picked up by following the road over the dam (information board and toilets in the car-park at the far end on the R) and turn L through a gate in the perimeter fence; the walk allows a return to the starting point.

*1 Bench Tor*
Bench Tor is depicted as 'Benjay Tor' on the first edition OS one-inch map of 1809 and an old deed denotes a North and South Bench Tor. Looking down into the valley from the

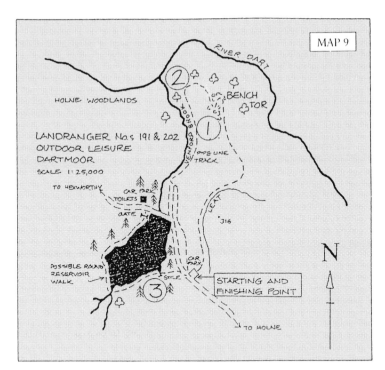

MAP 9

RIVER DART

HOLNE WOODLANDS

BENCH TOR

LANDRANGER No.s 191 & 202
OUTDOOR LEISURE
DARTMOOR

SCALE 1: 25,000

TO HEXWORTHY

CAR PARK
TOILETS

GATE

PIPE LINE
TRACK

VENFORD BROOK

LEAT

·316

POSSIBLE ROUND
RESERVOIR
WALK

STILE

CAR
PARK

STARTING AND
FINISHING POINT

N

TO HOLNE

*Bench Tor and the Double Dart Gorge.*

*A common moorland moss.*

north pile, granite (L) gives way to metamorphic rock (R). Opposite is Mil Tor from where the old local custom, known as the 'Rolling of the Waggon Wheels' took place on Midsummer Day on and off until the 1950s. Here, wheels were sent on their way down to the river some 600 feet (183 m) below. Few ever reached the bottom, being stopped by clitter and trees in Miltor Wood.

The unusually loud noise of the river here is described as being the 'cry of the Dart'.

2 *Holne Woodlands*

The wooded slopes below Bench Tor are part of a Site of Special Scientific Interest, known as Holne Woodlands, which extends for 2557 acres (1035 ha) across both sides of the River Dart Valley and the River Webburn. The whole site is important for its ancient semi-natural oak woodland. On the higher valley slopes the trees become more stunted and scattered and the woodland gives way to open moorland—a mosaic of bracken, heather, bell heather, gorse and moor grasses.

The woodland bird population includes raven, buzzard, great spotted woodpecker, wood warbler and pied flycatcher. The woodland edges are frequented by redstart and, on the adjoining moorland, stonechat and whinchat breed. Far below, dipper and grey wagtail nest alongside the river. The river also provides suitable conditions for the spawning of salmon and trout.

The National Park Authority owns 175 acres (71 ha) of Holne Woods, on the south side of the valley running west from the tor. Up to seventy or so years ago these woods were being commercially managed for charcoal, bark and firewood. That management having stopped, the woods today are predominantly of even-aged oak which is increasingly subject to die-back and windblow and because it is unfenced against grazing livestock on the moor, regeneration is severely hindered. To ensure their survival the National Park Authority explores the most appropriate and acceptable methods of management.

3 *Venford Reservoir*

Venford Reservoir dam, built of Dartmoor granite from quarries nearby and at Merrivale, was completed in 1907. The reservoir was originally constructed to provide water for Paignton which was fast becoming a popular seaside resort. By 1925 this supply proved insufficient and further water had to be piped to the reservoir from the River Swincombe, a distance of 5 miles (8 km); the spillway where this water enters the reservoir can be seen close to the dam.

# 1.7

# PEW TOR AND VIXEN TOR

STARTING AND FINISHING
POINT
Large car-park on the B3357 at the
top of Pork Hill on R 3 miles (5 km)
from Tavistock; 1½ miles (2.5 km)
west of Merrivale (191-531751).
LENGTH
3¼ miles (5 km)
ASCENT
Mostly level walking between
885–1040 ft (270–317 m) above sea
level.

This route offers wide unbroken views over much of south-west Dartmoor, Plymouth Sound and south east Cornwall and of the beautiful wood-and-torscape of the Walkham valley.

## ROUTE DESCRIPTION (Map 10)

Head to the westernmost end of the car-park for the granite plinth which supports a brass-made depiction of the panorama ahead. This structure was erected by the Royal Town Planning Institute to commemorate the seventieth anniversary of the Institute and to contribute to the enjoyment of the countryside. Turn L from the car-park and continue straight on (due south) to pick up a well-defined track which is flanked on the R for a short distance by a series of large boulders. Continue straight over the leat and, where the track passes close to a field boundary wall on the R, bear L along a small path making for the leaning granite cross known as Windy Post, sometimes known as Beckamoor Cross. The faces of this chamfered cross look almost due north and south. Here several trans-Dartmoor packhorse tracks converge which linked the eastern border country towns of Chagford and Ashburton with Tavistock.

Cross over the Grimstone and Sortridge Leat next to where a branch leat leads off by the cross (1). Continue straight on to Feather Tor which rises to 1028 feet (313 m) above sea level. The immense amount of clitter surrounding the tor indicates its primeval dimensions. Continue straight on to Pew Tor (2), a prominent landmark from afar, crossing over the branch leat on the way and keeping this on the L thereafter.

After an exploration of the summit area go left downslope and follow a former cart track keeping a boundary wall on the R and Heckwood Tor above on the L. Pass Heckwood Quarry on the L, noticing a large, dressed granite block; this was shaped for the 1812 Plymouth Breakwater and was abandoned due to a flaw. Vixen Tor comes into view straight ahead.

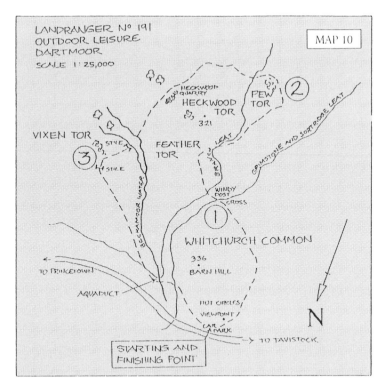

Cross over the Beckamoor Water at the ford and ascend the hill ahead for a stile leading into Vixen Tor Newtake. Go over the stile and go straight on up the hill keeping the rock pile immediately on the R *(3)*. The tor is on private land and permitted access to it has been granted provided that no fires are lit, no one camps here and dogs are not taken into the newtake. From the tor bear L, keeping your back to the Walkham Valley and leave the newtake by way of a stile provided by the National Park Authority in 1987. Continue straight on following Beckamoor Water upstream keeping the combe with its extensive evidence of tin streaming on the L. Go to the top of the gully whereupon a small aqueduct carries the Grimstone and Sortridge Leat over Beckamoor Water. Bear L and go over the lower, north slope of Barn Hill, cross over a leat diversion channel, keeping the main road on the R, and return to the car-park.

### 1 The Grimstone and Sortridge Leat

The Grimstone and Sortridge Leat was built some five centuries ago. Manor houses and farms are the main terminals and there are more delivery points on this leat than on any other on Dartmoor. The leat is taken from the River Walkham below Great Mis Tor and returns to the river 7 miles (11.3 km) further on. Running parallel with the leat,

Previous page: *Pew Tor from Feather Tor.*

Above: *The medieval Windy Post Cross, standing beside a 500-year-old leat.*

from its take-off point to the Windy Post, is a dry leat which is believed to have been cut in the 1870s to serve Tor Quarry. Local commoners objected to the scheme, which was subsequently aborted.

2 *Pew Tor*

Pew Tor stands some 1000 feet (305 m) above sea level. Here nature and man have created a wilderness of granite. On the summit pile are many shallow hollows known as rock basins. There were those, particularly during the first half of the last century, who believed that such phenomena were Druidical Seats of Judgement. Rock basins are, in fact, a natural formation produced by the combined effects of frost, wind and water.

3 *Vixen Tor*

Vixen Tor is a spectacular rock pile of ramparts and bastions overlooking the River Walkham valley. It is the highest tor on Dartmoor from the ground to its top—93 feet (29.3 m) on its south face. Writers in the last century noted that, from the north, this granite outcrop 'resembles the Egyptian Sphynx in a mutilated state'; today, and somewhat more prosaically, moormen see the anthropomorphic northern face as 'an old man who has turned his back on his wife'.

# 2.8

# HAY TOR AND HOUND TOR

STARTING AND FINISHING POINT
Small car-park on east side of Saddle Tor, off the main Bovey Tracey to Widecombe-in-the-Moor road (191-754764). 4 miles (6.4 km) west of Bovey Tracey, 2.5 miles (4 km) east of Widecombe-in-the-Moor.
LENGTH
6¼ miles (10 km)
ASCENT
Two climbs: about 250 yards (229 m), ascent 188 ft (57 m) to the summit of Hay Tor; ⅓ mile (0.5 km), ascent 197 ft (60 m) from Becka Brook on approach to Houndtor deserted settlement site.

The tors on the most eastern moorland block of the National Park dramatically reveal Dartmoor's granite face. The familiar outlines of Haytor Rocks, Saddle Tor and the nearby Rippon Tor can be seen on the skyline from many parts of south and east Devon. Hay Tor attracts many thousands of visitors each year and it and the surrounding Down (1089 acres, 441 ha) have, since 1975, been owned by the National Park Authority.

The Tor and the nearby Low Man offer the best climbing routes on Dartmoor.

## ROUTE DESCRIPTION (Map 11)

Facing Hay Tor, go uphill half L from the back of the car-park in the direction of an immediately visible upright bondstone. Continue over the brow of the hill and here there are several small disused granite quarries. Bear R here along a path which then skirts close to the road and continues up the south side of the brooding Lower Man. Keeping Lower Man to the L, turn L between the two bosses of the Tor *(1)* and then go half R to pick up a clear path leading down to the fenced-in Haytor Quarries. On reaching a track (before a solitary granite post and three weather-battered Scots Pine trees) go L to the workings. Go through a gate on the perimeter fence and turn L to explore the quarry and its ponds *(2)*. Retrace your steps to the gate, then go L following the perimeter fence and spoil down and, at the bottom of the slope, go L to pick up the granite tramway. Stretches of the tramway have suffered from erosion. The National Park Authority has undertaken restoration work in some places; walk parallel to the tramway to help the recovery process. Follow the tramway, passing a set of granite points, until reaching a junction between this branch line and the main line to Holwell Tor. Turn L at the junction and follow the tramway through a shallow cutting and down to its terminal

Following page: *Crane winding gear, Haytor Quarries.*

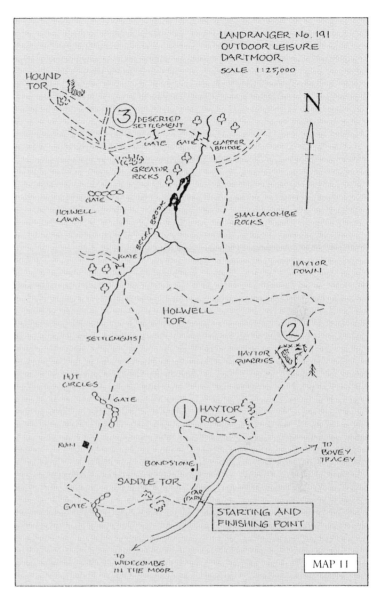

beyond the sheer worked face of Holwell Quarry. Retrace your steps back up the tramway passing a level spoil area on the L, a ruined building on the R and a set of granite points; keep on the L fork, and by the next set of points—near several small rowan trees—take the narrow path on the L which leads to the summit of Smallacombe Rocks. Views here of the Becka Brook valley are outstanding. Continue straight on over the summit and then bear half L on a path which leads to the valley bottom. On the way down this path unites with a public bridlepath (coming in on the R). Continue straight on here (PBS 'to Houndtor'). The path now enters the valley bottom woods where alder, blackthorn, rowan, hawthorn, birch and oak grow in wild profusion and natural confusion.

Cross over the clapper bridge at the Becka Brook and continue straight on up the steep valley side passing through a wooden gate. At the top of the hill Greator Rocks are close by on the L. The path here continues straight on down to the pre-Conquest settlement site of Houndtor *(3)*. From the village go straight on to Hound Tor, a massive tor steeped in superstition and legend. On reaching the summit, go through the central avenue of the tor and then bear half back L. Make for the R side of Greator Rocks, passing through a gap in the low banks of former field boundaries and keeping the settlement site down on the L.

Keeping the tor on the L (although it is well worth a slight detour here to explore these rocks) continue half R following a small path which leads to a wider track to a gateway in the enclosure wall ahead. The gateway carries a small information board and a fingerpost. On reaching the gate, the information board draws attention to the Agreement made between the landowner and the National Park Authority which allows access, along defined paths, through Holwell Lawn. A smaller sign here informs us that 'There may be a bull in this area at certain times. He will be a beef bull, running with cows or heifers, and in these circumstances is considered not to be dangerous.' Having being thus reassured, go through the gate and turn L onto a path waymarked 'Haytor Down'. At the next waymark post turn L downslope, again waymarked 'Haytor Down'. Go through the small wooden gate and follow the path to the R through the trees to the Becka Brook. Cross the infant river and go on up-slope to a path running parallel with the valley. Here, turn R and follow the path through the bracken. After several hundred yards it is necessary to go half L up to the clitter slope, below several outcrops, to avoid very boggy ground; drier ground here through the bracken allows easier passage up the valley. Continue round (L) the clitter slope and, with Rippon Tor in view ahead, make for the enclosure wall. The wall does a slight 'dog leg' to the L and here is a gate with another small access agreement information board. This agreement allows access, again on defined paths, through the Emsworthy enclosures. Go through the gate (waymarked 'Footpath to Common nr Hemsworthy Gate') and continue straight on along the path (waymarked red) passing the tumbled-down walls and field ruins of Emsworthy on the R. Turn L at next path junction (waymarked 'To Saddle Tor') and leave the Emsworthy enclosures via a gate. Continue half L for the summit of Saddle Tor and drop down to the car-park.

Previous page: *Hound Tor.*

Above: *Hound Tor, with Hay Tor in the distance.*

*1 Haytor Down and Haytor Rocks*

Haytor Down and Haytor Rocks, an area of 1089 acres (441 ha) was bought by the Dartmoor National Park Authority (Devon County Council) in 1975 to help protect the area from the consequences of its own popularity. The tor itself has been popular with the people of Devon for over a century and it now attracts many thousands of visitors each year.

*2 Haytor Quarries and Tramroad*

Haytor Granite Tramroad opened on 16 September 1820. Along its 10 mile (16 km) length, the quarried granite, valued as a building stone, was conveyed in horse-drawn trucks to the Stover Canal for subsequent transport. It had a full active life for some 40 years.

*3 Houndtor*

Houndtor deserted settlement today comprises the substantial remains of a cluster of buildings—four dwellings and their ancillary structures—and an outlying farmstead a short distance to the north west. The whole settlement, a Scheduled Ancient Monument, is surrounded by prehistoric enclosures.

# 2.9

# Cox Tor—White Tor—Staple Tors

This walk begins by traversing the dramatic, bench-like slopes of Cox Tor. A prehistoric stone row, standing stone and stone circle and an eighteenth-century suicide's grave add further human dimension to this imposing landscape.

The walk enters the Merrivale Firing Range from White Tor to Roos Tor. Firing times will need to be checked (see pages 311–12).

## Route Description (Maps 12, 13)

From the middle of the car-park cross over the road and head for the summit of Cox Tor *(1)* keeping a spring and wet flush area on the L. At the head of the spring bear half L and begin to zig-zag to the summit. Continue over the crest of the tor passing a prehistoric stone cairn and go straight on. With Higher Godsworthy directly ahead go half L down the slope tacking round the clitter slope to the road. Cross the road and by the corner of a large field go through the gate (PBS). Follow the edge of this field (boundary on the R) and enter another field which contains a large outcrop on the L. Soon the bridlepath divides; take the right fork and follow through the field of rough grazing, until the far north western corner. Here go through the gate, go R and follow the walled track down to Great Combe Tor.

From the tor go half R and follow the boundary wall down to the Colly Brook. At the brook bear L and follow downstream passing a series of small, and several large, waterfalls. At the lowest, largest fall follow the path which leads half L away from the river. Cross over a small leat and pass an artificial pond. Cut down the slope half R and go over the footbridge crossing the Colly Brook. Ignoring the paths to L and R continue straight on up slope and, at the cottage, go L through a gate and follow this track to the lane.

Cross the lane and tack up, half R, to the summit of Smeardon Down. Go R along the crest and pass Boulters Tor

STARTING AND FINISHING
POINT
Large car-park on the B3357 at the top of Pork Hill, 3 miles east of Tavistock; 1½ miles (2.5 km) west of Merrivale (191-531751).
LENGTH
7½ miles (12.25 km)
ASCENT
One climb: ¾ mile (1.2 km), ascent 384 ft (117 m) to Cox Tor summit; and three climbs of ⅓ mile (0.5 km) in length; ascent 382 ft (100 m) to Smeardon Down; 289 ft (88 m) to White Tor; and 112 ft (34 m) to Roos Tor.

*Following page: In Peter Tavy Combe.*

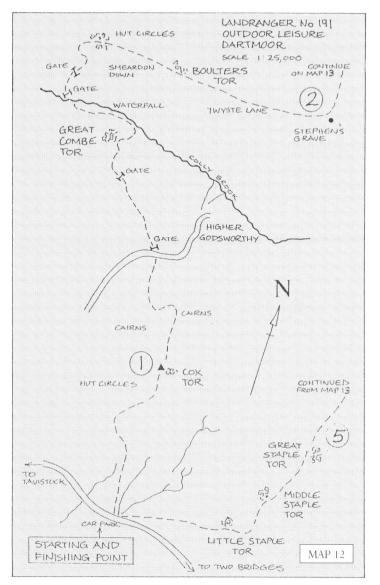

(L), where tor and stone walling appear as one. Continue along the clearly-defined, walled peat track (Twyste Lane) which separates the enclosures ahead. On reaching the open moor continue along the track to Stephen's Grave (R) *(2)*.

At the grave go L and follow the bridlepath keeping stone walls on L. Before the wall bends away half L turn R and go up-slope, passing a prehistoric enclosed settlement and the outcrop of Lower White Tor; then make for White Tor *(3)*, a riot of clitter, crags and the coursing of an Iron Age hill fort. Continue along the summit and head in the same direction to the 'Long Stone' Standing Stone, on Langstone Moor *(4)*. From this menhir follow the stone row to its northern end and retrace

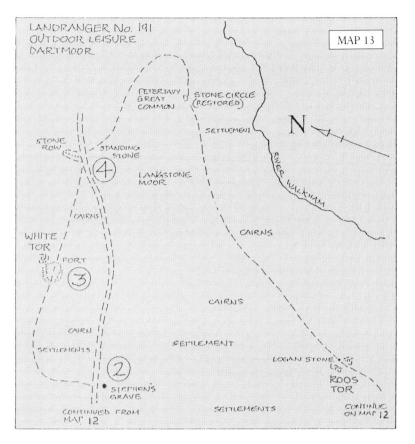

Map showing: LANDRANGER No. 191 / OUTDOOR LEISURE DARTMOOR — MAP 13. Features labelled: PETERTAVY GREAT COMMON, STONE CIRCLE (RESTORED), SETTLEMENT, STONE ROW, STANDING STONE, LANGSTONE MOOR, CAIRNS, WHITE TOR, FORT, CAIRNS, RIVER WALKHAM, CAIRN, SETTLEMENTS, SETTLEMENT, LOGAN STONE, ROOS TOR, STEPHEN'S GRAVE, SETTLEMENTS, CONTINUED FROM MAP 12, CONTINUE ON MAP 12.

your steps back. With your back to the stone row ignore the peat track and go half L along a path skirting Langstone Mire and head for Langstone Moor Stone Circle flanked by Great Mis Tor. From the stone circle, with this tor on the L, continue along the slowly-rising ridge ahead for Roos Tor, keeping the River Walkham down on the L and keeping above a prehistoric settlement group on the valleyside. From Roos Tor, which is surrounded by a ring of bond stones, the torscape of the Walkham Valley is spectacular.

Continue on in the same direction for Great Staple Tor. Rock basins, vast clitter slopes and an avenue between the remnant stacks—this is one of Dartmoor's greatest tors (5). Continue on down to Middle Staple Tor and thence continue straight on keeping to the L of Little Staple Tor for an exploration of the abundant worked stone in this area. Cut right to Little Staple Tor and then continue on downslope towards the road crossing over the extensive tin working gulleys. Follow the road for the return to the car-park.

*1 Cox Tor*

During the Quaternary period, which began some 1.7 million

*Previous page: View west from Boulter's Tor, showing Peter Tavy Church (left) and Mary Tavy Church (right).*

years ago, there have been at least 17 cold phases during which most of the British Isles was affected by the repeated advance and retreat of vast ice sheets. These ice sheets from the north reached Devon only once, but the cliffs of Bideford Bay halted the southern advance of that ice sheet and Dartmoor, therefore, escaped glaciation. However, it has been affected by a variety of cold-climate weathering and erosion processes during these phases, processes which subtly still go on today.

Frost shattering and riving of exposed bedrock, together with the subsequent downslope transfer of material has resulted in marked benches (so-called cryoplanation or antiplanation terraces) on some Dartmoor slopes. Cox Tor reveals a staircase of at least five such terraces, the metamorphic (altered) rocks here being particularly susceptible to this process. Similar forces have been at work on Smeardon Down and White Tor.

2  *Stephen's Grave*

At Stephen's Grave a simple stone is a memorial to John Stephen whose death occurred in October 1762. He was a young man of Peter Tavy who was driven to take his own life by the unfaithfulness of the girl to whom he was betrothed. His ghost was said to haunt the area, which disturbed the inhabitants of Peter Tavy so much that the parson was asked to lay the ghost; this he did on a night when a terrible storm was raging. For many years the stone pillar was leaning and insecure until it was set up on a plinth by the Dartmoor Preservation Association in May 1936.

3  *White Tor*

White Tor is a prehistoric fortified stronghold, dating from the Iron Age, and its siting around a tor is unique. A double line of stone ramparts encircle the tor and in many places, especially on the east side, outcrops of rock are incorporated in them. These ramparts enclose about 1½ acres (0.6 ha). The fort appears to have been a place of refuge in times of danger rather than being permanently occupied. On the south west slope of the tor are two oval shelters and at the west end another; these may have been shepherds' shelters.

4  *The Stones of Langstone Moor*

At the head of Langstone Moor mire is a dispersed collection of prehistoric monuments including a standing stone, a stone row and a stone circle. The menhir, known as the 'Long Stone', stands 9 feet (2.7 m) above the ground and is the southern terminal stone to a ruined stone row—some 110 yards (101 m) long—which was discovered in 1893. A few hundred yards away to the south east is the Langstone Moor

*Approaching Langstone Moor along Twyste Lane.*

Stone Circle. This impressively-sited circle, also known as the 'Ring-of-Stones', was re-erected towards the end of the last century and it then comprised sixteen stones. During World War II the monument was severely damaged by troops training on the moor. Today, only six stones stand to their full height, four are fallen and broken and six are stumps with their heads deliberately knocked off and laying on the ground nearby. The Long Stone too was used for target practice—the marks of gunfire are visible on it. All these monuments are of epidiorite, an altered igneous rock, and not of granite like most Dartmoor prehistoric remains.

5 *Great Staple Tor*

Great Staple Tor consists of remnant stacks on either side of a natural avenue, these piles being described as 'steeples' and likened to the Colossi.

The rocks here assume fantastic shapes and some are precariously poised. 'Staple Tor Tolmen' comprises a pile of four huge granite blocks. Tolmens are stones with holes in them and as such were thought to possess magical properties.

# 4.10

# SHAPLEY COMMON— GRIMSPOUND—HAMEL DOWN—CORNDON TOR —BIRCH TOR

STARTING AND FINISHING POINT
Shapley Common (191-698835).
From Moretonhampstead follow B3212 towards Princetown for just over 4 miles. Pass over cattle grid and turn immediately R into large car-park on the next bend.
LENGTH
16¼ miles (26 km)
ASCENT
Four climbs: 1½ miles (2.4 km), ascent 433 ft (132 m) to Hookney Tor; ⅓ mile (0.5 km), ascent 260 ft (79 m) to Hameldown Tor; 1¼ miles (2.0 km), ascent 636 ft (194 m) to Corndon Tor; 1 mile (1.5 km), ascent 357 ft (109 m) to Birch Tor.

This circular route allows a walk along all of the continuous, north to south running ridge comprising Shapley Common, Hamel Down, Dunstone Down and Bittleford Down—a distance of 5½ miles (8.8 km).

The walk includes four steep climbs and traverses open moorland. It follows, in part, a riverside footpath and a right of way through a conifer plantation. It also includes some 1½ miles (2.5 km) lane and road walking.

## ROUTE DESCRIPTION (Maps 14–17)

From the car-park cross over the road to follow the path rising up over Shapley Common, keeping the stone wall boundaries well to the L. On these lower slopes the route passes three massive prehistoric hut circles. Follow a prehistoric boundary work (a reave) up the slope until it peters out and head for the summit pile of Shapley Tor. Follow a clear path to Hookney Tor (1) crossing straight over a fallen, redundant stone wall.

A once severely eroded path drops down to the huge circular prehistoric settlement of Grimspound situated on the southern slopes of the Grims Lake Valley (2). The combination of horses' hoofs, walkers' boots and rain run-off had created a linear scar running down from the tor. The National Park Authority undertook the extensive, but subtle, restoration work here. Pass through the 'village' of Grimspound and leave the main gateway in the south-east wall for a short but steep climb straight ahead to Hameldown Tor.

The walk continues southwards along the ridge of Hamel Down to Wind Tor, a distance of 3 miles (5 km) and offers views of south-east and west Dartmoor and of south Devon.

Keep the OS Triangulation Point on the tor to the R and go straight on following a wide track which passes the remains of Hamel Down Cross (on R) *(3)* and the summit, prehistoric burial cairns of Broad Barrow, Single Barrow and—keeping Blackaton Down improved enclosure on the R—Two Barrows and Hameldown Beacon *(4)*.

From Hameldown Beacon the path descends to the enclosures of Kingshead and Coombe lying above Widecombe-in-the-Moor *(5)*; keep the wall on the L and continue straight on (fingerpost, 'To Widecombe'). Where the wall eventually bends around and drops down to the L the path divides; go straight on ignoring track waymarked 'To Widecombe'. Cross the lane, which drops down to Widecombe-in-the-Moor, and go straight on over Dunstone Down. Where the track divides bear half R for the small outcrop of Wind Tor. Continue straight on (south) over Bittleford Down and turn half R on approaching field boundaries. Cross over the lane and cut straight over a further area of common until reaching the Jordan and Shallowford Lane. Go R onto the lane and follow to the crossroads where there is a small medieval cross (R); turn L and continue along the lane, passing Drywell (on R), to the hamlet of Jordan.

*Prehistoric hut circle, Shapley Common.*

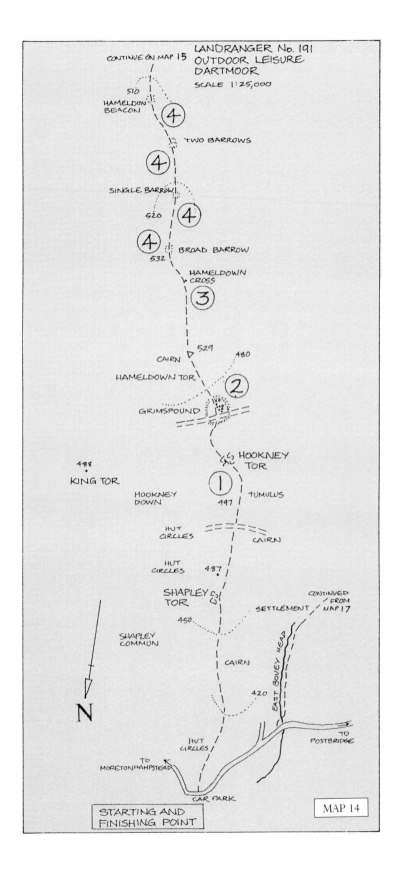

LANDRANGER No. 191
OUTDOOR LEISURE
DARTMOOR
SCALE 1:25,000

CONTINUE ON MAP 15

510
HAMELDON
BEACON
④

TWO BARROWS
④

SINGLE BARROW
520
④

④
532
BROAD BARROW

HAMELDOWN
CROSS
③

CAIRN
529
480
HAMELDOWN TOR
②
GRIMSPOUND

HOOKNEY
TOR

488
KING TOR

①
HOOKNEY
DOWN
447
TUMULUS

HUT
CIRCLES
CAIRN

HUT
CIRCLES
487

SHAPLEY
TOR
SETTLEMENT
CONTINUED
FROM
MAP 17

450

SHAPLEY
COMMON

CAIRN

EAST BOVEY HEAD

420

HUT
CIRCLES
TO
POSTBRIDGE

TO
MORETONHAMPSTEAD
CAR PARK

N

STARTING AND
FINISHING POINT

MAP 14

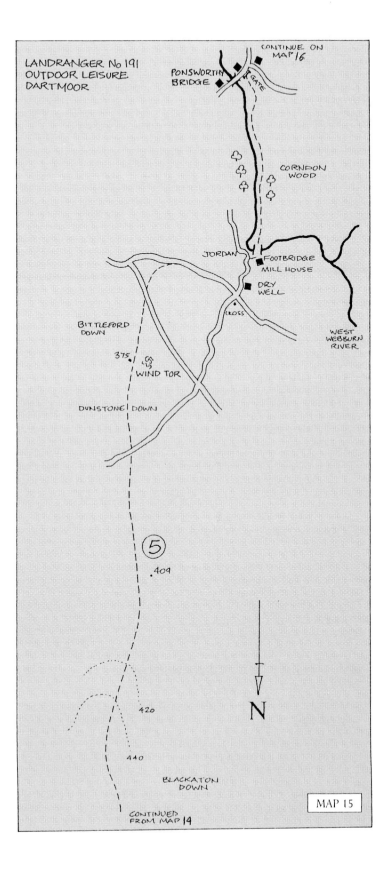

LANDRANGER No 191
OUTDOOR LEISURE
DARTMOOR

CONTINUE ON MAP 16

PONSWORTHY
BRIDGE

GATE

CORNDON
WOOD

JORDAN

FOOTBRIDGE
MILL HOUSE

DRY
WELL

CROSS

BITTLEFORD
DOWN

WEST
WEBBURN
RIVER

375.

WIND TOR

DUNSTONE DOWN

⑤

.409

N

420

440

BLACKATON
DOWN

MAP 15

CONTINUED
FROM MAP 14

At Jordan, ignore a turning on the L, and carry on for a short distance along the lane signposted 'No through road'. At Mill House and Jordan Cottage go left (PFS 'County Road at Ponsworthy ¼ ml'). The footpath goes between the two cottages and over a footbridge which spans the West Webburn River. After the bridge take an obvious path keeping the river to the L. Follow the riverside path, ignoring a wide forestry track on the R which climbs above Corndon Wood. On reaching the end of the footpath at Ponsworthy, go through the gate by the cottage. If you want the village post office and stores (a sign describes it as 'a brandy to boot laces village shop') turn L, cross the ford, and go L again; the shop is on the R just above the road bridge which crosses the river. Otherwise, at the lane go R and walk up the lane to Lock's Gate Cross.

At the crossroads go straight on (highway sign 'Dartmeet and Princetown') taking the path running parallel to the lane on the R side verge. Where the field boundaries end abruptly to the R, follow the path round and ascend Corndon Tor (half L).

From the summit of Corndon Tor are fine views including one of the ancient tenement of Babeny. Pass a prehistoric stone cairn and continue straight on along the crest of the ridge heading for two more massive stone cairns. Go roughly straight on but slightly to the left, crossing several prehistoric reaves and head in line with the distant Fernworthy Forest which edges its way over the furthest horizon. Bear half L when Riddon and Wild Goose settlements come into full view and walk down-slope to reach a well-defined track; turn R and follow to the lane. Go L onto the lane and follow. Continue straight on at Cator Green T junction (highway signed 'Bellever'). After about a further ¼ mile (0.4 km) of lane walking, at the far end of a large beech shelter-belt, go through a gate immediately on the R and keep on the bridlepath across Cator Common heading for Soussons plantation; a PBS confirms the route halfway over this open area.

On reaching an ancient track which leads to Pizwell (on the L) *(6)* go through the gate and cut straight over to the road heading for a large ride within the conifer plantation. On the other side of the road is a small area which escaped coniferization and here is a fine prehistoric cairn circle tucked closely to the plantation perimeter. Retrace your steps to the lane. Go left along the lane past Ephraim's Pinch *(7)* and at the granite gate posts, around the next bend, go half L on a path through a clear-felled pine wood. This leads onto open ground to pick up a track to Soussons Farm, a Forestry Commission holding on a lease from the Duchy of Cornwall which is tenanted out.

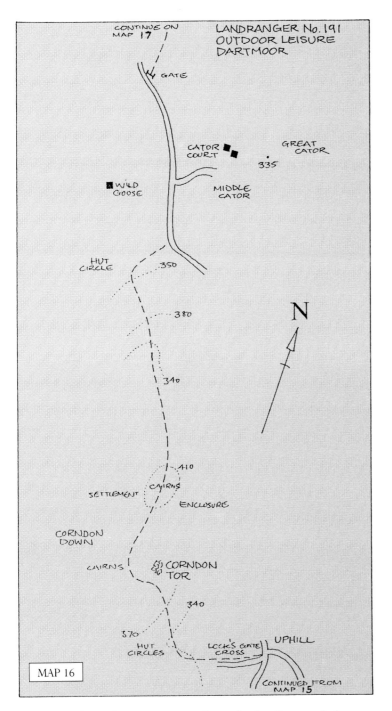

At the farm do not turn R through the farmyard, but go through the gate and turn R (PFS 'Challacombe'). Follow the edge of the field round and follow the fence line up the hill. At the top of the field go through a gate and turn R onto a track running parallel with a stone wall (on R). Cross the stone bridge over the stream and follow the path straight on. At the next gate

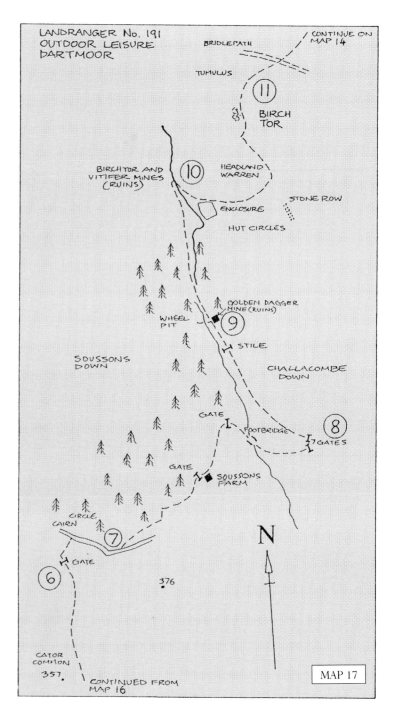

LANDRANGER No. 191
OUTDOOR LEISURE
DARTMOOR

BRIDLEPATH

CONTINUE ON
MAP 14

TUMULUS

(11)

BIRCH
TOR

BIRCH TOR AND
VITIFER MINES
(RUINS)

(10)

HEADLAND
WARREN

STONE ROW

ENCLOSURE

HUT CIRCLES

GOLDEN DAGGER
MINE (RUINS)

WHEEL
PIT

(9)

STILE

SOUSSONS
DOWN

CHALLACOMBE
DOWN

GATE

FOOTBRIDGE

(8)

GATES

GATE

SOUSSONS
FARM

N

CIRCLE
CAIRN

(7)

GATE

(6)

376

CATOR
COMMON

357.

CONTINUED FROM
MAP 16

MAP 17

continue in the same direction (towards Hamel Down ridge) and when Challacombe Farm, a Duchy holding, comes into view go through a gate and turn immediately L to go through another gate to follow a footpath (PFS 'Bennett's B3212 Cross'—as spelt on the OS map) *(8)*. Keeping on this path continue around the lower slopes of the bracken-infested western flank of

Challacombe Down. On reaching the forest edge, go over a stile (PFS) passing the remains of Golden Dagger (tin) Mine *(9)*. After a ruined building on the L, a small overgrown path drops down and crosses the infant river, via a small granite bridge, and leads up to the walled structure of a disused wheel pit—well worth a visit, but take care as it is quite deep. Retrace your steps to the footpath, turn L and head upstream along the valley bottom. Where the path emerges from the forest go straight on and pass the stream-side willows; ignore paths to the L and R. A path-bridlepath junction is soon encountered; continue in the same direction (PBS 'Bennett's Cross B3212') on what can be a muddy stretch. The small fenced-in areas, by the bridlepath, here warn us of disused mining shafts—keep well away. Go through the gate, continue straight on along the bridlepath for about 550 yards (503 m) to reach a relatively broad level area in the valley bottom. Here are the remains of the Birch Tor/Vitifer Tin Mines complex *(10)*. On reaching this level ground a line of telegraph poles cuts the valley bottom. On encountering the first pole on the R, walk 75 yards (64 m) and then follow the track (a bridlepath) leading off on the R uphill. This track runs roughly parallel with the lines of telegraph poles on the L and the wall of an abandoned enclosure on the R for a short distance.

Where the bridlepath levels out continue in the same direction until the prehistoric triple stone row on Challacombe Down ridge is immediately on the R. Here, turn L to leave the bridlepath and follow a small path weaving its way through bracken and heather and bilberry to Birch Tor *(11)*. From this granite pile much of the walk so far accomplished comes into view. Continue straight on along the path over the summit passing a cairn and a small granite warren bondstone on the L. At the west–east running bridlepath go R and follow until reaching another warren bondstone on the R, next to some tinners' trial pits and gullies. Leave the bridlepath here, turning half L (the orientation of a trial gully working here gives the direction needed; there is no path to follow across the down). With the Widecombe-in-the-Moor to Challacombe Lane in view go to East Bovey Head to encounter the source of the river. A walk in summer here to reach the combe floor will mean some bracken-wading. Keep the infant river to the R and follow the left bank downstream. On reaching the Moretonhampstead to Postbridge road cross over the river by the road bridge to avoid boggy ground. Continue along the left verge of the main road to return to the car-park.

*1 Hookney Tor*

The 360-degrees view from the Hookney Tor is magnificent. A 20-mile (32-km) north to south span of Dartmoor includes

Brent Hill, Ryder's Hill, Caters Beam and Eylesbarrow on the southern moors and the lofty skyline of Cut Hill, Whitehorse Hill, Hangingstone Hill, High Willhays, Yes Tor, and the smooth-domed skyline of Cosdon Hill, to the north west. Due north the Exmoor range can be seen on the distant horizon. Shallow leats have been cut by tinners on the tor's southern flank to collect hillside drainage and stream flow from Grims Lake; this water was conducted to the huge gerts of Headland Mine for washing out lodes.

2 *Grimspound*

Grimspound is probably the best known collection of prehistoric hut circles—24 in all—on Dartmoor and lies 1530 feet (470 m) above sea level. Some believed this four-acre (1.6 ha) site to be a temple of the sun, others a fortified settlement. Despite its massive enclosing wall, clearly the village's position on the slopes of a hill flanked by tors was not defensive.

The surviving remains of this village have been altered by subsequent peoples. For example, the vast perimeter wall, now about nine feet (2.5 m) in width, has been restored as regards its height in the recent past and what appears to be an entrance on the lower, west side, is the result of generations of tinners and moormen and, for the last hundred years, visitors, passing through.

3 *Hamel Down Cross*

The rudely-fashioned Hamel Down Cross bears on its east face:

HC
DS
1854

This inscription refers to the name of the cross and the Duke of Somerset. At that time the Duke owned Natsworthy Manor in the East Webburn valley and it was he who had the ancient cross adapted as a manor boundstone. Further on along the ridge more 'DS stones' were set up including one on each of the four barrows to the south of the cross.

4 *Hamel Down and the Beacon*

Around 2000 BC stone rows and small cairns appear to have been succeeded by the large cairns and barrows which can be striking features of the Dartmoor skyline. These were burial mounds of the more important families, some of whom were buried with copper or bronze weapons. On Hamel Down, at about 1735 feet (529 m) above sea level, is a cemetery consisting of four sizeable barrows.

In a mid-sixteenth-century document specifying the

Opposite: *A small wood near Ephraim's Pinch.*

Following page: *Headland Warren and Birch Tor.*

Natsworthy Manor bounds, Hameldon Beacon appears as 'Fyerbicken'. Tradition records that this signal hill was fired when the Armada was sighted in the English Channel.

5 *Widecombe-in-the-Moor*
Widecombe-in-the-Moor lies within the sweeping vale of the East Webburn River. To the west of the village the ridge of Hamel Down separates this valley from that of the West Webburn. St. Pancras Church, known as 'the cathedral of the moor', was built in the fourteenth century on the site of an earlier church and then was enlarged and the 120-foot (36.6-m) tower added in the fifteenth or early sixteenth century. The magnificence of the tower is attributed to the financial support of tin miners who exploited all the surrounding valleys for the rich ore.

6 *Pizwell*
Pizwell was first documented as a tenement cluster of three farms in 1260. Previous to this date it is known that families living here had to use the parish church at Lydford on west Dartmoor until dispensation was granted, by Bishop Bronescombe, to use the church at Widecombe-in-the-Moor—a distance of 3½ miles (5.6 km), being considerably shorter than the distance to Lydford. The route to Widecombe became established as one of the many church paths on Dartmoor.

7 *Ephraim's Pinch*
Ephraim's Pinch is reputed to be so-called after a man named Ephraim who laid a wager that he could carry a sack of corn from Widecombe-in-the-Moor to Postbridge, a distance of 5 miles (8 km), without dropping it. After 3½ miles (5.6 km) he reached this spot and he found the *pinch* too much for him and threw his burden on the ground thus losing his bet.

*Challacombe Farm*
A shrinkage of the medieval hamlet here has occurred either because of the Black Death or because of climatic deterioration. The hamlet once had at least seven dwellings but is now occupied by a farmhouse and two cottages.

The slopes of Challacombe Down are infested with bracken. Bracken is believed to have spread in recent years on a wide scale not just on Dartmoor but throughout the world. It is known to be carcinogenic to cattle, and possibly to man, and is ecologically poorer than the moorland plant communities it takes over; it also looks at its best when dead. The Duchy of Cornwall, with the co-operation of its tenant farmer at Challacombe and the National Park Authority are undertaking an extensive and detailed series of bracken control experiments.

9 *Golden Dagger Mine*

The last tin mine to work on Dartmoor was at Golden Dagger. Underground work had stopped at the time of the First World War, but exploitation of the waste heaps left by earlier generations of tinners continued until 12 November 1930 when the firm operating at that time closed the mine.

The mine almost certainly had a medieval origin but the first record of the name 'Golden Dagger' dates from 1851.

Along the path through the plantation there are remains of old buildings, a wheelpit, leat systems and three circular buddles where crushed tin ore was concentrated. On the opposite side of the (Redwater Brook) valley another wheelpit can be seen; this, together with the remains of the Mine Captain's House, was consolidated by the National Park Authority in March 1982 to prevent further deterioration. Not all the shafts have been filled in so do not venture off the paths.

10 *Birch Tor tin workings*

Some of the most extensive tin working activity on Dartmoor took place in the Birch Tor area. Here are the waste heaps of alluvial workings, or streamworks, in the valleys and the vast man-made gullies where lode ore was exploited by open cast workings and later by shaft mining. Two separate mines, Birch Tor and Vitifer existed here but for most of their working lives from 1858 they operated as one. Some of the open cast workings are probably medieval in origin and deep shafts were sunk in the bottom in the eighteenth and nineteenth centuries. The first record of a mine here dates to 1750. The foundations of the mine carpenter's shop, blacksmith's shop, the 'Miner's House'—where workers could stay for a week in dormitories—the Mine Captain's House and several cottages still survive. The remains of wheelpits and dressing floors containing the foundations of buddles can also be seen.

11 *Birch Tor*

Birch Tor itself stands 1598 feet (487 m) above sea level. Below the tor are four enclosures known as 'Jan Reynolds' Cards' or the 'Aces'. In the southernmost, the miners grew vegetables and in others the warreners of Headland Warren grew furze as food for rabbits. Legend has it that Jan Reynolds was carried off by the Devil for playing cards in Widecombe Church and dropped the four aces as he was taken over Birch Tor. From the tor several warren boundstones bearing the letters 'WB' will be encountered.

# WALKS IN THE EXMOOR NATIONAL PARK

*Allerford Bridge*

# 1.11

# A Circuit of Dunster Park

STARTING AND FINISHING
POINT
Car-park on south side of Dunster
Castle near Gallox Bridge (181-
990433).
LENGTH
3 miles (4.8 km)
ASCENT
700 ft (213 m)

A pleasant walk on the edge of Exmoor's most attractive small town through woods and a one-time deer park belonging to Dunster Castle. Deer may still be seen, but they are no longer confined to the park. There are fine views of the Castle, and the walk passes through two prehistoric earthworks.

## Route Description (Map 18)

Leave the car-park on the south side of Dunster Castle, and take the short footpath going downhill to the ancient crossing of the small river Avill known as Gallox Bridge *(1)*. Cross the bridge and walk past a thatched cottage to Park Gate, a junction of several tracks.

Take the track signposted 'Timberscombe 3, Luxborough 5 via Croydon Hill'. This is a broad, gently-rising track through mixed woodland and is waymarked yellow and blue. Where the track levels out, ignore a gated path L. The route to follow is straight ahead and is waymarked. Take the L track at a fork. This rises further and bears L and is the Old Coach Road *(2)*. At a sharp bend to the L, leave the track for a viewpoint a short distance to the R *(3)*.

Return to the track and continue along it. About 150 yds (137 m) further on, turn acutely L up a climbing path, and 5 yds (4.5 m) before reaching a gate and stile pass through a hedge gap R and climb steeply up a path through young trees. The path reaches open moorland where there is much bracken. To the R of the path are the earthworks of a prehistoric enclosure *(4)*.

Carry on along this airy ridge path, descend to a saddle and climb beyond to Bat's Castle *(5)*. Pass through this earthwork and go down the other side on a broad grassy track towards a larch plantation. About 150 yds (137 m) into the plantation, at its far end, there is a path junction. Pass through a gate called Withycombe Hill Gate and turn L, ignoring a signpost before the gate reading 'Dunster'.

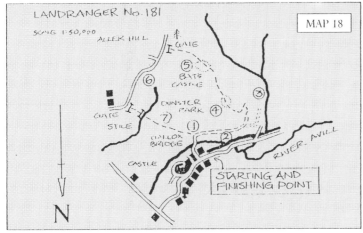

*Bridge over the River Avill, looking towards Dunster deer park.*

Follow this rough track downhill. The beech hedge on your L is known as the King's Hedge *(6)*. After nearly 1 mile (1.6 km) of walking down this track with the ancient wall on your L, where the track bends sharply R, turn L through a gate at a signpost reading 'Public Path Dunster'.

*Dunster Castle stables.*

The way is obvious across several fields through rolling parkland. This is the most recognizable section of the old deer park *(7)*. The outward leg of the route is eventually met, where you should turn R past the thatched cottages for Gallox Bridge and the start of the walk.

*1  Gallox Bridge*

A two-arched packhorse bridge once called Doddebridge. Carts used the ford. 'Gallox' means gallows, and there may have been a gallows nearby, or it could have been sited on the top of Gallox Hill, or both! Look for the smart little dipper flitting from stone to stone in the river.

*2  The Old Coach Road*

This was begun as a gently-graded carriage-way by Mr George Luttrell in the last century, and was meant to run from Dunster Castle to the Luxborough road, but funds ran out, and construction stopped at the viewpoint.

*3  The viewpoint*

The viewpoint at Black Ball is a delightful area of heather and scattered Scots' pine. Views extend up the Avill valley to Wootton Courtenay and Dunkery Beacon.

*4  Gallox Hill earthwork*

A small enclosure of less than 1 acre probably dating to Iron Age times, say 2,000 years ago. This is a good place for whortleberries in early September.

*5  Bat's Castle*

The origin of the name is not known, but its age is probably similar to its neighbour on Gallox Hill. It may have been refortified in the Civil War.

*6  King's Hedge*

The origin of the name is not known. Some authorities say it marked the boundary between the Royalists and the Parliamentarians in the Civil War. There are place names on Dartmoor known as the King Way, the King Wall and King's Gutter.

*7  Dunster Deer Park*

In medieval times deer were kept to the north-east of Dunster, but in 1755 Henry Fownes Luttrell emparked 348 acres to the south of the Castle. The purpose was what we would now term 'amenity', and the animals were culled and eaten. There are some fine old oaks still to be seen, and the views of Dunster Castle from this angle show it to its best advantage.

# 1.12

# DICKY'S PATH AND DUNKERY BEACON

STARTING AND FINISHING
POINT
Webber's Post car-park (181-
903438).
LENGTH
6 miles (9½ km)
ASCENT
1000 ft (303 m)

An open moor walk in two parts. Most of the first half uses Dicky's Path which passes along the northern slopes of Dunkery Beacon just above the tree line. The second half traces the high ridge of the Rowbarrows, Dunkery Beacon, Kit Barrows and Joaney and Robin How. As this is a high-level walk a day of good visibility is recommended. This walk is entirely on land owned by the National Trust as part of the Holnicote (pronounced 'Hunnicut') Estate *(1)*.

## ROUTE DESCRIPTION (Map 19)

From the informal National Trust car-park at Webber's Post *(2)*, walk uphill beside the Dunkery Beacon road—the more easterly of the two minor roads which converge here—to a point 100 yards (91 m) beyond the double bend where on the R (west) of the road is a PFS marked 'Dicky's Path to Stoke Pero' *(3)*.

This delectable route undulates beguilingly westwards across the northern skirts of the Dunkery massif, and is well marked and used, so yard by yard route instructions are unnecessary. In one's progress from east to west the minor valleys of Hollow Combe, Aller Combe, Sweetworthy Combe and Bagley Combe are encountered, each with their own little stream. Between Aller Combe and Sweetworthy Combe the walker will come across two fenced-off ancient monuments, and there is another beyond the beech hedge on the lower side *(4)*.

This is a good walk to observe birds as the path is constantly entering woods and leaving them for more open country. The habitats are therefore frequently changing *(5)*. Views to the north across the rolling tree-clad hills towards the Bristol Channel are best seen in late October or early November when the leaves are turning.

Immediately after crossing the small stream which flows down Bagley Combe—the fourth small valley since leaving the

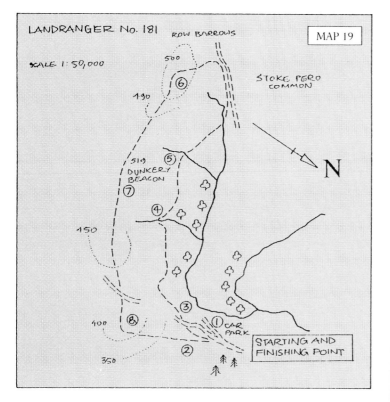

road—turn up a path L by a single Scots pine tree, and walk slanting uphill towards the road. When nearly at the road follow it up parallel with it and to the east. Where the path meets a National Trust informal pull-in beside a bend in the road, take the broad track heading south-east to the summit of Rowbarrows *(6)*. From here a broad path leads due east to Dunkery Beacon exactly 1 mile (1.6 km) away *(7)*. Now walk slightly north of east to the twin cairns of Kit Barrows, the next high ground further on, and from here descend to the road and continue north-east to the prominent cairn-bearing spur of Robin How and Joaney How *(8)*.

Walk north, downhill, for 50 yards (45 m) or so, and Webber's Post with its scattering of cars becomes visible due north and in line with Porlock.

1 *The Holnicote Estate*
   The 12,420 acres (5,030 hectares) of the Holnicote Estate were given to the National Trust in 1944 by Sir Richard Acland, and extend from the sea to well south and west of Dunkery Beacon.

2 *Webber's Post*
   A kind of breathing space on the steep road up from Horner and Luccombe where it divides. One branch twists its way to

Previous page: *Sweetworthy Combe.*

*Dunkery Beacon, Exmoor's highest point.*

Cloutsham and Stoke Pero and the other climbs to the shoulder of Dunkery Beacon. The place is named after Tom Webber, a well-known staghunter in the last century.

3 *Dicky's Path*
This may have been named on Sir Richard Acland's 21st birthday in 1927, but is likely to be much older. It was the custom of the Acland family to name walks and rides after people, animals and events.

4 *Settlement sites*
The Sweetworthy settlement sites are little understood. No excavation has been carried out, but it is presumed they belong to the Iron Age.

5 *Bird life*
Some of the birds seen along here are the green woodpecker, redstart, stonechat, buzzard and kestrel.

6 *Rowbarrows*
Exmoor's second highest point (after Dunkery Beacon) at 1674 feet (510 m). Several large Bronze Age cairns survive. The track along this watershed is probably an ancient one.

7 *Dunkery Beacon*
Exmoor's highest point at 1704 feet (520 m). A toposcope provided by the AA indicates the chief places seen on a clear day. The suffix 'Beacon' points to its use in early times as a fire signal station.

8 *Robin How and Joaney How*
'How' is Norse for a barrow, and there are actually three close together, and others on the hill slope. Robin and Joaney seem to be nineteenth-century names.

# 2.13

# SELWORTHY AND HURLSTONE POINT

**STARTING AND FINISHING POINT**
Selworthy church car-park (181-920467).
**LENGTH**
6½ miles (10.4 km)
**ASCENT**
1500 ft (457 m)

A walk through unusual woods to the rugged promontory of Hurlstone Point, returning over the breezy eminence of Selworthy Beacon and past the Iron Age hill fort of Bury Castle.

## ROUTE DESCRIPTION (Map 20)

Leave the car-park and enter Selworthy Green *(1)* to the west of the church. Go down the path, and 5 yards (4.5 m) past the National Trust shop and information office turn R over a small stone footbridge signposted 'Bossington Hurlstone' into woods. After 20 yards (18 m) turn L over a stile and bear L ignoring a path going up R. After 250 yards (228.5 m) ignore a path going down to the L. A further 150 yards (137 m) on a cross path is met, but the correct route is to continue contouring. The path now runs along the edge of woods at the top of several fields, and a good view opens up to the south.

At a fork Catherine's Well (or Katherine's Well) appears on the R *(2)*. Bear L, still keeping along the top of fields. At Holnicote Combe, continue to contour, ignoring paths up and down to R and L, and the way is now along a broad track. At the next signposted cross path continue to contour following the 'Bossington' PFS.

When you reach a timber-loading area, take the lower of three facing tracks signposted 'Agnes Fountain Bossington'. This is Allerford Combe. Arriving at Agnes Fountain *(3)* one finds six paths meet at this spot, and there is a seat. Take the centre path heading north signposted 'Hurlstone Point Lower Path'. From here on the route will pass through extensive groves of ilex trees *(4)*. A path comes up from the L to join our track, and 100 yards (91 m) further on a path descending on the L can be ignored. At Lynch Combe the route goes through a gate and crosses an up and down path. Carry on through another gate signposted 'Hurlstone Point'. There are more ilex here. Yet another gate is entered in Church Combe, and there is a good example of

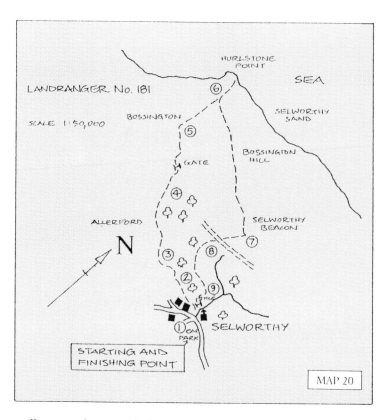

walling on the L, and the woods are left behind. A path goes down L to Bossington.

A good view is now seen *(5)*. As the route bears round to the R the view changes, and some scree slopes will be noticed. The foot of Hurlstone Combe is crossed—our return route—and a path is met coming up from the beach. A narrow path climbs to the rocky tip of Hurlstone Point where there is a coastguard lookout *(6)*. Once round the corner the path degenerates, so walkers are recommended to return when they have had a look. Landslips sweep the area and smooth grassy slopes at 45° make for dangerous walking.

Retrace your steps to the foot of Hurlstone Combe and walk up this dry valley. This is a long slog, but is not excessively steep. At the top, continue up the spur ignoring paths to the L and R and following the signpost 'Coast Path Minehead'. After 200 yards (182.8 m) a wartime track is met and this should be followed. A cairn is seen on Bossington Hill to the R. 30 yards (27.4 m) beyond a PFS pointing R and saying 'Lynch Combe' bear L at a fork. Here Selworthy Beacon comes into view ahead, and should be aimed for. There are fields on your L. At the summit of Selworthy Beacon *(7)* the view should be appreciated before leaving this elevated spot.

Descend by the track which approaches the summit at 45° to

*Allerford Bridge.*

the south from our own approach from the west. This track leads to an open glade of pine trees. The earthworks of Bury Castle—soon to be visited—are visible to the left at the edge of open land. The stone memorial hut *(8)* near the road should be seen, then the path through the trees followed by Bury Castle *(9)*. This earthwork bears a sign 'Bury Castle Iron Age Fort', and from this notice a path descends steeply, enters woods, and zigzags over a stile and down through the woods. Turn L at the main path and walk steeply down to a five-bar gate and a footbridge over a stream. 5 yards (4.5 m) beyond, climb the stile beside the stream. Recross it, and 10 yards (9 m) beyond you rejoin the outward path. Recross the stream for the last time and you are on Selworthy Green.

*1 Selworthy church and Green*

The white-walled church, so boldly placed on the south-facing hillside, is a landmark from many viewpoints. Conversely, the panorama from the church steps is unsurpassed in Somerset. Within, the features to look for are the window tracery, the richly-decorated wagon roof in the south aisle, carved bench ends, and fifteenth-century pulpit with sounding board and hour glass.

The thatched cottages round Selworthy Green were built

in 1828 to accommodate estate pensioners who were kitted out in red cloaks. The inspiration for the contrived appearance of cottages round a green was Blaise Hamlet, on the outskirts of Bristol, also now in the care of the National Trust. One of the cottages is now a small National Trust shop and another serves teas in the summer. There are lavatories at the foot of the Green.

2 *Katherine's Well*

A natural spring probably named after St Katherine or St Catherine, and thought to have special properties.

3 *Agnes Fountain*

Like Katherine's Well, a spring, probably named after St Agnes.

4 *Ilex trees*

The extensive groves of evergreen oak (*Quercus ilex*) were originally planted in 1815. It is unusual to find so many together. The ground beneath, being so shaded by year-round heavy green leaves, is devoid of weed growth.

5 *The view*

The low-lying land is the highly fertile Vale of Porlock. Porlock Weir is at the far end and beyond are the wooded slopes of Culbone and Glenthorne trailing off to the Foreland in the distance. Porlock is to the L and the round chimneys of Bossington can be seen below.

Left: *A prehistoric cairn (right) on the summit of Selworthy Beacon.*

Above: *Bury Castle.*

6 *Hurlstone Point*

This rugged promontory has also been called Hurststone, Hustone and Huntstone Point. The coastguard lookout has been boldly embellished with the stone walls and small turrets of a castle.

7 *Selworthy Beacon*

At 1012 feet (308 m) the highest point on this detached piece of Exmoor. Like Dunkery Beacon, it was used as a fire signal station in times of emergency during medieval times.

8 *Stone memorial hut*

Sometimes known as the 'wind and weather hut', this is a memorial to the 10th Baronet, Sir Thomas Dyke Acland (1787–1871). He was fond of walking this way on Sundays, and some of the quotations with which he entertained his family are inscribed in the hut.

9 *Bury Castle*

An Iron Age earthwork where defences employed the tip of a spur above Selworthy.

# Walks in
# the Lake District
# National Park

*Church Beck, Coppermine Valley*

# 1.14

# ALCOCK TARN

STARTING AND FINISHING
POINT
Grasmere village. Park at the NPA car
park in Broadgate (SE-337077).
LENGTH
3½ miles (5.6 km)
ASCENT
990 feet (300 m)

No one could possibly claim that Alcock Tarn is the most beautiful stretch of water in the Lake District; nor is it the largest or the most spectacularly sited. For reasons such as these, this route is neglected by many who walk the fells around Grasmere. This is a shame, for as you continue a little beyond the tarn onto Butter Crag, you have a splendid panorama of the head of Grasmere valley.

## ROUTE DESCRIPTION (Map 21)

Directly opposite the car park entrance, there is a wooden footbridge which crosses the River Rothay (PFS 'riverside path'). Cross the bridge and follow the broad footpath along a field boundary, winding around behind the houses. At a point where the footpath is intersected by a wide track, continue straight across (following the 'riverside path' sign again) and you will find yourself walking along the riverbank. Follow the path around the fields until you emerge onto the road beside St Oswald's Church *(1)*.

Turn L and go through the churchyard. Once back on the road, turn L again and follow the road back towards the A591. At the junction, go straight across and along a narrow lane directly in front of you. This takes you into Town End; after a few yards you cannot fail to notice that you are passing Dove Cottage on your left *(2)*.

Continue uphill, past the houses and keep a close eye on the stone wall on your L; as it ends, notice the large, flat-topped boulder *(3)*. Follow the road past the small pond until you come to the junction at How Top Farm. Turn L and follow the road for 100 yards (91 m) until you come to a bench and a path off to your L (PFS 'Alcock Tarn'). Turn L and follow the path uphill and into the trees. Shortly past a gateway for Wood Close, on your L, the path forks; keep R, past a National Trust sign for 'Brackenfell'. The path becomes steep and rough. You climb up to a kissing gate. Go through and keep to the path bearing along the stone wall on your L. You begin to ascend between two

*Looking towards Grasmere during the ascent to Alcock Tarn*

stone walls and eventually reach a point at which there is a small metal gate on either side of you. Do not go through either of them, but if you look to your L you get an excellent view of Helm Crag. Keep climbing and as the path flattens out towards Grey Crag look out for a metal gate in the wall on your L. Cross via the stile alongside and follow the path across a beck to Alcock Tarn.

Not the most spectacular tarn that Lakeland has to offer—in fact, it is part-artificial. Tucked away behind Grey Crag it is isolated from the views in a secluded fold in the fellside. Follow the footpath past the tarn and cross the stile at the far end. The path continues directly ahead, skirting an area of bog and running alongside a stone wall on your L. As you leave the wall and pass a large cairn you can see Greenhead Gill ahead of you. A few yards farther on you come out onto a rocky outcrop at Butter Crag and a glorious view of Grasmere valley. The panorama hits you unexpectedly and makes the steep climb to Alcock Tarn worthwhile. From this point you can see well up into Easedale (though not the tarn itself, unfortunately) and beyond that to Sergeant Man, Great Gable and the Scafell range.

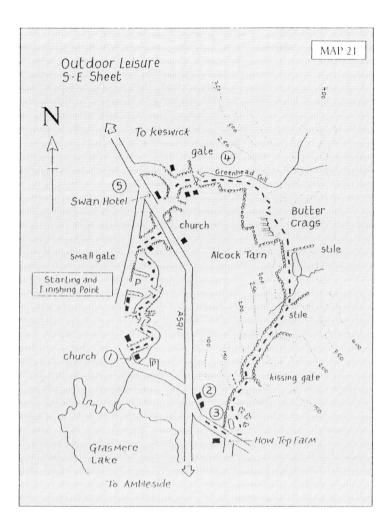

Outdoor Leisure
5-E Sheet

N

To Keswick

MAP 21

gate (4)

Greenhead Gill

(5)

Swan Hotel

church

Butter Crags

small gate

Alcock Tarn

stile

Starting and Finishing Point

P

stile

church (1)

P

kissing gate

(2)

(3)

How Top Farm

Grasmere Lake

To Ambleside

When you are ready, continue past the crags, bearing slightly to the L and descending steeply in a series of broad zigzags. Disregard the occasional sheep track which comes in from the side. The path drops very quickly to the gill, arriving at a stone wall on your L. Follow the wall down to the gill *(4)* and then turn L and follow the beck downhill. After 200 yards (182 m) you will reach a footbridge. Cross the beck and go through the farm gate in the wall on your L. This brings you onto a rough track which you should follow downhill until you emerge onto a peaceful minor road. Turn L and follow the lane until you meet the A591, arriving next to the Swan Hotel *(5)*.

Turn L along the road for 100 yards (91 m) until you come to Our Lady of the Wayside Church. Cross the road at this point and in the wall on the other side you will find a clearly defined footpath, running between two fields (signed: Pedestrians only).

*Grasmere village and Helm Crag from Butter Crag*

Go down the path and follow it across the fields to the village. You come back onto Broadgate; turn L and follow the road until you path the Rothay Garden Hotel on your L. Then turn L, through a small wooden gate and follow the path around the park to rejoin the river. Turn R along the bank and the path takes you straight back into the car park.

1 *St Oswald's Church*

Grasmere Church dates back to the thirteenth century and is today most famous as the resting place of William Wordsworth. Inside the church itself there is a memorial to the poet, but it is the grave—in the north-east corner of the little churchyard—which attracts the crowds. He lies here with his sister, Dorothy, wife, Mary, and other members of his family. Alongside is the grave of Hartley, son of Samuel Taylor Coleridge.

St Oswald's remains one of the few churches in the Lake District to conduct an annual rushbearing service. This ancient ceremony commemorates the day when the old rushes were removed and the church floor strewn with new. Today, the ceremony is enacted by a small procession of children from the village; the girls wear crowns of flowers and the boys carry crosses made from rushes.

Rushbearing ceremonies can also be seen at Ambleside, Urswick, Musgrave and Warcop—always between late June and early August. In addition to Grasmere, the Warcop rushbearing is particularly worth trying to see.

2 *Dove Cottage*

Dove Cottage was originally built as an inn, the *Dove and Olive Branch*, sometime around the early seventeenth century. In 1799, it became the home of William and Dorothy Wordsworth, who rented it from a local farmer for £5 a year (plus an additional 7 shillings annual window tax, which one wag of the period described as daylight robbery). William married in 1802 and had three children at the cottage. His wife's sister, Sarah Hutchinson, also lived with the family and, by 1808 the house was becoming rather crowded. They moved across the valley to a newly-built house called Allan Bank.

The early, day-to-day life of the Wordsworths, with its simple philosophy of 'plain living and high thinking', was recorded by Dorothy in her journal. The poetry William produced whilst living here includes some of his best and most well-loved work.

The house was first opened to the public in 1899, having been bought by the Dove Cottage Trust, which still maintains it to this day. It has been furnished with much of William's original furniture and visitors receive a guided tour of the house and grounds. On a quiet morning, before the crowds arrive, it is sometimes possible to wander around by yourself and get a sense of what it must have been like in Wordsworth's time.

Next door to the cottage there is a modern museum which, in addition to telling the story of Wordsworth's life and work, features a number of special exhibitions throughout the year, related either to the area or the period in which Wordsworth lived. The Trust also runs a bookshop and a restaurant.

3 *The Coffin Stone*

This flat-topped boulder, just above Town End, stands on the old coffin track to Rydal. The dead were brought along this route on their way to Rydal church, Grasmere at that time having no churchyard of its own. The bearers would rest their load on this stone before continuing along the track; hence its name—Coffin Stone.

4 *Greenhead Gill*

Greenhead Gill was the setting of one of Wordsworth's best-known poems, *Michael*. Written whilst the poet lived at Dove Cottage, it sets Wordsworth's ideals of the nobility of the statesman farmer against the worldliness of the city-dweller. It tells the tale of a shepherd's son leaving the valley for the city, to redeem his father's estate.

5 *The Swan Hotel*

Originally the Swan Inn, this establishment had its part to play in the life of Wordsworth. It was during a visit to Wordsworth, in 1805, that the poet and novelist, Walter Scott grew into the habit of frequenting the Swan Inn for breakfast. Objecting to the monotonous diet of porridge at Dove Cottage, he used to sneak out of his bedroom window, whilst the rest of the household thought he was still asleep, and repair to the Swan for something more substantial.

# 1.15

# CAT BELLS

---

Cat Bells—the delightful name derives from the wild cats which once roamed this district. This prominent, hump-backed ridge to the west of Derwent Water must be one of the most popular routes in the Keswick area. The views are splendid and the stiff climb onto the ridge gives you a fine sense of accomplishment. For the complete experience, catch one of the Keswick launches to Hawes End in order to begin the walk. The return route brings you back to the jetty through a delightful National Trust woodland on the shore of Derwent Water.

## ROUTE DESCRIPTION (Map 22)

Disembark at Hawes End onto a rickety, wooden landing stage. Walk straight up the beach and into the trees to join a footpath. Turn R, to cross a footbridge then R again at the fork in the path. This brings you to a kissing gate. Go through onto a cart-track and turn R for a few yards, then L and through another kissing gate, into a small conifer wood. By now your ears should have recovered from the racket of the launch trip. The path climbs though the wood to join the Portinscale road.

Follow the road uphill, over the cattle grid, until you come to a junction. Turn L (signed: 'Grange $2\frac{1}{2}$') and follow the road for 100 yards (91 m) until you come to a footpath on your R. Leave the road and start to climb the side of Cat Bells. Follow any diversion signs you may encounter if footpath maintenance work is in progress.

The path zigzags uphill very steeply but after a short distance you begin to get a good view over the lake. This provides you with an excellent excuse to stop now and then to catch your breath. The footpath becomes rough and loose in places as it climbs sharply towards the top. Just below the summit you scramble up a rocky outcrop; look out for a slate plaque mounted in the rock (1).

Once you have attained the summit, you have a superb panorama of Newlands Valley and the northern fells. The route along the ridge is obvious.

*Opposite Derwent Water and Skiddaw from Cat Bells (note erosion—this is a very popular route)*

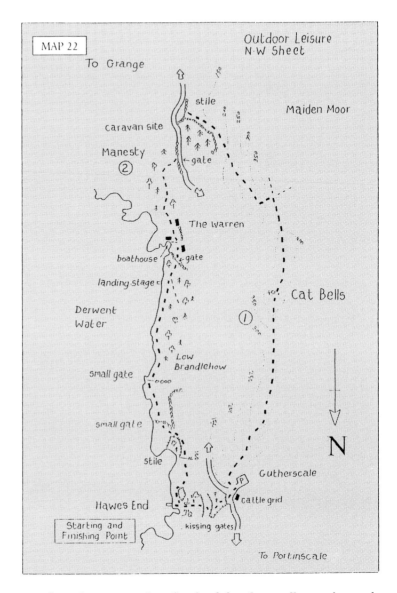

After almost a mile of splendid ridge walking, the path descends to a wide, flat area with Maiden Moor looming ahead. At the junction of tracks, turn L and begin a steep descent down a series of step-like terraces. The path is well-laid and follows a broad zigzag pattern until it begins to level off as you draw close to a group of larches. Ignoring any incoming paths, follow the track down to a stile in a stone wall. From this point you have an excellent view of the Jaws of Borrowdale.

Cross the stile and join the road. Turn L and follow the road, past Low Manesty caravan site, until you come to a farm gate in the wall on your R (signed: 'NT Manesty Woods'). Turn R and follow the track through the woods (2).

After a $\frac{1}{4}$ mile (0.4 km), the track leads you to a small bay

*Approaching the summit of Cat Bells*

beside the lake. You pass a slate house, called The Warren, and 200 yards (182 m) farther on come to a fork in the path, beside a boathouse. Go L to pass a small bungalow and the path then bears R, through a stone wall and back into the trees. Take the R-hand path at the next fork and you find yourself on a very attractive woodland route along the shores of Derwent Water.

Continue along the shore, through a kissing gate at Low Brandlehow, and across a field. As you come within sight of Hawes End jetty, the path leaves the shore to divert around a bed of reeds and you encounter a strange, curved bench, following the line of the fence. This is actually a walk-way, as the path suffers from frequent flooding in winter.

Beyond the reeds, you take the lower path across a field to arrive at a stile. Cross and continue through the woods back to the jetty.

*1 Memorial Plaque*

This is a memorial to Thomas Arthur Leonard, 'founder of Co-Operative and Communal Holidays and "father" of the open-air movement in this country'. Leonard was born in 1864 and, whilst a minister in Lancashire, founded the Co-Operative Holidays Association, in 1892. This organization was the direct forerunner of the Countrywide Holidays Association. It sought to provide houses and residences— either leased or bought—for its members. The CHA thrives to this day. (See address in Appendix.)

*2 Manesty Woods*

A very old woodland originally purchased by the National Trust in 1908. The first property in the Lake District ever bought by the Trust lies at the northern end of this walk; Brandlehow Park, acquired in 1902.

# 2.16

# HAYSTACKS

STARTING AND FINISHING
POINT
Gatesgarth Farm; park on the
roadside, next to the beck
(NW-195150)
LENGTH
4½ miles (7.2 km)
ASCENT
1720 feet (520 m)

Haystacks is an attractive little summit; an easy romp on a hot summer's day with plenty of time to spare to find a little cafe in Keswick and relax, with the feeling of a walk well done. Do not bother with Fleetwith Pike—a minefield of intersecting tracks and ruts, courtesy of the Buttermere and Westmorland Green Slate Company. The descent via Warnscale Beck is far superior, a scenic stroll past a number of delightful cascades.

## ROUTE DESCRIPTION (Map 23)

Gatesgarth Farm stands at the head of Buttermere Lake, beside the Honister Pass road. Between the entrance to the farm and the road bridge, there is a small gate (PBS 'Buttermere and Ennerdale'). Go through and follow the track past the farm, keeping to the river. The track goes through another gate and heads across the fields to a farm gate. Go through and bear slight R, following the river until you come to a pair of farm gates. Go half-L, past the farm gates (not through them—sign on the gates: Please keep to footpath) and walk along the edge of a field, leaving the river behind you. The lake comes into view on your R and ahead of you is Buttermere Fell, with a good view L to Haystacks and Warnscale. After 150 yards (136 m), you arrive at another farm gate in a fence in front of you. Carry on through the kissing gate alongside and continue across the fields. 'Buttermere' literally means 'the lake by the dairy pastures' and at this point on the walk, it is easy to see why.

As you draw closer to a stone wall, the path crosses Warnscale Beck by means of a wooden bridge. Go through the kissing gate in the wall ahead of you.

The track now forks two ways (look out for public footpath sign). R takes you along the lake shore, so instead bear half-L, up a series of steps. The path is quite steep and eroded in places, but has recently been subject to maintenance work; follow any footpath diversion signs and adjust your route with the aid of a map, where necessary. You start to gain height very quickly and soon have good views opening up behind you of the lake and village.

One hundred and fifty yards (136 m) beyond the wall, you will encounter a junction of several footpaths. Turn L so that you climb alongside a wire fence on your L. This fence marks the boundary of a conifer plantation. A few yards farther on, the path crosses a beck via a small wooden bridge. Keep climbing; the footpath becomes very rough in places. Disregard a footpath joining you from the R, about 200 yards (182 m) up from the beck.

As you climb, the route is marked by piles of stones which eventually lead you to a wire fence running across the path. Cross the stile and continue along a broad track, heading up into Scarth Gap. The rocky cliff on your right is High Crag.

The route follows a broken stone wall on your L and then begins to zigzag sharply to Scarth Gap. An old, broken wall comes down the fellside in front of you; as you approach, there

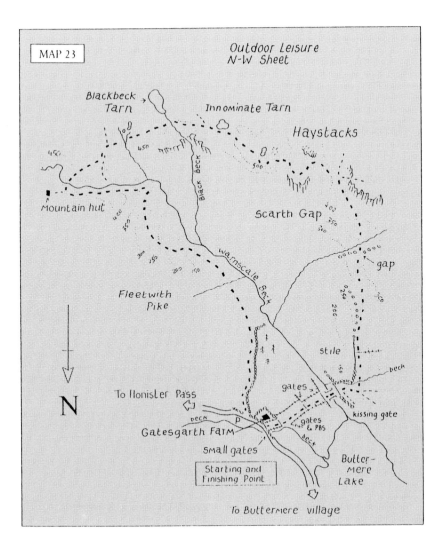

MAP 23

Outdoor Leisure
N-W Sheet

are so many boulders in the vicinity that it becomes difficult to follow the path. Look for a small cairn beside the wall and cross by the gap alongside. Cross a tiny beck and once across a further stretch of boulders you will see a line of stones stretching in front of you, marking the way.

The piles of stones lead you up through Scarth Gap and you arrive on a sloping, grassy hillside. Continue up the slope to a junction of four footpaths. From this point you can look down upon the conifer forests of Ennerdale and across to Pillar and Kirk Fell. On your R is Seat and the long ridge of High Stile and Red Pike. Turn L at the junction and begin the steep climb up the side of Haystacks. Once again, the going is rough underfoot in places and as you climb the path becomes indistinct in places; watch out for the piles of stones marking the route. Just below the summit, you have a short scramble up scree before arriving at a rock face. Bear L and the path takes you round the crag in a series of natural steps. On clear days you will start to get brilliant views out towards Cockermouth and the Solway Coast. The cone-shaped mountain on the horizon is Criffel, in Scotland. The path opens up onto a mossy fellside, dotted with heather and you get a magnificent view along the ridge to Red Pike.

Once on level ground, the path wanders along the eastern edge of the summit, forming a muddy little plateau before you come to the rocky summit itself.

The summit cairn stands to one side of a cleft in the rocks, with a tiny tarn formed below. It offers wonderful all-round views and the cleft itself provides good protection from the wind.

Continue past the cairn and follow an obvious path across the rocks towards a small, sheltered tarn below you. This is called Innominate Tarn, somewhat confusingly as its name means that it hasn't a name at all. The path bears L of the tarn and heads downhill across open fellside. This area acts as a good water table and so can be boggy in places almost all year round. Follow the footpath to pass Blackbeck Tarn; Black Beck itself drops away on your L through a dramatic cleft in the rocks, which gives you a good vantage point to look down to Buttermere.

As you walk across this wide, open moor, you can see Grey Knotts and Brandreth on your left and, on a busy afternoon, you will probably also see fellwalkers making their way towards Great Gable, just to the south of you.

Ahead of you are the Honister slate quarries, disfiguring Fleetwith Pike. Half a mile (0.8 km) or so beyond Blackbeck

*Buttermere and Crummock Water from the summit of Haystacks*

*Quarry building above Warnscale Beck*

Tarn, the path drops to Warnscale Beck.

The beck is quite wide and fast and drops away on your L in a series of waterfalls. Crossing the beck, bear L across muddy ground and go uphill a short distance to join a major track. If you turn R, this will take you past the mountain hut (known as 'The Ritz' by the grafitti on its door) and down to Honister Pass. At one time there was also a good alternative descent along the ridge of Fleetwith Pike, but in recent years the fellside has been so badly chewed up by the quarries that finding the path has become a difficult and tedious task.

Go L and follow the beck downstream. You pass a 15 foot (4.5 m) cascade on your L where the beck drops to a strikingly green pool before plunging into a dramatic gorge.

The path is a steep descent, the ground being rough and loose in places. There are odd rowan and gorse bushes dotted about, otherwise the fellside is harsh and rocky.

Once the path levels off at Warnscale Bottom, it becomes harder to distinguish and you have to follow the lines of stones. It winds through bracken and becomes a flat, easy route back towards the farm.

# 2.17

# GREAT  GABLE

STARTING AND FINISHING
POINT
Car park at Honister Hause
(NW-225136).
LENGTH
5¾ miles (9.2 km)
ASCENT
2200 ft (666 m)

Although the summit of Great Gable is rather flat and boring, being little more than a boulder field, the approach march around Brandreth is superb and the views from the summit are exhilarating. The starting point, at Honister Hause, gains you over 1100 feet (335 m) before you even leave the car, making this a splendid long afternoon walk.

## ROUTE  DESCRIPTION (Map 24)

At the end of the car park, next to the slate works, there is a farm gate and alongside a short flight of stone steps (PBS 'Great Gable, Dubs'). Cross the stile at the top of the steps and, after 5 yards (4.5 m) cross another stile to emerge onto the roadside. Turn L and follow the road for 40 yards (36 m) until you come to a green iron gate at the entrance to the slate works *(1)*. Go through the small, wooden gate alongside (signed: Public Bridleway) and bear R, past the buildings. Shortly beyond the buildings there is a sign on your L—'Danger quarry road, advised alternative route'—and the track forks. Go L, up a steep slate track.

As you climb, look right across the valley to Dalehead and the Yew Crag Quarries (now disused). If you look carefully you will be able to see a stretch of railway track coming straight down the fellside.

After climbing 400 feet (120 m), the track begins to level off across grass-covered fellside and climbs to a dismantled tramway. Carry straight on, over the first of the old sleepers lying across the path and up onto the embanked section. After 20 yards (18 m) you will see an obvious path on your L, marked by a line of small cairns. Turn L onto this path and follow it across open moorland. The cairns are at very regular intervals and after ¼ mile (0.4 km) you begin to have good views down to Buttermere and Crummock Water. The path ascends steadily at a gentle gradient but becomes very rough underfoot.

As you approach the ridge, almost 1 mile (1.6 km) from the tramway, a number of minor paths begin to split off. Keep to the main path and you come to the remnants of a boundary fence – now marked only by a line of rusty fence posts. At the fence, turn R and follow the line of posts downhill for 120 yards (109 m) until you come to a strong path cutting across the line of the fence in front of you. Turn L and follow the path, marked by lines of stones. The footpath becomes broad and eroded as you follow it over the ridge.

You are now walking at the very head of Ennerdale. Ahead of you are Great Gable and Kirk Fell (the latter with its very distinctive flat summit) and if you look to your R and behind a little, you can see the forest of Ennerdale and Black Sail Youth Hostel *(2)*.

You are walking down a broad, rounded fellside until you come to Stone Cove, directly beneath Windy Gap. This area is well-named and is a riot of boulders and scree. You pass a large cairn on your left and 20 yards (18 m) beyond that come to a small gill. A path goes L, along the gill to Windy Gap. Do not follow this but keep straight on to cross the beck and follow a very obvious path across the boulder field. The sombre bulk of Gable Crag looms above you on your L as you pick your way across the boulders and climb up to Beck Head.

This is a rocky, level area with good views down Ennerdale and back along the route you have just followed. You have a tremendous feeling of isolation here with mountain peaks stretching away into the distance on all sides.

As you attain the plateau there is a steep path running up the ridge of Great Gable, on your L. Although not the OS right-of-way, this route is easy to follow (by eye if not by foot, being very steep and rugged). Across the boulders there is a line of tiny cairns to mark the way up. After a final scramble to the top, you are greeted by a boulder field and a short walk to the summit cairn *(3)*.

Although the actual summit of Great Gable is not a great deal to boast about, it commands some of the finest views of any peak in the Lake District. The landscape is dominated by mountains. A short walk to the south of the main cairn and you will encounter another large cairn, known as the Westmorland Cairn *(4)*.

Walk away from the summit cairn in a north-easterly direction and you will pick up a line of stones to mark the route off Great Gable and down to Windy Gap. As you drop over the side the path becomes very steep and rocky. As you descend, Styhead Tarn comes into view (invariably surrounded by tents during the Duke of Edinburgh Award season). Once down at

*View of Wasdale Head from Wesmorland Cairn on Great Gable*

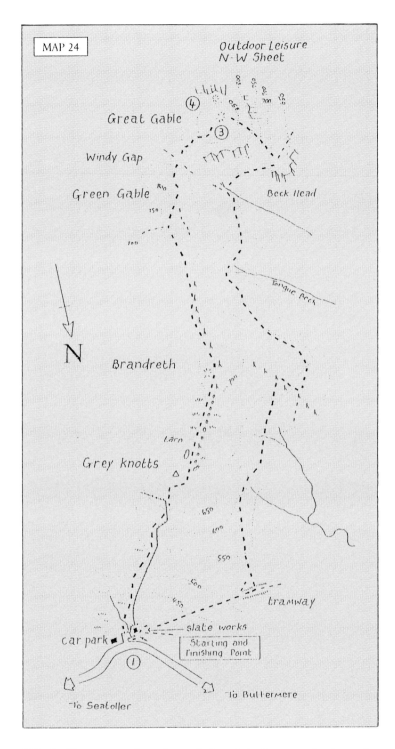

Windy Gap, a very broad, eroded path before you leads to the summit of Green Gable.

Mercifully, this ascent is quite short. Green Gable lives up to its name, a grassy, rounded fell, in marked contrast to Great

Gable which is almost devoid of vegetation. A clear footpath leads off the summit, marked by cairns. After 200 yards, (182 m) the path forks. Bear half-L across a flat, open fellside, following the cairns towards Brandreth. You pick up another line of fence posts and, as you approach the summit of Brandreth, the stones peel off to the L. Keep to the fence posts until you reach the rocky summit. From Brandreth, head north-east again, towards Grey Knotts and a straight, eroded path in front of you. The path is marked by piles of stones once more and you begin to run along another line of fence posts. Walk past a number of small tarns and the path takes you amongst rock outcrops at the summit of Grey Knotts.

The fence line turns sharply R, around an outcrop topped by a cairn. The path at this point is indistinct, so keep with the fence and follow it steeply downhill until you meet a wire fence in front of you, coming up from the valley. Go to the L of the new fence and you will come to a wooden stile. Cross the fence and continue downhill with the wire fence on your L.

You should keep to the fence at all times and follow a steep descent across a grassy fellside, back towards the slate works. The path is muddy in places, but otherwise easy to follow and you soon come within sight of the car park. Follow the path down through the yard at the back of the works, cross the quarry road and through a small wooden gate to re-enter the car park.

*1  Honister Quarry*

The quarries at Honister have been producing the distinctive green slate (in great demand as a high grade building material) for over 300 years. At one time, the blocks of stone were brought down the fell on wooden sleds until the tram ways came into use towards the end of the nineteenth century. Today, the stone is carried down by lorry, but the final 'dressing' of the slate—working it into the required shape— is still largely accomplished by hand. In recent years the Buttermere and Westmorland Green Slate Company Ltd has enjoyed a boom in business, with export orders from all over the globe.

*2  Ennerdale*

Ennerdale is the only one of the sixteen lakes to lack a metalled road travelling its length. Probably because of this, the valley remains a quiet, peaceful place where it is easy to get away from the crowds of central Lakeland. Cars are only permitted as far as Bowness Knott, at the western tip of the lake—thereafter the valley is the exclusive preserve of the walker.

*Looking back at Great Gable from Brandreth, on the return route*

The valley was heavily afforested during the 1930s, causing an uproar of protest which forced the Forestry Commission to take a more sympathetic approach to seeding the fells. In recent years, they have also opened up the head of the valley to walkers, with the Nine Becks Walk and the Smithy Beck Trail. Walk leaflets are available at Bowness Knott car park.

At the head of the valley stands Black Sail Youth Hostel. Completely inaccessible by car, it is little more than a mountain hut, with a total of eighteen beds.

3 *Summit Cairn*

On the north side of the summit cairn there is a bronze plaque which bears a relief map of the summit and the following inscription:

'The Fell and Rock Climbing Club.
In glorious and happy memory of those whose names are inscribed below, members of this club who died for their country in the European War, 1914–1918. These fells were acquired by their fellow members and by them vested in the National Trust for the use and enjoyment of the people of our land for all time.'

The club purchased just over a thousand acres—shown on the plaque—in 1923 and the memorial was unveiled the following year. The Fell and Rock Climbing Club continues to hold a commemorative service every year on this spot, on Remembrance Sunday.

4 *The Westmorland Cairn*

Just south of the summit there stands a large stone cairn, built in the 1870s by Edward and Thomas Westmorland. It marks what they felt to be the finest view in the Lake District. As you stand here, looking down over Wasdale, it is hard to disagree.

# 3.18

# FAIRFIELD

STARTING AND FINISHING
POINT
Car park at Cow Bridge, just north of
Brothers Water on the Kirkstone Pass
road (NE-404133).
LENGTH
10½ miles (17 km)
ASCENT
2515 ft (762 m)

Everyone has their favourites but this walk is difficult to surpass. It begins with an easy 'approach march' along the beautiful sylvan valley of Dovedale and returns via St Sunday Crag, the impressive southern wall of Grisedale Valley. St Sunday is one of the best ridge walks in Cumbria—superb on a clear, sunny day when you can look right across High Street to the Pennines.

## ROUTE DESCRIPTION (Maps 25–27)

Cross Goldrill Beck by the road bridge, walking into the woods and away from the main road. Immediately on your L there is a farm gate and a kissing gate. Go through and begin walking along a delightful wooded cart-track which leads past Brothers Water *(1)*. This is an extremely pleasant way to begin an ascent of one of the Lake District's most popular summits.

*Looking towards Ullswater from St Sunday Crag*

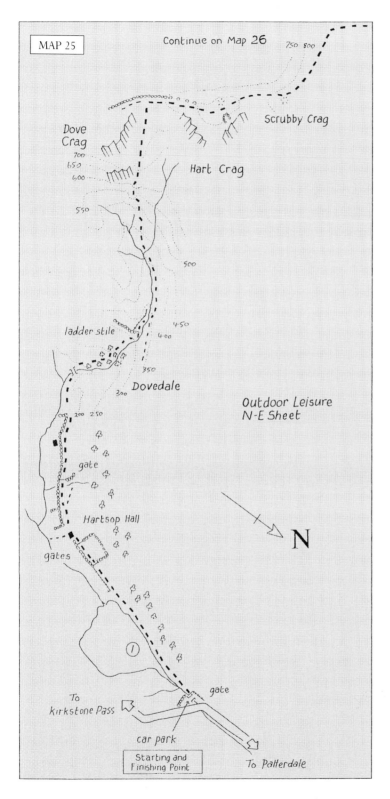

MAP 25

Continue on Map 26

750 800

Scrubby Crag

Dove Crag

700

650

600

Hart Crag

550

500

ladder stile

450

400

350

Dovedale

300

200 250

Outdoor Leisure
N-E Sheet

gate

N

Hartsop Hall

gates

①

gate

To
Kirkstone Pass

car park

Starting and
Finishing Point

To Patterdale

*Looking west from Fairfield*

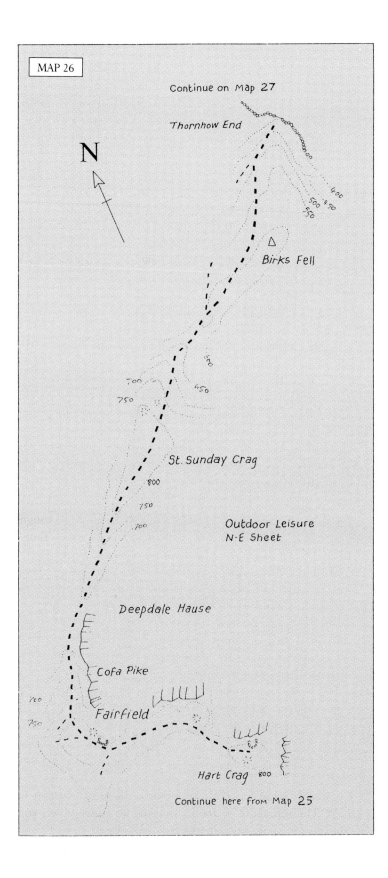

MAP 26

Continue on Map 27

Thornhow End

N

400

500 450

550

Birks Fell

600

700

750

650

St. Sunday Crag

800

750

Outdoor Leisure
N·E Sheet

700

Deepdale Hause

Cofa Pike

760

Fairfield

750

Hart Crag    800

Continue here from Map 25

Just beyond the end of the tarn, the track goes through a wooden farm gate and you start to approach Hartsop Hall, now a farm. Go through another gate and the track bears round behind the farm. Ignore the turning on your L, which leads to Sykeside Farm and campsite, and continue straight on to another group of farm buildings. You come level with sheep-pens on your L and another turning, signed for Kirkstone Pass. Continue past the buildings and, at the next fork, bear slightly L, ignoring the old mining track on your right.

The track crosses a beck and then through another farm gate in a stone wall ahead of you. You are following a wall on your L and pass a large bank barn. As you begin to bear away to the west of High Hartsop Dodd (not as high in 'feet' as Hartsop Dodd, but higher up the valley) you cross a level, fellside field and come to Dovedale Beck. Cross the footbridge which stands just below the line of trees and turn R, to follow the path upstream.

Dovedale is an attractive, wooded valley. The path climbs steadily, passing a number of pretty waterfalls along the way. Once above the trees, you climb to a drystone wall. Cross via the ladder-stile and, 100 yards (91 m) beyond the wall, the path rejoins the back alongside a wire fence. The fence forces you to cross the beck, using the stepping stones. Once over, go straight up the other bank to join a wide track coming in from your R. Turn L along the track and you are heading towards the dramatic cliff of Dove Crag at the head of the valley. The track climbs steeply above the level of the stream and you begin to approach a scree, below the crags. The track becomes a rough path which in turn degenerates into a scramble up a short stretch of scree and rock. Keep to the R-hand side of the scree—marked by a series of small cairns—and you regain a grass path and climb onto open fellside. Continue uphill to the ridge and you encounter a stone wall in front of you, with good views of the Langdales and the Scafell range. Turning round, you can see across the ridge of High Street to the Pennines.

Follow the wall R, away from Dove Crag, keeping to the Hartsop side of the wall. You come to a boulder field and the wall vanishes, to be replaced by a line of small cairns. Follow the path through the boulders. At the top of Hart Crag, the path becomes more obvious. Follow the ridge as it makes a dramatic sweep up to the summit of Fairfield. Looking to your R, you can see the barren, empty valley of Deepdale, contrasting oddly with the lush vegetation in Dovedale.

It is an easy stroll across Rydal Head to the broad summit of Fairfield. The top sports a good stone shelter from which you can admire the views and shelter from the wind.

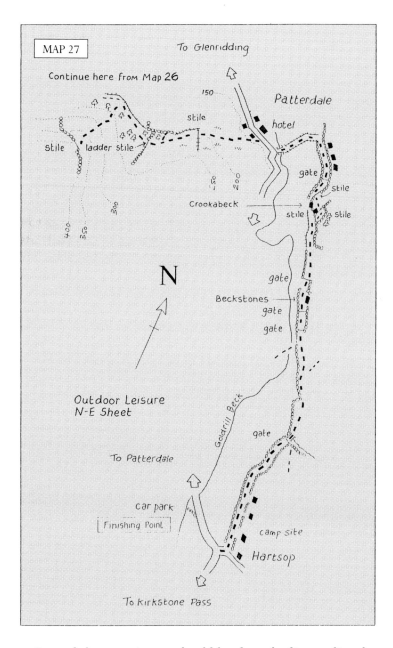

MAP 27

To Glenridding

Continue here from Map 26

150

Patterdale

stile

hotel

stile

ladder stile

stile

gate

stile

Crookabeck → stile stile

50

200

300

400

300

N

gate

Beckstones →

gate

gate

Outdoor Leisure
N-E Sheet

Goldrill Beck

gate

To Patterdale

car park

Finishing Point

camp site

Hartsop

To Kirkstone Pass

Beyond the summit, you should head north, disregarding the path which bears L and down to Grisedale Tarn. The path drops steeply down Cofa Pike and suddenly you are confronted by the superb ridge of St Sunday Crag.

Walk onto the ridge past a castellated rock on your R and there is a tremendous view of Grisedale Tarn, to your L. You may be lucky enough to cover this part of the route when a low-flying jet passes below you, hugging the contours of Grisedale valley; being able to peer into the cockpits is quite common for ardent fellwalkers. Continue up to the summit.

As you begin to descend the other side of St Sunday Crag, Ullswater opens up before you. The path bears L across the broad, rolling ridge of Birks Fell, keeping to the Grisedale side and you drop steeply over the northern end of the ridge to descend to a stone wall. Look for a section of wooden fence in the wall and cross at the stile. Continue downhill, bearing slightly L, following the cairns.

This part of the walk can be hard on the knees as it drops quite steeply in places and is loose underfoot. Distract yourself by paying attention to the good views opening out in front of you. After another 500 yards (455 m) you arrive at a wire fence. Do not go through the gate but turn R and follow the fence. It joins a stone wall after a short distance and the path begins to bear away slightly but still curving round to the L. Rejoin the wall and keep it on your L until you meet another wall, coming in at right angles from your R. At the junction of the two walls there is a broken farm gate and a ladder stile. Cross the stile and the path bears half-L, across a bog. After 50 yards (45 m), the path splits. Take the R-hand fork over a rock outcrop and the path winds downhill towards another wire fence. Continue over the stile, across a beck and keep R to follow the path to a barn.

*Looking east along the ridge towards St Sunday Crag*

You join a farm road which bears R around the barn to bring you into Patterdale village, almost opposite the White Lion Hotel.

A suitable pause for refreshments follows. Then cross the road to the pavement and turn R until you come to a small road bridge on your L, crossing Goldrill Beck. Walk over the bridge and continue up the lane towards a group of houses.

You arrive at a T-junction. L goes to Side Farm, so turn R (PBS 'Hartsop'), following the lane past a number of pretty cottages. 150 yards (136 m) beyond the last cottage (Rooking End), you come to a farm gate and once through the lane deteriorates into a rough track. You pass a pair of wooden barns on your L and a hay barn on the R. Just past the barns, look out for a stile in the stone wall on your L. Leave the track here, crossing the stile (PFS 'Hartsop') and following a permissive path across a field for 80 yards (73 m) until you meet up with a stone wall. Turn R along the wall, cross another stile in a section of wooden fence and the path bears round the back of Crookabeck Farm to rejoin the main track. Once on the track, turn L (signed: 'Hartsop') and follow the track.

After a further $\frac{1}{2}$ mile (0.8 km) of the track, three more farm gates and after passing through Beckstones Farm, the track forks two ways. Keep straight on—the R-hand fork leads down to the river at Deepdale Bridge. A little further along the track you pass a footpath on your L which leads to Angle Tarn. Continue along the track until you arrive at Angletarn Beck, which runs across the track in front of a farm gate. Ford the beck and go through the gate. Eventually, after passing a campsite full of log cabins on your L, you come to a metalled lane. Go half-R and follow the lane towards Hartsop village. At the next junction turn R until you reach the main road. Turn R again and follow the road for $\frac{1}{4}$ mile (0.4 km) to arrive back at Cow Bridge.

*1 Brothers Water*

Most people agree that there are sixteen lakes in the Lake District, but the actual identity of the sixteenth seems to come and go out of fashion. Today it seems to be settled that it is Elterwater, but at one time Brothers Water had the position. Once called Broadwater, the name was changed in the nineteenth century after two brothers were drowned here, whilst skating.

# 3.19

# THE OLD MAN OF CONISTON

STARTING AND FINISHING
POINT
Main car park in Coniston village
(SW-304976)
LENGTH
10 miles (16 km)
ASCENT
3320 ft (976 m)

Coniston's 'Old Man' is actually a reference to the mountain's summit cairn; 'man' is the old word for cairn. 2635 feet (803 m) high, this is the southernmost of the major central Lakeland fells. The glorious view from the top takes in both mountains and seascape. The mountain has been so extensively mined in the past and is now so full of holes that it has been described as like 'a maggoty old cheese'. This route, however, avoids most of the unsightly elements and makes an exciting approach to the summit via Buck Pike and the ridge above Dow Crag.

## ROUTE DESCRIPTION (Maps 28, 29)

Leave the car park via the main entrance and turn L, past St Andrew's Church *(1)* and over Church Bridge. Immediately over the bridge, turn R along a minor road (signed: 'Sun Hotel') beside the Bridge House Cafe. Within 20–30 yards (18–27 m) you have left the village and the traffic behind you and you are walking along a pleasant, tree-lined lane. Continue past the Sun Hotel until you come to a road junction, with an old stone well in the wall opposite. Turn R and follow the road uphill for a short distance. The road bears sharply L (signed: 'Old Man, Walna Scar and Seathwaite'). The road continues uphill. Ignore any side roads and keep straight ahead. You are following a nice, wooded stream on your L and there are glimpses of Coppermines Valley to your R.

As the trees begin to thin out, the road bears L. Ignore the gate (PFS 'Coppermines Valley') in the wall in front of you and keep with the road. Another 10 yards (9 m) farther on, the road turns R again and in front of you is a track to Heathwaite. Stay with the road and the view opens out as you climb uphill. There are fields on either side of you. The old hedge on your L shows distinct signs of the hedgelayer's art.

Three quarters of a mile (1.2 km) from the village, you come

*Old Wheelhouse, Coppermines Valley*

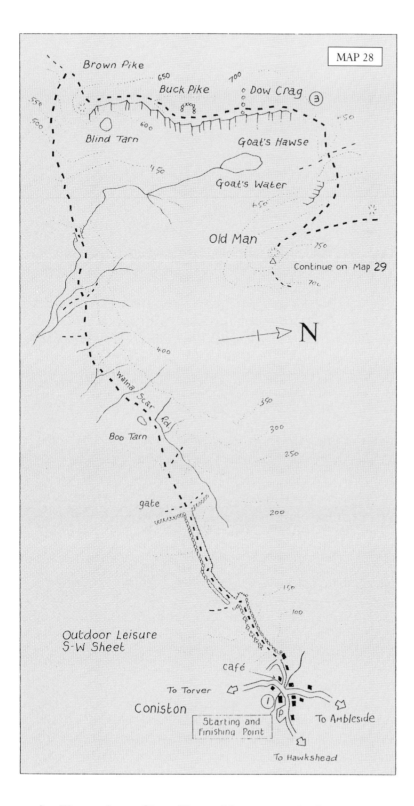

MAP 28

Brown Pike

650

700

Buck Pike

Dow Crag ③

550

600

600

Blind Tarn

450

Goat's Hawse

450

Goat's Water

450

Old Man

750

Continue on Map 29

700

N

400

Walna Scar Rd

350

300

Boo Tarn

250

gate

200

150

100

Outdoor Leisure
S-W Sheet

café

To Torver

Coniston

①

Starting and
Finishing Point

To Ambleside

To Hawkshead

*Low Water, a glimpse of Levers Water and Coppermines Valley from the summit
of Coniston Old Man*

to an iron farm gate across the road. Once through, you are on open fellside. Ignoring the track heading R, continue straight ahead. The tarmac peters out and you are on a rough track. Half a mile (0.8 km) on, you will pass another track going R—access road to Bursting Stone Quarry—which you should ignore. Continue past Boo Tarn—little more than a pond on your L, but a good spot for dragonflies.

The track deteriorates as you climb, getting rougher underfoot, though still quite easy to follow. On your L the view has opened out to give a tremendous panorama across to the coast. The 'lighthouse' on the hill above Ulverston is the Hoad Monument. The industrial buildings on the far side of Morecambe Bay form Heversham power station.

One mile (1.6 km) from the gate, the path crosses a beck via a slate footbridge and then splits three ways. Keep straight on and after another 400 yards (274 m) you cross another beck, this time by means of a stone packhorse bridge (somewhat disfigured by iron handrails). From this point there are good views down to Coniston Water; the white house which figures so prominently on the far shore is Brantwood, John Ruskin's home (2).

Once beyond the packhorse bridge, the track begins to zigzag steeply uphill, leaving the flat, open moorland and beginning to climb up into the crags, with impressive views to Blind Tarn screes on your R and, a little further round, the Old Man. This route is known as the Walna Scar Road, an old packhorse route.

You arrive on a flat, moorland ridge. Go R, following an ugly, eroded scar up onto Brown Pike. The views become more impressive the higher you climb.

Continue along the ridge, the footpath being very straightforward and easy to follow despite encountering slate scree. The going gets rougher as you approach the boulder-strewn summit of Buck Pike, but from the shelter at the top you command wonderful views across the Duddon to the west coast of Cumbria. Below you, to the south, is Blind Tarn and to the north-west, the rounded summit of Old Man.

Ahead of you now is almost 1 mile (1·6 km) of very impressive ridge walking. The footpath, once you climb towards the summit of Dow Crag, becomes indistinct. Keep to the ridge, crossing an old stone wall at one point. As you reach the summit of Dow Crag, Goat's Water comes into view on your R and ahead of you looms Coniston Old Man.

A very rocky descent follows and as you descend, the footpath picks up again. The climb down to Goat's Hawse is overshadowed by the vast, rounded summit of Old Man on your R. At the Hawse, there is a distinct footpath R to Goat's Water and a less distinct one L. Keep straight ahead, following a great,

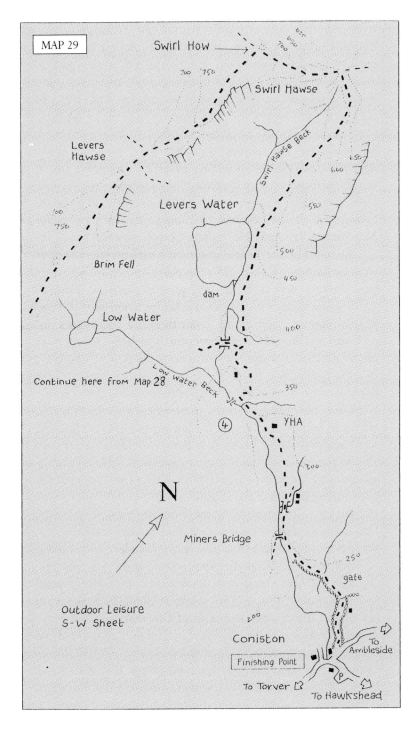

MAP 29

Swirl How

Swirl Hawse

Levers
Hawse

Levers Water

Swirl Hawse Beck

Brim Fell

dam

Low Water

Low Water Beck

Continue here from Map 28

④

YHA

**N**

Miners Bridge

gate

Outdoor Leisure
S-W Sheet

Coniston

Finishing Point

To
Ambleside

P

To Torver

To Hawkshead

eroded scar up the grassy flanks of the Old Man. The path is
very steep to begin with and then, within 300 yards (273 m) of
the summit cairn, it levels off and joins a path coming in from
your L. An easy walk follows along the ridge above Goat Crag to
the cairn.

The view from the cairn—one of the tallest in the Lake District—can be stunning on a clear day, stretching out to the coast, to Ingleborough in the east and to the Furness peninsula to the south. Closer to hand, the large rock face above Goat's Water is Dow Crag *(3)*. (The blue rectangular shape at the foot of the crag is a mountain rescue box.)

From the summit, retrace your steps along the ridge until you reach the path at which you ascended from Goat's Hawse. Bear half-R and follow the path—marked by cairns—along a wide, moorland ridge, to the cairn at the summit of Brim Fell. From here, follow the ridge in a northerly direction towards Levers Hawse. The footpath has become an easy, grassy track with impressive views all round. As you descend past Levers Hawse, there is a striking view of Lever's Water below you.

From Levers Hawse, there is another $\frac{3}{4}$ mile (1.2 km) of superb ridge walking before you climb to the rocky summit of Swirl How. The 8 ft (2.4 m) high summit cairn is most impressive.

From the cairn, bear R down a steep, rough ridge (Prison Band). As you scramble over the rocks, look for signs of quartz beneath your hands. Prison Band extends for perhaps 700 yards (637 m) before depositing you on a grassy 'saddle' between Swirl How and Wetherlam. Turn R and begin the gentle descent to Levers Water.

Although it can be boggy in places, depending upon the time of year, this is a very easy path to follow, keeping the tarn in view the whole time. Situated in a classic, glacial corrie, Levers Water is surrounded by crags on almost all sides—the only opening to the east being the outflow to Coniston and Coppermines Valley. As you reach the rubble-strewn shore of the tarn, work round to the dam and descend L of the beck, below Kennel Crag. As you cross over a small beck, look at the channel—or 'leat'—on your L, once used to take off water to power the mining machinery. Coppermines Valley, a desolate wasteland to some, a rich example of industrial archaeology to others, opens out below you *(4)*.

Five hundred yards (455 m) below Levers Water, the path comes to a snaking L turn and in front of you is a small wooden bridge, crossing Levers Water Beck. Ignore the bridge and continue L. The path becomes a disc slate-covered track, passing slagheaps on your L, as you work down towards the Youth Hostel. The track continues past the Youth Hostel, and past a row of converted miners' cottages on your L. Another 500 yards (455 m) farther on from the Youth Hostel, cross a beck coming in from your left via a concrete bridge. Three hundred yards (273 m) beyond that, you arrive at Miners Bridge, which spans the main beck. The rocks hereabout are very pale and the beck falls below Miners Bridge to form a milky-white waterfall. Don't cross the bridge, but continue down the track. The beck on your R descends via a series of waterfalls, foaming rapids and deep pools before cutting through the rock to form a deep ravine thickly overgrown with alder. The track crosses a cattle grid and descends to become a metalled lane. Follow this downhill to emerge in the village at Yewdale Road, beside the Black Bull Inn.

### 1 St Andrew's Church

St Andrew's Church was built some time during the sixteenth century and is rather a fine building which stands at the centre of the village. The churchyard contains the tomb of Coniston's most famous resident, John Ruskin. There is also a small museum named after him in Yewdale Road. Just as you leave the car park, you should cross to a stone seat on the green opposite; this commemorates Donald Campbell who died on Lake Coniston in 1967 whilst attempting the world speed record in 'Bluebird'.

*Church Beck, Coppermines Valley*

*Low Water from Coniston Old Man*

2 *Brantwood*

This was the home of John Ruskin, art-critic, writer, philosopher and champion of many of the social causes of his day. He lived here from 1872 to 1900 and originally purchased the property, site unseen, from one William Linton, for £1500, declaring that 'any place opposite Coniston Old Man must be beautiful'. The house originally consisted of a modest cottage, built by Thomas Woodville around 1797. Ruskin acquired 'a mere shed of rotten timbers and loose stone' but transformed it into a beautiful home which he stocked with books and paintings—including works by Turner, of whom he was an early champion. Ruskin lived the last thirty years of his life at Brantwood and it is now, in accordance with his wishes, open to the public. It must be one of the most beautifully-sited houses in England, with magnificent views across the water to the Old Man.

3 *Dow Crag*

This was once a tremendously popular spot for rock climbers, although in recent years they seem to have favoured the crags of Langdale and Borrowdale. It had an important part to play in the early development of rock climbing as a sport. The first recorded ascent of Dow Crag was made by Walter Haskett Smith and J. W. Robinson, in 1886.

4 *Coppermines Valley*

Digging for copper around Coniston probably dates back as far as the Romans. The first serious impact on the area was made during the sixteenth century by German engineers of the Company of Mines Royal, brought down from Keswick to begin digging for copper. With increasing industrialization, the mines began to dig deeper into the earth and, by the mid-nineteenth century, were reaching depths of over 1000 feet (300 m). They began to decline shortly afterwards as the cost of pumping water from the deep shafts became uneconomic. The mines finally closed at the end of World War I. A railway was built to connect the village with the main line at Broughton and carry ore and slate to the coast.

# WALKS IN
# THE NORTHUMBERLAND
# NATIONAL PARK

*Track from Trows to Windy Gyle*

# 1.20

# Hadrian's Wall Country

STARTING AND FINISHING
POINT
Housesteads car-park (87–793684)
Located by the B6318 road, midway
between Greenhead and Chollerford.
LENGTH
4½ miles (7 km)
ASCENT
450 ft (140 m)

This circular walk offers an opportunity to explore the most complete Roman Fort in Britain and to experience the scale and grandeur of Hadrian's Wall, the Roman Empire's North-West Frontier. Surmounting a natural defensive line of basaltic cliffs, the Wall's location offers spectacular views into the Tyne Valley and north towards the windswept landscape of moor, lough and forest.

## Route Description (Map 30)

Leave the car-park via the archway in the Information Centre, through two gates and on uphill towards Housesteads Fort *(1)* (admission charge for entry). Walk on between the fort and museum, then on to the R-hand end of the trees seen ahead. Climb the stone steps turning L onto the path which continues through the woodland. You are now walking along the top of Hadrian's Wall *(2)*, perched high on Housesteads Crags *(3)*. Soon after leaving the trees the path descends from the Wall to pass to the L of Milecastle No. 37 and on alongside the Wall beyond. A backward glance after climbing onto Cuddy's Crags is a classic view of the Wall. Descend into Rapishaw Gap to cross a ladder stile just before the path joins the Pennine Way. Continue straight on alongside the undulating Wall until a small plantation on the L and a PFS are reached. The view straight ahead is of Crag Lough, one of four lakes to be seen on this walk.

   Cross a stile in a fence and turn immediately to the R through a gate, to pass to the R of Hotbank Farmhouse *(4)*. Go through a gate at the end of the buildings seen ahead. Walk on keeping R at each fork in the track and through a gate in a wall on the skyline. The grassy track continues straight on then bears R at an indistinct junction and on to the L of a plantation. Pass a derelict wall (to your L) and then a limekiln *(5)* to reach a ladder stile in a wall. The scene to your L is of Greenlee Lough with

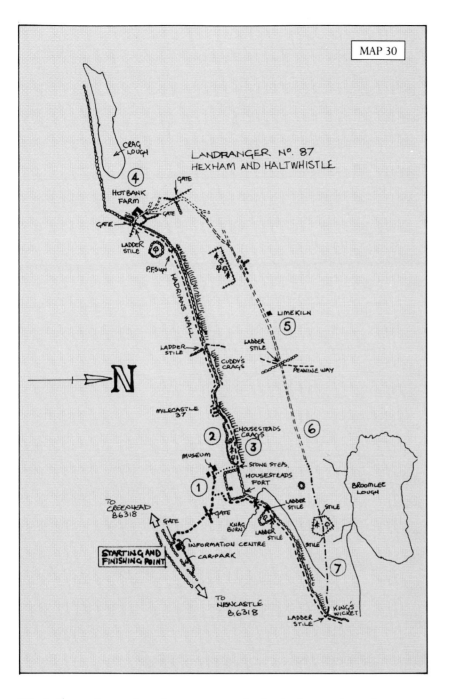

MAP 30

LANDRANGER Nº 87
HEXHAM AND HALTWHISTLE

CRAG LOUGH

④ HOTBANK FARM

GATE

GATE

GATE

LADDER STILE

P.F.SIGN

HADRIANS WALL

N

LIMEKILN

⑤

LADDER STILE

LADDER STILE

CUDDY'S CRAGS

PENNINE WAY

MILECASTLE 37

② HOUSESTEADS CRAGS

③

⑥

MUSEUM

STONE STEPS

① HOUSESTEADS FORT

TO GREENHEAD B6318

GATE GATE

KNAG BURN

LADDER STILE

LADDER STILE

STILE

BROOMLEE LOUGH

STARTING AND FINISHING POINT

INFORMATION CENTRE

CAR-PARK

STILE

⑦

TO NEWCASTLE B6318

LADDER STILE

KING'S WICKET

Wark Forest beyond, and to your R a barbarian's-eye-view of the impregnable Wall. Cross the stile and straight ahead (not to the L on the Pennine Way) along a green track for ½ mile (800 m), giving fine views of Broomlee Lough and the wavelike landform *(6)*. The track becomes vague before descending into a depression and out again on a narrow path to a woodland plantation. Cross the stile into the wood, walk through the trees and out over another stile. Follow the path across the wet grassland *(7)* to the ladder stile at King's Wicket on the Wall.

Climb the stile and turn R alongside the Wall again for about ½ mile (800 m). Look to your L to see Grindon Lough before crossing two ladder stiles, one at each end of a wood. Cross the Knag Burn by the stone slab bridge and up to the Fort. Turn L following the Fort wall. In front of the main entrance turn downhill on the gravel path to return to the car-park.

1 *Housesteads Fort*

This 5-acre (2-hectares) fort was constructed by Emperor Hadrian to garrison up to 1,000 soldiers stationed on this section of Wall. One of twelve built, it has been described as the most complete example in Britain, and includes barracks, granaries, hospital, bathhouse and flushing latrines, all confined within a rectangular curtain wall with towers and gates.

Adjacent to the south gate a civil settlement grew to serve the fort; buildings included shops, workshops and inns. A pair of skeletons were found under the floor of a house, a sword tip lodged in the ribs of one, giving the building its name: Murder House.

2 *Hadrian's Wall*

The Wall is probably the most important Roman structure in Britain. Built after AD 122 on the orders of Emperor Hadrian, this frontier between the Empire and the Barbarians stretched from coast to coast across the country. It took the soldiers six years to build; the vallum (a ditch and mounds) and the forts were later additions. Hadrian carefully planned the Wall using naturally defensive features as well as looking at the availability of local building materials. Its dimensions are impressive: 9 ft 6 in (2.9 m) wide, 21 ft 6 in (6.5 m) high and 73 miles (117 km) long. The 80 Roman mile length was punctuated by protected gates called Milecastles and between each of these were two turrets.

3 *Whin Sill wildlife*

The dry, well-drained grassland encourages scented thyme and rarer wild chives, whilst on the cliffs and screes heather, bilberry, rock rose and parsley fern, together with the mountain ash, all flourish away from the grazing sheep. Jackdaws, wheatears and kestrels all find nesting places in the cracks and crevices of the dolerite cliffs.

4 *Hotbank Farm*

A typical Northumbrian farm steading; its name may have been derived from Holt or Hott—a clump of birch trees—on a bankside.

*Housesteads Fort*

5 *Limekiln*

This well-preserved nineteenth-century limekiln still shows the triangular arches and corbelled stonework of the inverted pots. Lime was burnt with coal in the pots for use on the land to sweeten sour or acid soil.

6 *Landform*

Hadrian's Wall appears to run like a rollercoaster along the cliff edge of the Great Whin Sill. The Sill was formed 295 million years ago as molten rock was forced between compacted layers of limestones, sandstones and shales. Earth movements after this time tilted the rocks and final shaping by Ice Age glaciers produced the parallel waves or ridges dominated by the Whin Sill escarpment. The poorly drained troughs between the ridges now hold the shallow loughs and peat-filled mires so characteristic of this landscape.

7 *Wet grassland*

Poorly drained soil encourages rushes to grow, together with the tall-stemmed marsh thistle. The tiny yellow flowers of tormentil can cloak the ground in summer growing alongside the tall, daisy-like mugwort. In spring these areas resound with the calls of skylarks, lapwings and of course the curlew—the symbol of the Northumberland National Park.

# BETWIXT MOOR AND FOREST – THE CHIRDON BURN

STARTING AND FINISHING
POINT
Chirdon Burn Bridge lay-by
(80–783850)
From Bellingham take the Kielder
Reservoir road turning L at the
junction at Lanehead. Cross the
bridge over the Tyne, turn sharp L
on a minor road. Cross the
Chirdon Burn bridge in ½ mile
(800 m).
LENGTH
8½ miles (14 km)
ASCENT
900 ft (275 m)

The walk focuses on the lower reaches of the beautiful Chirdon Burn. The ascent across pathless moorland with its attractive rocky outcrops provides spectacular views across the Chirdon Valley and towards Kielder Forest and its reservoir. The route continues through the maturing conifers of Wark Forest before dropping down to the picturesque buildings of Allerybank. A forest track joins a quiet, single track road which follows the tree-fringed Chirdon Burn as it tumbles past Dally Castle and Mill on its way to meet the river North Tyne. A walk of many contrasts.

## ROUTE DESCRIPTION (Maps 31–33)

From the lay-by turn R and along the road which bears L away from the Chirdon Burn. At the next bend turn R and through a recessed gate. Walk straight on past a single ash tree with the riverside and fence to the R. Birks (1) can be seen in the trees across the river. Just before the Wall is reached, turn L and through a gate in a fence. Walk on for 30 yds (27 m) and turn R through a gate in the wall. Follow the sunken track uphill with the low mound to your R until it levels out, briefly to view the remains of Dally Castle (2) next to the farmhouse across to the R. Continue uphill bearing away from the Chirdon Burn. As it climbs, the track becomes almost lost in the heather and bracken of Snabdaugh Moor (3). A series of waymarking posts may assist in route-finding. After crossing two narrow streams, walk up to the R of a low, bracken-covered mound to a marker post on the skyline. Walk to the trees and buildings of Whitchester Farm seen ahead. Go through the gate in the wall and on through another gate between the farmhouse and outbuildings. Turn R, then across the yard and through another

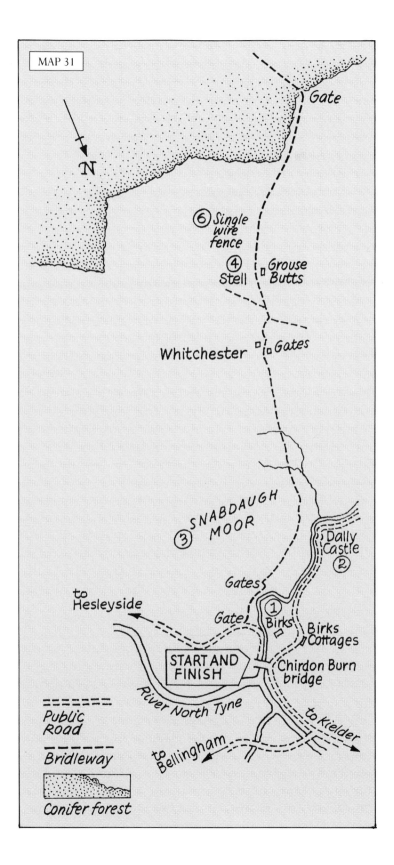

MAP 31

N

Gate

⑥ Single
wire
fence

④ Grouse
Stell Butts

Whitchester Gates

SNABDAUGH
MOOR

③ Dally
Castle
②

Gates

to
Hesleyside

Gate ① Birks

Birks
Cottages

START AND
FINISH

Chirdon Burn
bridge

River North Tyne

to Kielder

to Bellingham

=======
Public
Road

— — —
Bridleway

Conifer forest

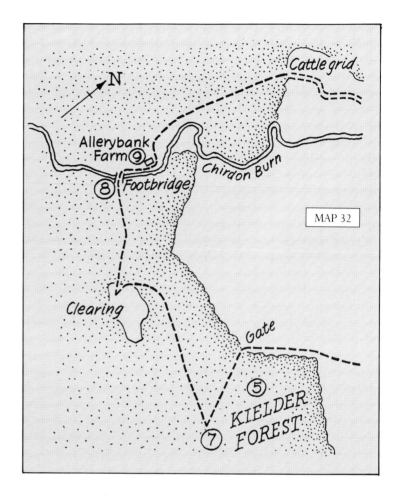

gate. On reaching the next gate by some trees to the R, go through it and turn immediately L through another gate. Walk on across a stream and up through a gate in the wall. The track continues between two fence lines, then as they part bear R to a sign post. Walk straight on ignoring the sign's directions, across a small bridge and after 50 yards (45 m) bear R away from the track, uphill to the stell *(4)*. There is no sign of a path on this section. Continue on the same line uphill passing to the R of a low rock outcrop. Stop on reaching the edge of the next outcrop which has a line of stone shooting butts on top.

The wide views over Kielder Forest *(5)* are impressive. Look for a single-strand wire fence leading away from the outcrop. Follow this fence *(6)* across wet moorland to the corner of the forest. On reaching the clearing continue to the angle in the fence. Go through a gate and turn L down the wide forest-fire break then straight on down the forest road. Just after the road begins to climb, turn back half R along another road between the conifers *(7)*. Continue along the road for ¾ mile (1.2 km) as it winds through the trees and across an unplanted clearing.

At the point where the road crosses a stream at the forest edge, turn R off the road down the L-hand fire break between the trees. At times, the walking and route-finding is difficult as the fire break narrows and becomes overgrown. Walk straight on until the corner of an old wall is reached. Walk on with the wall on your R until it becomes obscured by trees. At this point turn L up the wide fire break. After 30 yds (27 m) turn R along another wide break which leads to the footbridge across the Chirdon Burn *(8)*. Cross the bridge and turn R along the track to Allerybank Farm *(9)*. At the end of the outbuildings turn L to follow the track behind the house.

Walk uphill, then around the forest edge on an overgrown track. At the top of the hill take the R fork. After entering the trees the track bears L past several ride junctions to eventually reach a forest road. Turn R downhill, keeping straight on at a junction of roads until a cattle grid is reached. Continue on, along the metalled road and through a gate next to the farm of The Bower. Follow the tree-lined road *(10)* for 2½ miles (4 km) passing Dally Castle *(2)*, its Farm and Mill, Birk's cottages to a 'T' junction. Turn R over the humpbacked bridge to the lay-by.

1 *Birks*

Originally a farmhouse built in 1836, the house was greatly extended later in the century. The name is probably derived from birch or where birch trees grow.

2 *Dally Castle*

The history of the castle is obscure, but its probable that it was built by Sir David Lindsay of Lothian around 1237 on land belonging to Alexander II of Scotland. So little now remains, except for a few courses of finely dressed stone, it is difficult to imagine how it may have looked at the time. However, it is clear that the castle had bowmen's loop holes and corner turrets and may have been occupied until the sixteenth century, as a helmet and sword of this period were found inside the walls. Stone from the castle was used to build the picturesque Cornmill in the eighteenth century.

3 *Moorland wildlife*

The sandstone outcrops give a clue to the leached and acid nature of the soils. Plants like heather and tormentil grow well whilst in the wetter areas you will find jointed rush and the pink, cross-leaved heath. During summer, the adder likes these areas in its search for food, but will be found near rockier areas in spring and autumn.

4 *Stell*

A circular sheep pen built of local stone: changes in sheep husbandry have left many stells in Northumberland derelict.

*Chirdon Burn and Birks*

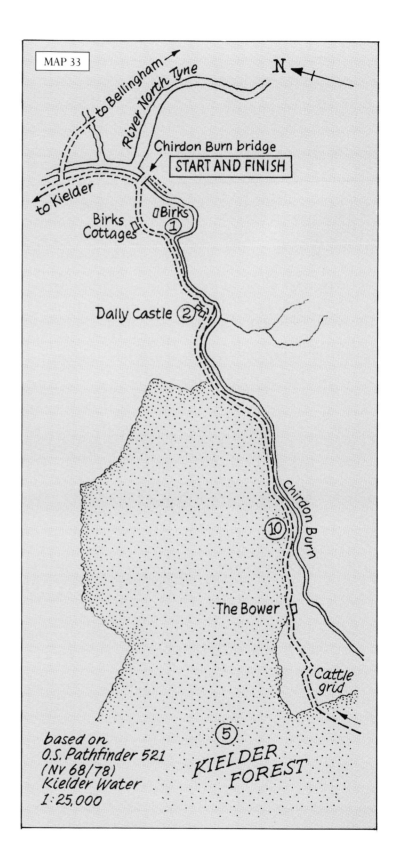

MAP 33

to Bellingham

River North Tyne

N

Chirdon Burn bridge

**START AND FINISH**

to Kielder

Birks

Birks Cottages

①

Dally Castle ②

Chirdon Burn

⑩

The Bower

Cattle grid

based on
O.S. Pathfinder 521
(NY 68/78)
Kielder Water
1:25,000

⑤

KIELDER FOREST

5 *Kielder Forest*

Covering an area of approximately 125,000 acres (50,000 hectares), it is considered to be the largest man-made forest in Western Europe. The land is owned by the Forestry Commission. Starting in 1926, to date more than 200 million trees have been planted, over 70 per cent of them being Sitka spruce from western America. Trees reach maturity after forty to fifty years, so much of the forest is being felled and restocked in a more sympathetic way in both landscape and wildlife terms. Whilst Kielder Reservoir is hidden from view, the barn-like roof of the valve tower is just visible between the trees.

6 *Boundary stones*

Several low stone boundary markers may be found a short way from the fence. Inscribed with the letters C & W their purpose in past centuries was to pinpoint the boundary of two landholdings, presumably Chirdon and Whitchester.

7 *Conifers*

The mature Sitka and Norway spruce trees are easily told apart. Sitka has a blue cast to its needles whereas the Norway's are green. In a good cone year, crossbills will be seen and heard everywhere and roe deer are often glimpsed browsing along a ridge at any time.

8 *Chirdon Burn*

Rising deep in the forest the burn winds and tumbles over many cascades on its way downstream. The peaty brown water supports a wide variety of bird life such as the heron, goosander, dipper and grey wagtail, whilst the fringe of deciduous trees resounds with the calls of flycatchers, tits and woodpeckers in spring.

9 *Allerybank*

This cluster of farm buildings nestled by the Chirdon Burn got its name from the bankside alder trees that still flourish here.

10 *Roadside wildflowers*

In summer the banks and verges abound in a purple haze of scabious flowers mixed with horsetails, marsh woundwort, orchids and betony. Great burnet is also present; here it is close to its northern limit in Britain.

*Common spotted orchid*

# WINDY GYLE AND THE BORDER RIDGE

---

**STARTING AND FINISHING POINT**
A parking area at the junction of single track roads (80–860114), located 6½ miles (11 km) north-west of Alwinton in Upper Coquetdale.
**LENGTH**
10½ miles (17 km)
**ASCENT**
1650 ft (500 m)

Steeped in the bloody history of conflict between England and Scotland, these now quiet, windswept hills provide a unique atmosphere for this walk. Starting in remote Upper Coquetdale, the route climbs through the Cheviot Hills on an ancient drove road before turning along the Border Ridge itself. A brief step into Scotland leads to Windy Gyle (2040 ft, 619 m), the highest point on the border with the exception of the flank of the Cheviot itself. The panoramic view across the seemingly endless Cheviot foothills and into the river Tweed basin in Scotland are unrivalled in the area. The descent offers surprise views at every turn as it skirts the steep-sided valleys of the Usway and Barrow Burns. Choose a clear day for greatest appreciation of the walk and ease of route-finding.

## ROUTE DESCRIPTION (Maps 34–37)

Leave the parking area *(1)* and cross the road bridge over the Rowhope Burn. Almost immediately bear R through a gate and up the track called The Street *(2)*. Cross the stile by the gate and on, with a fence to the R. Where the track bears L, walk on staying close to the fence. The first view of our objective, Windy Gyle, now looms over the farmhouses of Rowhope and Trows to your R. Avoiding a gate in the fence to your R, continue to rejoin the track. Pass through a gate and on for ¾ mile (1.2 km) past Hindside Knowe and over The Slime, aptly named after heavy rain. Continue along the track until a gate is reached next to an apparently discouraging sign. It reads 'Danger Keep to the Path, Uncleared Military Target Area. Do not touch anything, it may explode and kill you'. Please note the wording of the sign, but have no fear; just press on like the many who have used this public bridleway before you. Just before Swineside Law the track passes the end of the fence and provides fine views up the steep-sided valley of the Rowhope Burn. As the clear, green track climbs onto Black Braes, it divides into numerous sunken

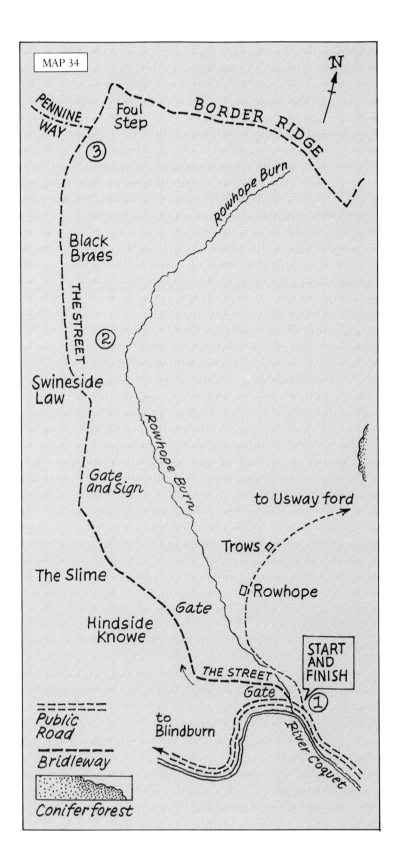

MAP 34

N

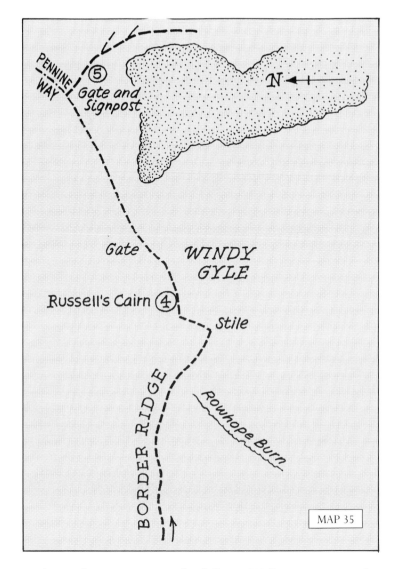

trackways but reunites at the hilltop. Walk on to meet the Pennine Way *(3)* at a fence corner. Continue straight on with the fence alongside on your L. Pass along a sunken trackway until the gate is reached at Foul Step.

Turn R in front of the gate and up the indistinct path by the fence. After descending into a small valley bear R then L onto the clear path which climbs to meet the fence again. Carry on along the path towards Windy Gyle seen ahead. Cross the narrow ridge and as the final ascent begins cross the stile by the gate into Scotland. Gradually bear away to the L from the fence and climb to the summit Cairn *(4)*. From Russell's Cairn continue on in the same direction now descending to rejoin the fence. Go through the gate by a large cairn and on downhill over peat hags, past a marker post and across a ladder stile.

Turn R at the signpost, down the sunken track of Clennell Street *(2)*. Pass the sign (Salters Road) staying on Clennell Street then over the stile by a gate. Walk on bearing R past a PBS on the wide, grassy track between forestry plantations. After 1 mile (1½ km) the track drops steeply towards the Hepden Burn. Continue around the hillside until the gravel road is reached. Cross the road and along the fence line ahead, ignoring first a stile then a gate on your L. Pass through the gate which lies across the obvious track ahead. Just after the gate, bear L away from this track along a narrow hillside path above the Usway Burn down to your L. Clennell Street can now be seen climbing the valley side opposite on its way to Alwinton. The path rejoins

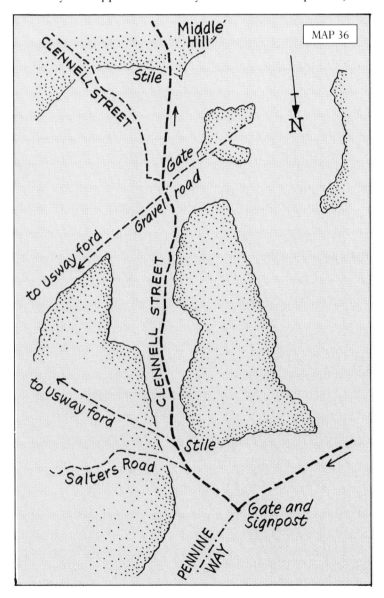

*Looking towards*
*Windy Gyle*

the track just before the forest plantations of Fairhaugh. Cross the stile into the forest and on uphill. At the top of the rise take the L fork down the narrow forest track. The Usway Burn and Fairhaugh farmhouse *(5)* are soon reached. Opposite the house the track joins another track at a bend. Bear R uphill and at the top cross the ladder stile out of the plantation. Press on along the hillside and then down to the valley floor of the Barrow Burn to the R. The track soon climbs the valley side again which leads to the buildings of Lounges Knowe *(6)*.

Pass the old school and through the gate ahead onto a tarmac track. After another gate, cross the footbridge. Bear R then L past the end of the old farmhouse of Barrow Burn and on, keeping L at a junction of tracks in the haymeadow *(7)*. Go through the gate ahead and turn R along the main valley road. Pass Windyhaugh Farm on the opposite bank of the river Coquet *(8)* then some sheep pens on route to the parking area.

*1 Slymefoot*

On this small flat car-park where the Rowhope Burn enters the Coquet there once stood a notorious public house called 'The Slymefoot'. During the eighteenth century, sheep farmers gambled and drank great quantities of 'innocent' whiskey which was produced locally in illicit stills carefully hidden along nearby streams. Being 'innocent' or 'duty free', this whiskey was a real 'Mountain Dew'; prized far and wide, it encouraged much smuggling activity.

*2 Drove roads*

The Street is one of several ancient trading routes crossing these border hills. Much used over recent centuries by Scottish drovers taking stock to market in England, they probably date back to pre-Roman times. Clennell Street and the Salters Road are other examples encountered on this walk.

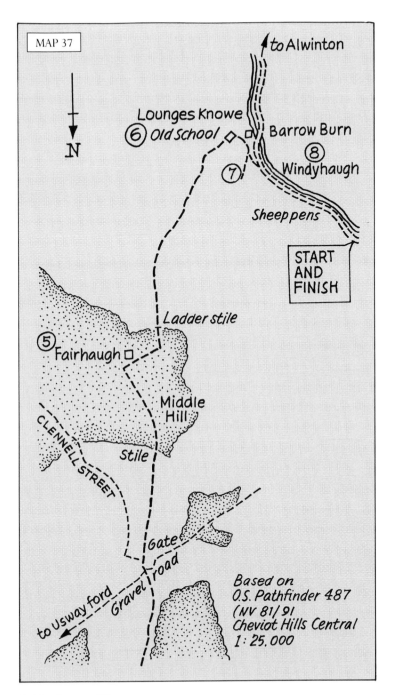

MAP 37

N

to Alwinton

Lounges Knowe
⑥ Old School ◇   □ Barrow Burn
                              ⑧
                    ⑦    Windyhaugh

Sheep pens

START
AND
FINISH

Ladder stile

⑤ Fairhaugh □

Middle
Hill

CLENNELL STREET

Stile

Gate

to Usway ford    Gravel road

Based on
O.S. Pathfinder 487
(NV 81/91
Cheviot Hills Central
1:25.000

*3  The Pennine Way*

This long-distance footpath, when opened in 1965, marked the beginning of a series of National Trails in Britain. From Edale in the Peak District to Kirk Yetholm in Scotland the route covers 250 miles (402 km) in all. This challenging northern section provides walkers with 27 miles (43 km) of remote, uncompromising, moorland walking.

*Russell's Cairn*

### 4 Russell's Cairn and Windy Gyle

Between the fourteenth and sixteenth centuries chronic warfare existed between England and Scotland, the effects of which were felt greatest along the Border counties. A military zone existed then and to exert control a unique system of administration was set up on both sides of the Border. This involved the appointment of Wardens of the Marches (or Border areas) who were required to meet at pre-arranged places on the border to hand out harsh penalties to law breakers who feuded or raided. It was at such a meeting at the Border crossing of Clennell Street that Lord Francis Russell was killed; the Bronze Age burial cairn on Windy Gyle now bears his name in commemoration.

This wild and lonely hill has a chilling atmosphere in more than one sense of the word. Amongst the heather on the summit a mountain plant grows; the aptly named cloudberry has large green leaves that shrivel in summertime to reveal sweet-tasting, bright orange berries known locally as Noops.

### 5 Fairhaugh

In the sheltered valley of the Usway Burn (pronounced Oozy Burn) the white walls of Fairhaugh shine brilliantly against the deep-green shades of burnside trees and nearby conifers of Kidland Forest. Once a remote sheep farm, little remains unplanted except for the small flat meadow (or haugh) by the burn.

### 6 Lounges Knowe

Prior to the opening of the school in 1879, it was the custom for the teacher to live with each shepherd in turn, staying one week for each child in the family, in exchange for his board and lodgings, a small wage and the obligatory social banter at the fireside in the evenings.

### 7 Hay meadows

Surrounding Barrowburn farmstead are some of the best traditionally managed hay meadows in the National Park. They contain a wide variety of wild flowers, including cranesbill and yellow hay rattle. The tiny black day-flying moth, the chimney sweeper, will often be seen in summer sunshine. The hay produced in these meadows will be taken out to storage huts on the hills and fed to the sheep during winter.

### 8 River wildlife

The fast flowing Coquet is a haven for birds such as the dipper, grey wagtail and common sandpiper who all nest along its banks in spring. The small heath butterfly is often found on the grassy banksides in summertime along with wild flowers like maiden pink, harebell and thyme.

# WALKS IN
# THE NORTH YORK MOORS
# NATIONAL PARK

*Cliff top path near Hayburn Wyke*

# THE WHITE HORSE WALK

**STARTING AND FINISHING POINT**
Sutton Bank car-park (100-515830)
on the A170 from Helmsley to Thirsk.
**LENGTH**
3¼ miles (5 km)
**ASCENT**
200 feet (60 m)

This short walk offers some of the finest views in Yorkshire. From 900 feet (270 m) up on the edge of the moors you can see across the Vale of York to the mountains of the Yorkshire Dales. The route is obvious throughout the walk and the climb and descent are along stepped paths.

## ROUTE DESCRIPTION (Map 38)

From the car-park near the Information Centre, cross over the main road and turn R towards the edge of the escarpment. Turn L along the track beside the wire fence. A path leads off here to the view indicator *(1)* if you wish to visit this point. Continue on the track beside the wire fence and you soon find yourself walking along the top of a cliff. Below and to the R is Lake Gormire *(2)*, nestling among the trees, and beneath you is the steep hill descending to Thirsk *(3)*. Continue along the cliff top for about ¾ mile (1.2 km), then fork R down the steps. At the bottom bear L on the path which offers views of the crags and continue on the main track which gradually sweeps L through mixed woodland to a gate into a car-park.

Above you at this point is the vast Kilburn White Horse *(4)*. At the foot of a series of steps are two memorials to the building and maintenance of the White Horse. Climb the steps and turn L at the top passing above the White Horse. From this point there is an excellent view south *(5)*. Follow the cliff-top path back to Sutton Bank car-park. On your R is the glider station with sailplanes often soaring overhead.

*1 View indicator*
From this excellent view-point the indicator points out the directions of numerous places, including Knaresborough Castle nineteen miles (30 km) away, Richmond twenty-four miles (39 km) and Great Whernside on the skyline thirty-two miles (52 km) to the west.

*Glider over Sutton Bank*

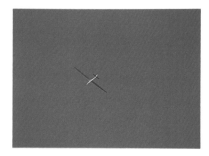

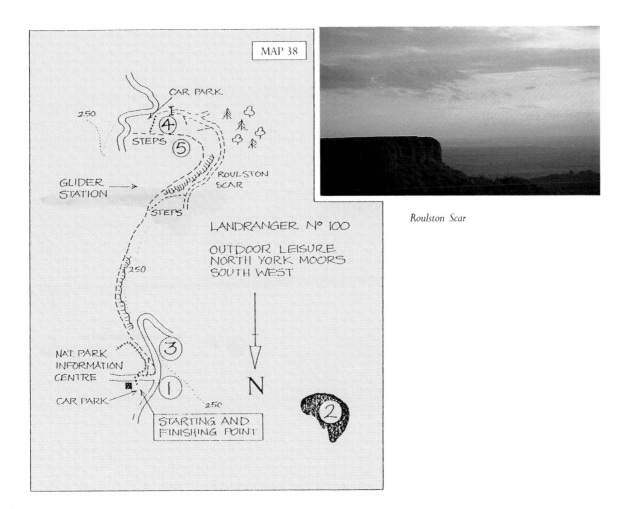

Roulston Scar

2 *Lake Gormire*
The lake is set below the steep crags of Whitestone Cliff. It is an unusual lake, as it has no feeder stream or outlet and according to local folk lore is bottomless. The Garbutt Wood Nature Trail from Sutton Bank car-park explores the area above the lake.

3 *Sutton Bank Hill*
Nowadays the steep 1 in 4 hill is used regularly by vehicles heading to and from the moors and coast, but in the 1920s the hill was used for motor trials with only the best men and machines reaching the top.

4 *Kilburn White Horse*
The massive hill figure is 314 feet (95 m) long and 229 feet (70 m) high and was cut out on the hillside in 1857. It was the idea of Thomas Taylor and John Hodgson, the village schoolmaster, who with thirty-three local men marked out and cut the figure. Unlike the hill figures in southern England, the base is limestone, not chalk, so to keep its white

*Kilburn White Horse*

colour it requires regular maintenance. The figure is visible up to seventy miles (113 km) away.

5 *The view-point*

Among the many things to be seen from this view-point is the picturesque village of Kilburn, which contains the workshops of Robert Thompson the woodcarver, whose furniture carries a mouse as its trademark. Looking further afield the view extends over the patchwork quilt of fields, which was originally the Forest of Galtres, to York in the distance.

# THE HOLE OF HORCUM

STARTING AND FINISHING
POINT
Saltergate Bank car-park (94/100-
852937) on the A169 Pickering to
Whitby road.
LENGTH
5 miles (8 km)
ASCENT
600 feet (180 m)

This is a walk of delightful contrasts. The first mile of the route skirts the top edge of the natural hollow of the Hole of Horcum, offering fine views. The heather-covered Levisham Moor, spectacular in August, is crossed to Dundale Pond. Here the scenery changes to quiet woodland in the valleys of Dundale Griff and Levisham Beck. The return through the centre of the Hole of Horcum gives an opportunity to grasp the size and structure of this natural basin.

## ROUTE DESCRIPTION (Map 39)

From the large car-park cross over the road, and in front of you is the vast hollow of the Hole of Horcum *(1)*. Turn R along the track which skirts the top of the hollow and descend to join the road near the sharp bend of Saltergate Bank *(2)*. Continue straight on to a stile and gate which give access to a broad track over Levisham Moor. After a mile (1.6 km) the track descends slightly to Seavy Pond then continues through the heather for another mile to Dundale Pond *(3)*. At this pond turn L down Dundale Griff. The path down the valley continues on the R bank of the stream which quickly leaves the level moorland and cuts deeply into the tree-lined valley.

As you approach the valley bottom you pass two small valleys on your L with the quaint names of Pigtrough Griff and Water Griff, but you continue to a junction of tracks in the valley with a wooden signpost *(4)*. Turn L over the stream to a footbridge over Levisham Beck. Turn half L after crossing the bridge and continue with a wall on your R and the stream on your L. After about 300 yards (275 m) you cross over a stile and the path continues over the fields crossing two further stiles to Low Horcum Farm *(5)*. Pass the farm on your R and continue into the head of the valley. Cross over a stile, and when the stream bears L carry straight on. The path begins to climb out of the Hole of Horcum, leading into a gully up the western edge of the hollow and continuing fairly steeply up to a stile and the road on Saltergate Bank. Turn R back along the edge of the Hole of Horcum to the car-park.

*The Hole of Horcum*

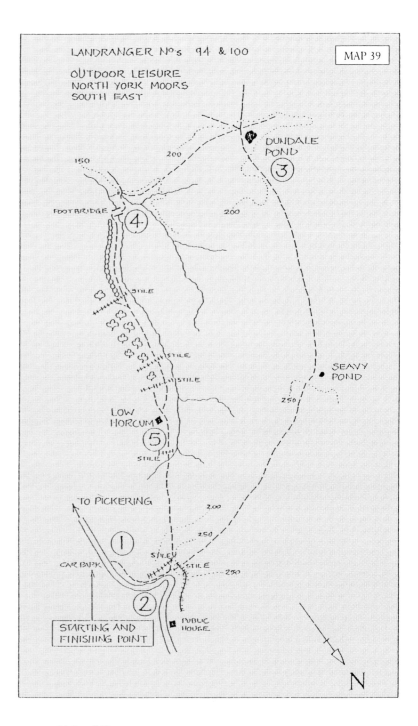

*1  Hole of Horcum*

The vast hollow is a ¼ mile (1.2 km) wide slice taken out of
the surrounding moorland. Legend says that Giant Wade dug
the earth out of the hollow with his hand and threw it at his
wife; he missed, and the hill of Blakey Topping two miles to
the east was formed. The land was in fact undermined by

springs many thousands of years ago and the resulting debris was washed down Levisham Beck.

2 *Saltergate Bank*

At this point on the hill there is an excellent view northwards to the Ballistic Missile Early Warning Station at RAF Fylingdales. This station gives the famous four minute warning of nuclear attack to Britain and fifteen minutes to the United States. The station also tracks satellites out in space. At the foot of the hill is the Saltergate Inn, a resting place for travellers crossing the moors. In time gone by there would be a variety of goods passing the inn including fish from the coast, lime to sweeten the acid soils and probably smuggled contraband. Behind the inn you can see the top of Newtondale Gorge, through which the North York Moors Railway threads its way.

3 *Dundale Pond*

This pond was probably built about 1230 when the land was given to the monks of Malton Priory as pasture for their sheep, cattle and horses. To this day common rights of Levisham Moor are owned by twenty-six local people who hold the various rights to graze over 2,000 sheep or a lesser number of cattle; the Right of Turbary (to collect turf for fires); the right of estovers (to collect wood); the right of piscary (to fish) and also the right to graze a limited amount of poultry and horses.

4 *Levisham Beck Woods*

The woods support a wide variety of birds. If you are lucky you may see tits, treecreepers, woodpeckers, blackcaps or a dipper winging its way just above the stream.

5 *Horcum*

The land at the bottom of the Hole of Horcum supported two farms up to about twenty years ago. The one at Low Horcum has been restored, but High Horcum, at the northern end of the hollow, has now disappeared.

# 2.25

# OSMOTHERLEY AND THE DROVE ROAD

STARTING AND FINISHING
POINT
Sheepwash car-park (100-469993).
Turn east off A19 Thirsk to
Middlesbrough road to Osmotherley.
Turn L in village on Swainby road for
1½ miles (2.5 km).
LENGTH
6 miles (9.5 km)
ASCENT
450 feet (140 m)

The Scottish drovers bringing their cattle south to the English markets in the eighteenth and nineteenth centuries used the ancient Hambleton Street. This clearly defined walk sets out on this track and then follows a woodland path leading across to the attractive village of Osmotherley. Here the Cleveland Way is joined for a circuit of Scarth Wood Moor, revealing extensive views to the west and north.

## ROUTE DESCRIPTION (Map 40)

From the car-park turn R up the road towards Swainby. When the road turns L turn R over a footbridge and follow the broad track up a short hill *(1)* continuing south alongside a plantation. After ¼ mile (1.2 km) turn R over a stile beside a gate with a fenced pond on your L. Walk down the broad ride between the trees crossing two other rides, pass a ruined building on your R then cross a lane to a gate. The track descends between trees following a stream on your L. Pass the ruins of Cote Garth on your R. Continue on the track to a gate which leads down to a tarmac road, turn R past the Youth Hostel and climb up to a junction. When you reach the junction, turn L down the road into Osmotherley *(2)*.

Return back up the road towards Swainby and turn L along Ruebury Lane, where there is a Cleveland Way signpost *(3)*. As the road swings R a fine view opens up across the plain below. There is an indicator pointing out places to be seen at the fork in the tracks. Your route lies to the L, but the track on the R leads up to the Lady Chapel *(4)* ¼ mile (1.2 km) away, a diversion well worth undertaking, returning to this point.

Continue on the broad track, pass Chapel Wood Farm on your L, and continue through two gates into a wood. Fork R on the Cleveland Way track which climbs steadily through the trees. At the top follow a stone wall on your R. Pass a GPO booster station screened by the woods, and a short while later

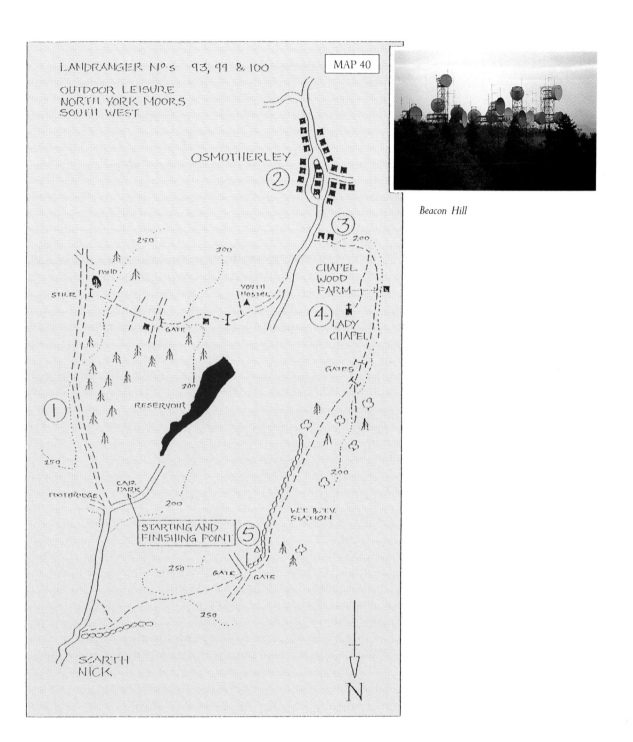

LANDRANGER Nºs 93, 99 & 100

OUTDOOR LEISURE
NORTH YORK MOORS
SOUTH WEST

MAP 40

OSMOTHERLEY

②

③

CHAPEL
WOOD
FARM

④ LADY
CHAPEL

STILE

POND

YOUTH
HOSTEL

GATE

250

200

200

200

RESERVOIR

GATES

①

150

CAR
PARK

FOOTBRIDGE

200

W.T.B.T.V.
STATION

STARTING AND
FINISHING POINT ⑤

250

GATE

GATE

250

SCARTH
NICK

200

N

Beacon Hill

you pass an OS obelisk on your R just over the wall *(5)*. Pass
through two gates and follow the broad track across the moor.
The finest views are now to the north across the Cleveland
Plain. The path eventually joins a wall descending to the road in
Scarth Nick. Turn R along the road back to the car-park.

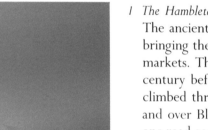

*1 The Hambleton Drove Road*

The ancient trackway became popular with Scottish drovers bringing their cattle south, on the hoof, to sell at the English markets. The trade reached its peak in the early nineteenth century before the railways took over the trade. The route climbed through Scarth Nick then passed the Chequers Inn and over Black Hambleton. It then split near Steeple Cross, one road continuing south to York while a south-eastern road led down Stocking Lane to Malton, continuing south over the Wolds and River Humber into Lincolnshire and Norfolk.

*2 Osmotherley*

This attractive village of stone houses stands on the edge of the moors overlooking the plain. In the centre of the village is the market cross and a stone table set on five short stone legs where produce for sale could be displayed. Fish was sold here as late as 1874. The church stands on the site of a Saxon church, but the earliest part of the present building is the Norman south doorway.

*3 The Cleveland Way*

The 112 miles (180 km) Long Distance Footpath starts at Helmsley and heads west to Sutton Bank and Kilburn White Horse. The route then turns north to Osmotherley, over the Cleveland Hills and Roseberry Topping to the coast at Saltburn. For the last fifty-two miles (84 km) the cliff top path is followed, passing through Whitby and Scarborough to finish at Filey Brigg.

*4 The Lady Chapel*

The small chapel is attached to a stone house set amidst trees. It was reputedly built in 1515 by Queen Katherine of Aragon, first wife of Henry VIII, for the recluse Thomas Parkinson.

*5 Scarth Wood Moor OS obelisk*

This is one end of the Lyke Wake Walk, the other end of the forty miles (64 km) moorland walk being Beacon Howe, above Ravenscar, on the coast. The route was devised by Bill Cowley and first walked in October 1955 by him and twelve other walkers. At peak weekends in the early 1980s over a thousand people at a time were completing the challenge. The track over the high moors is now very eroded, and large groups are being advised against undertaking the walk to give the path a chance to recover.

*Scarth Wood Moor*

# HACKNESS AND WHISPERDALES

---

STARTING AND FINISHING
POINT
Reasty Bank car-park (94/101-
964943).
Turn south off the A171 Scarborough
to Whitby road, north of the Falcon
Inn, towards Harwood Dale. Turn R
just before the village to Hackness.
The car-park is at the top of the
steep hill.
LENGTH
7½ miles (12 km)
ASCENT
450 feet (140 m)

The early part of the walk is through a conifer plantation, then across farmland. The descent to Hackness is through a deciduous wood rich in wild flowers in summer. The picturesque village of Hackness was the site of a convent established in the seventh century by St Hilda of Whitby, and there are parts of an Anglian cross in the church. The return is along peaceful Whisperdales with valley fields overlooked by conifer-topped heights.

## ROUTE DESCRIPTION (Map 41)

From the car-park on the eastern side of the road take the track which keeps to the top of the plateau—not the one marked with a PFS. There are views over Harwood Dale from the car-park. The track passes beneath the trees. After 600 yards (550 m) a path on your L leads in 50 yards (45 m) to a fine view-point over the fields to Scarborough Castle, but your route carries straight on along the plateau top. Eventually the track swings R to a road; cross the road coming in from your L and continue along the roadside for 50 yards (45 m) then turn L at a PFS. This narrower but still distinct track passes in a semi-circle beneath the trees to join the road further south. Turn R parallel with the road and turn L at the road junction to Silpho.

At the end of the wood pass Thieves Dike and 200 yards (180 m) later turn L at the PFS. Cross two fields keeping the hedge on your R. Turn L at the PFS along the edge of a field, then R at the next PFS along the edge of fields with a stone wall on your R. After crossing two stiles turn R to a stile and descend into a valley. Turn L down the valley (PFS to Hackness) and pass over a stile into a wood. The hillside track leads through the deciduous wood which has a wide variety of wild flowers *(1)*. On reaching the road descend the steep hill to a T-junction in Hackness. Your route lies to the R but you may wish to turn L and visit the church first *(2)*.

*Farmer's tombstone, Hackness*

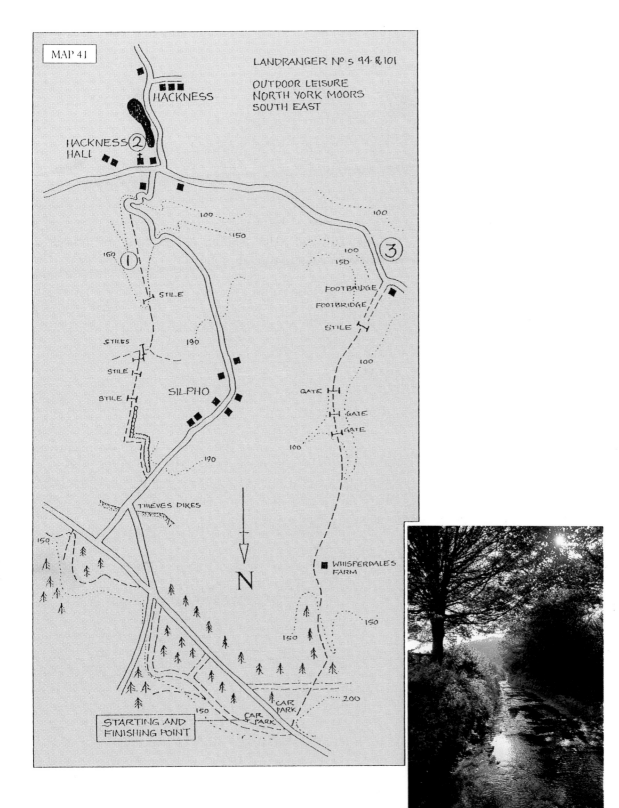

*Low dales ford*

Having turned R, you turn R again after 100 yards (90m) along the road signposted 'Low Dales and High Dales only'. This lane leads through the quiet pastoral valley for a mile (1.6 km); you may then encounter a flooded road *(3)*, so fork R over the footbridge and stile and follow the hedge on your L to Low Dales, walking parallel with the road.

At the fork in the road bear R, cross a footbridge over a stream, fork R again to another footbridge and then a stile. The track leads up the valley passing through gates and over stiles and then swings R around Whisperdales Farm; it then climbs steadily into a forest and sweeps R. At the next junction you can see a boundary marker inscribed 'SIL'; continue on your track back to the car-park at Reasty Bank.

1   *Hilda Wood*

The wood probably takes its name from St Hilda, the Abbess of Whitby Abbey who founded a cell of the Celtic abbey at Hackness. On a walk through the woods in the late spring you should find an interesting selection of wild flowers beside the path, including wood anemone, red campion, forget-me-not, wild garlic, bluebell, lesser celandine and primrose.

2   *Hackness Church*

The church stands on the site of a Celtic cell set up by Whitby Abbey. Begu, one of the nuns, saw the death of St Hilda in a dream and informed the other nuns hours before the news arrived from Whitby. A Benedictine house was founded on the site in the eleventh century. The present church on the same site contains a late Saxon chancel arch and some Norman work. Inside the church are two pieces of an Anglo-Saxon cross.

3   *Low Dales Ford*

This section of road is often flooded and must be the longest ford in Yorkshire.

*Autumn in Hilda Wood*

# 2.27

# THE PACKHORSE TRACKS OF COMMONDALE MOOR

## STARTING AND FINISHING POINT

Commondale village (94-662104).
Turn south off the A171 Whitby to
Guisborough road towards Castleton.
After 2½ miles (4 km) turn R to
Commondale.

## LENGTH

7 miles (11 km)

## ASCENT

600 feet (180 m)

The moorlands are crossed by many ancient paved tracks and this walk incorporates a number of these. This is an excellent moorland walk, with views of the sea from the high points. One part of the route is poorly defined and some easy compass work may need to be undertaken to reach Hob Cross. For this reason, it would be better walked on a fine day.

## ROUTE DESCRIPTION (Maps 42, 43)

From the village walk up the road towards Kildale and Stokesley. Pass the 'Commondale' village sign and 100 yards (90 m) later turn R along a track near a group of trees. Turn R at the PFS to Guisborough and a grassy track crosses open moorland and joins a short section of paved way *(1)*. Fork R shortly after joining the paved way, cross the moorland stream and the track climbs up the hillside and eventually joins a broader track. Continue straight ahead and in 50 yards (45 m) fork L on a track to a memorial *(2)*.

Rejoin the broad track, then follow a bearing of 352° magnetic, keeping a line of grouse butts on your L to reach a stone pillar inscribed 'Hob on the Hill' *(3)*. Then take a compass reading of 10° magnetic for ¾ mile (1.2 km) to Hob Cross, a stone with that inscription set on a mound. It stands on the moor about 100 yards (90 m) short of a stone wall. There are fine views over the moorlands to the coastline and sea beyond.

Turn R at Hob Cross on a narrow track marked with wooden posts with blue arrows. Cross under the overhead wires and continue to the paved Quaker Path. Turn half R along this fine exposed section of causeway, and when it ends continue along the path to the road. Lockwood Beck reservoir comes into view on your L. Turn R along the road.

At the first bend you can shorten the route by following a line of boundary stones across the moor; keep to the L of the wood and turn half R down the road into Commondale.

166

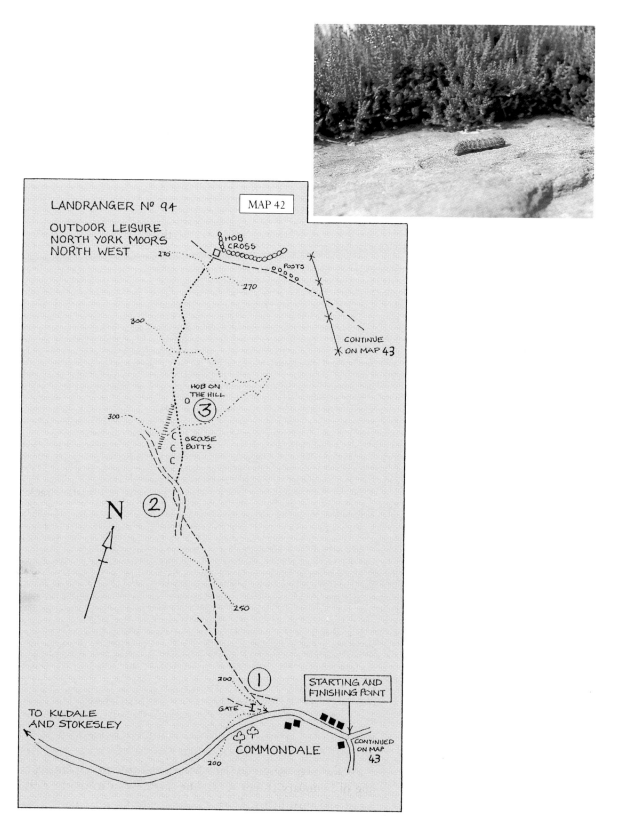

LANDRANGER Nº 94

MAP 42

OUTDOOR LEISURE
NORTH YORK MOORS
NORTH WEST

HOB CROSS

270

POSTS

270

300

CONTINUE ON MAP 43

HOB ON THE HILL

0

③

300

GROUSE BUTTS

C
C
C

N

②

250

①

200

STARTING AND FINISHING POINT

GATE

TO KILDALE AND STOKESLEY

COMMONDALE

200

Continued ON MAP 43

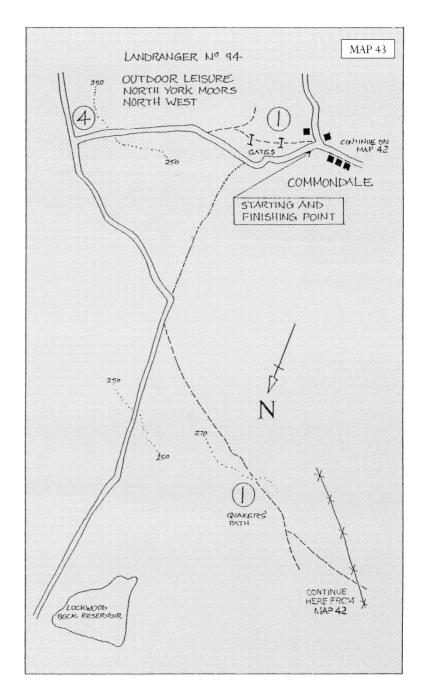

For the main route continue on the unfenced moorland road to the road junction where the base and shaft of White Cross *(4)* is situated. Turn R down the road towards Commondale and at the bend in the road bear L onto the paved way, turning half R along it towards Commondale. Short sections of the paved way *(1)* are missing, but the line of the route continues to a gate and then crosses two fields. Here the paving is covered with

*Hob on the Hill*

*The War Memorial, Commondale Moor*

grass, arriving at the crossroads in Commondale where you started.

*1 Paved ways*

The paved ways were used by pannier ponies as the stones were wide enough for ponies but not for wheeled vehicles. The paved sections were usually on the steeper slopes, where traffic would erode the surface, but a few of them ran for miles across the moors. The ponies carried their loads in panniers balanced on either side of their backs. A train of twenty to forty ponies were usually headed by a lead pony wearing bells. Moorland coal was moved by this method around Rosedale as late as the 1870s.

*2 War memorial*

The stone is a memorial to Guardsmen Robbie Leggott, who was killed in action in 1916, and Alf Cockerill, who died of wounds received during the First World War. It was erected by Hon. Margaret Bruce Challoner in the area where these two volunteers had spent their boyhood, one of them shepherding his father's flock.

*3 Hobs*

These were local folklore characters which were thought to be something similar to elves. Some were mischievous and others were helpful to the farmers. They were associated with various places on the moor and at least twenty-four were recorded by George Calvert in a manuscript written in 1823.

*4 White Cross*

This White Cross should not be confused with the White Cross known as Fat Betty at the head of Rosedale. The stone base and shaft stand on the old moorland road from Whitby. At this point the road may have split, one route going down the side of the Leven Valley to Stokesley, while a north-western route went along the Quaker Path to Guisborough.

# THE HERITAGE COAST PATH

STARTING AND FINISHING
POINT
Ravenscar car-park (94-980014).
Turn east off the A171 Scarborough
to Whitby road.
LENGTH
12 miles (19 km)
ASCENT
1000 feet (300 m)

South of Ravenscar stretch miles of peaceful coastline. The cliffs tumble away, sometimes to the sea or to the Undercliff, offering splendid views. There are two descents with easy access to the shore at Hayburn Wyke and Cloughton Wyke. The return is made along the disused railway track. The route-finding is simple throughout the walk.

## ROUTE DESCRIPTION (Maps 44, 45)

From the car-park turn L, walk down the road and turn R along Station Road *(1)*. After 50 yards (45 m) turn L at the end of the wire fence and follow the path down to the cliff top, then turn R. The savage coastline below was the scene of the shipwreck of the *Coronation* in 1913 and the *Fred Everard* in 1965 *(2)*. The path continues south along the cliff top for 3½ miles (5.5 km). Pass a coastguard station and continue with the Undercliff *(3)* below.

As you approach Hayburn Wyke on a clear day you can see Scarborough Castle and Filey Brigg in the distance *(4)*. Eventually the path passes over a stile and descends into Hayburn Wyke Woods *(5)* down a series of steps. Ignore the stile signposted to Staintondale and bear half L. The second footbridge in the wood crosses Hayburn Wyke Beck, and then a path to the L leads to the beach where there is a small waterfall.

Continue straight along the path which begins to climb up the hillside. Fork L at the two junctions and you will arrive back at the cliff-top path. After 1¼ miles (2 km) the path descends into Cloughton Wyke. At the bottom turn R up some steps and pass a small car-park. The track becomes a surfaced road. Cross a bridge and turn R over a stile, then descend to the former railway track and turn L. This was the route of the Whitby–Scarborough railway line *(6)*.

The track is followed all the way to Ravenscar passing on the way the sites of Hayburn Wyke and Staintondale stations. The climbing is hardly noticeable, but between Staintondale and

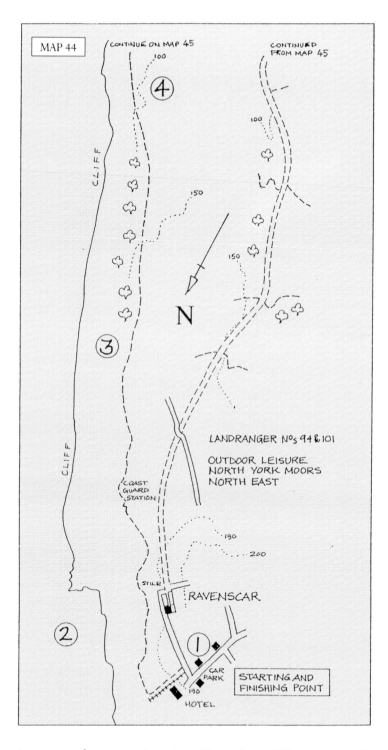

MAP 44

CONTINUE ON MAP 45

CONTINUED FROM MAP 45

LANDRANGER Nºs 94 & 101

OUTDOOR LEISURE
NORTH YORK MOORS
NORTH EAST

RAVENSCAR

STARTING AND
FINISHING POINT

Ravenscar the ascent is a 1 in 41 gradient. When you reach Ravenscar, pass over a stile beside the gate and take the track to the R of the platform; cross Station Square and turn L down Station Road, turning L again to the car-park.

*Cliff top path near Hayburn Wyke*

1 *Ravenscar*

The Raven Hall Hotel stands on the site of a Roman signal station. There were plans in the 1890s to develop the village into a major seaside resort; some building plots were sold but the scheme collapsed. The 600 feet (180 m) high cliffs which separated the proposed new town from the sea would have been a problem.

2 *The* Coronation *and* Fred Everard *shipwrecks*

The 3290 ton (3237 tonne) *Coronation* ran aground on 11 January 1913 in a snow storm. The distress signals went unnoticed in the storm, but the crew rowed a boat ashore and rigged a line and bosun's chair to take everyone off the ship. Various attempts were made to refloat the ship all through the spring and summer, but it was September before she was refloated and taken to Hartlepool. After all the effort the ship was burned out at Hartlepool a month later.

The 1542 ton (1567 tonne) motor vessel *Fred Everard* ran ashore at nearly the same place in a snow storm on 27 November 1965. The crew were saved by Whitby lifeboat. This ship broke up within weeks and parts of the wreck may be visible at low tide.

3 *The Undercliff or Beast Cliff*

This long shelf-like plateau lies some 200 feet (60 m) down

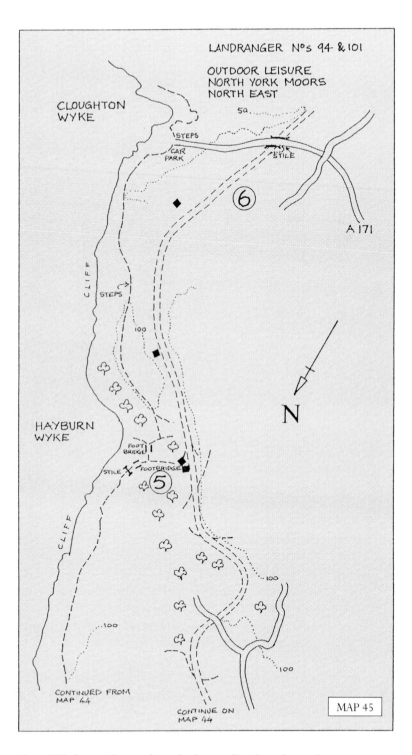

the cliff face. The undisturbed woodland and scrub now forms an interesting area for naturalists. It has been designated as a Site of Special Scientific Interest and may become a nature reserve.

4 *The Cleveland Way*

Filey Brigg is the end of the Cleveland Way and this is the first sight of the walker's goal.

5 *Hayburn Wyke Nature Reserve*

The nature reserve was created around the wooded banks of Hayburn Beck. The wood consists mainly of oak, with ash, hazel and hawthorn. Among the plants to be seen in early summer are woodruff, enchanter's nightshade, lady's mantle, common spotted orchid and wild honeysuckle. The chiff-chaff can be heard and there are treecreepers, blackcaps and redstarts.

6 *Whitby–Scarborough Railway*

The line was opened in 1885 and was one of the most scenic lines in Britain. It offered both moorland and sea views. The 21 mile (34 km) long route had eight stations between Scarborough and Whitby West Cliff; the line reached its maximum height of 631 feet (192 m) at Ravenscar, where it entered a tunnel. A number of stations on the line offered camping coaches for holidaymakers.

Previous page: *The waterfall, Hayburn Wyke*

# WALKS IN THE PEAK DISTRICT NATIONAL PARK

*Curbar from Baslow Edge*

# 1.29

# Stanton Moor

This small, attractive, heathery moor is covered with the
evidence of past civilizations, including many stone circles and
burial mounds. There are several interesting rocks, boulders and
quarries to be seen, but please take care near the quarry edges.

## ROUTE DESCRIPTION (Map 46)

Walk up the main street to a gate on the R (marked 'Barn
Farm') at the end of the houses, opposite Ann Twyfords quarry
(1). Go up the farm road and to the R of the farm to a stile.
Keep to the L of the fence to the gate and in the far corner of
the next field a stile leads to a fenced path. At the end of the
path turn half R over the stile, through the wall ahead at a gap
and up to join the road at a stile in the hedge. Go L on the road
for a few yards and turn R by the National Trust sign.

A fence follows the edge of Stanton Moor (2) for ½ mile

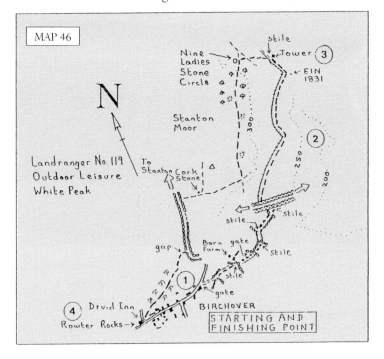

*Opposite* Stanton Moor

*The tower on Stanton Moor*

(800 m) before turning L at the large inscribed boulder (EIN 1831) in which footholds have been cut. After 150 yards (135 m), cross the fence at a stile behind the tower *(3)*. Go half R on the path which, in 200 yards (180 m), reaches Nine Ladies Stone Circle among the trees. Turn L and cross the open moorland for ½ mile (800 m) on a clear path. Turn R at the junction. Passing the Cork Stone, which can be ascended by means of metal rungs, the road is reached in ¼ mile (400 m). Turn L and just before the road turns L, go through a gap on the R and descend through the woods to the Druid Inn with Rowter Rocks *(4)* behind. Turn L back into Birchover.

*1  Ann Twyfords Quarry*

This is one of the few quarries still producing traditional millstones. They also manufacture grindstones which are used in engineering works, in glass bevelling and for knife sharpening. Large stones from the quarry are used in the manufacture of paper in crushing the wood to pulp and of course a lot of building stone is also produced.

*2  Stanton Moor*

On the eastern edge of the Peak District limestone, this outcrop of sandstone holds in its 150 acres (60 hectares) of heather-clad moorland one of the finest collections of Bronze Age remains to be found in the British Isles. Over seventy barrows are scattered across the moor, with examples of stone circles, cairns and standing stones; the best preserved is the Nine Ladies Stone Circle, 33 ft (10 m) in diameter, with its King Stone close by. This was once enclosed by a stone wall which has now been removed. A private museum at Birchover was established by J. and J.P. Heathcote, who from 1927 to 1950 excavated seventy cairns on the moor. Twenty-seven acres (11 hectares) of the moor were gifted to the National Trust in 1934.

*3  Tower*

At one time an inscription over the door read 'Earl Grey 1832' in tribute to the gentleman who carried the Reform Bill through parliament.

*4  Rowter Rocks*

This fascinating maze of caves, stairs and tunnels in the rocks is a delight to explore. Once thought to have connections with Druid culture, it was in fact the work of the local vicar, Thomas Eyre (died 1717), who built a study among the rocks and carved rooms, armchairs and alcoves. A rocking stone here was unseated by vandals – not recently however; it was the work of a group of fourteen young men on Whit Sunday in 1799.

# 1.30

# CHEE DALE

**STARTING AND FINISHING POINT**
Car-park on A6, Buxton–Bakewell road. Opposite Topley Pike Quarry (119-104725).
**LENGTH**
4½ miles (7 km)
**ASCENT**
500 ft (150 m)

Kingfishers and dippers skim the waters of the River Wye, which is crossed and recrossed many times by the huge arches of the disused Midland railway as it follows this narrow limestone valley. The old railway track is followed for a short way past the impressive cliffs of Plum Buttress, before descending to the river. At two places the path follows stepping stones in the river and after heavy rain these may become impassable, and you will have to retrace your steps. Therefore this walk is best kept for dryish conditions.

## ROUTE DESCRIPTION (Map 47)

Follow the track beside the river away from the A6 and under two of the railway arches. In ½ mile (800 m), just before a third arch, turn R up some steps to join the disused railway (PFS 'Monsal Trail') *(1)*. Turn R on the railway past Plum Buttress *(2)* which towers above on the R. At the next bridge over the river turn L down a little path to the river (sign 'Chee Dale'). Cross the footbridge and turn R down steps to the river-bank. Soon

*The River Wye, Chee Dale*

the cliffs close in, overhanging the river, and you take to the stepping stones. In ¼ mile (400 m) the river enters a gorge. Two footbridges allow the river to be crossed and recrossed by the Nature Reserve, bypassing the gorge. Again the cliffs close in and only the stepping stones allow further progress. The cliff beyond overhangs considerably, while opposite are the sheer cliffs of Chee Tor *(3)*, also popular with climbers. The foot of Flag Dale is reached, with two footbridges and a stile just before Wormhill Springs which gush forth from beside the path. The dale soon widens out and at an iron footbridge after ¼ mile (400 m), double back up the hillside.

The path, with a natural paving of bare limestone, climbs gradually up the hillside and then swings away from Chee Dale and up to a stile and walled track which leads to the road. Turn L beside the road for a few yards and then L (PFS 'Great Rocks') at a stile. Go through the farm to a very small gate in the wall,

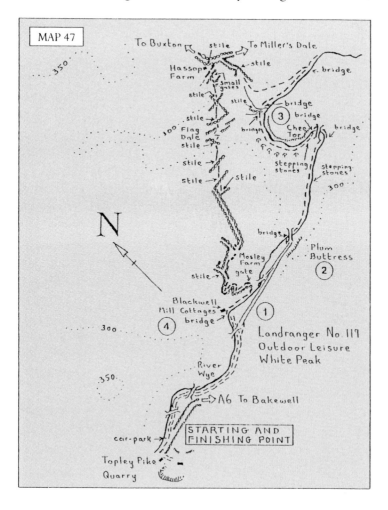

*Chee Dale from the Wormhill road*

half R to a similar gate and down to a stile in the corner. Continue in the same line to a stile above Flag Dale and zig-zag down into the dale. Climb steeply out of the dale to a stile and go straight ahead across the field to an indistinct stile. The next stile is to the R of the overhead lines and then, in the corner of the field beyond, a stile leads to a walled lane. Turn L down to the farm and R at the barn. Passing the farm, where the farm track turns R, turn L at a stile and zig-zag down the hill to a gate and under the railway. Turn R and walk beside the river to Blackwell Mill Cottages *(4)* to cross the river at a footbridge. The car-park is just over ½ mile (800 m) back up the track.

*1  The Monsal Trail*

The Peak Park Board negotiated with British Rail for twelve years before an agreement was reached which allowed the track to be put to new use in 1981 as the Monsal Trail. BR provided £154 000 towards the cost of repairs and although money is not yet available to improve the track surface in Chee Dale, making it rather rough walking on the old gravel ballast, it is a very attractive walk with spectacular views of the magnificent limestone cliffs.

The Buxton to Matlock railway, which reached Manchester in 1867, closed in 1968. The Great Rocks Dale to Doveholes section, however, is still in use, running through one of Europe's biggest quarries, principally for the supply of lime to the ICI works.

*2  Plum Buttress*

This is one of the finest limestone cliffs in the Peak District with several high standard climbs around 200 ft (60 m) in length, which ascend to the obvious horizontal slot, where the tiny figures of climbers will often be seen belayed. The routes then go over or around the overhanging face above.

*3  Chee Tor*

Another of Chee Dale's imposing limestone cliffs, whose most celebrated route is the Chee Tor Girdle. This, as its name indicates, traverses the cliff along the fault line, rather than, as is more usual with rock climbs, going straight up. This gives a rock climb of nearly 600 ft (180 m) in length, all of it exposed. The surrounding area is a Derbyshire Naturalist's Trust Nature Reserve.

*4  Blackwell Mill Cottages*

Surrounded by railway lines, these were built for railway workers and were serviced by a tiny railway station, Blackwell Halt, comprising one up and one down platform, each just long enough to take one carriage. The weir supplied Blackwell Mill, which has almost completely disappeared.

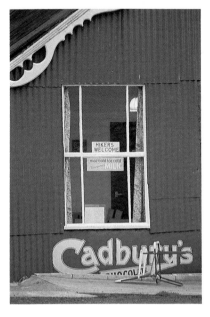

*Café near Chee Dale*

# 2.31

# WELLINGTON'S AND NELSON'S MONUMENTS

**STARTING AND FINISHING POINT**
Curbar Gap National Park car-park east of Curbar (119-261748).
**LENGTH**
6½ miles (10.5 km)
**ASCENT**
850 ft (260 m)

*Birchen Edge near Nelson's Monument*

This visit to the matching monuments to Nelson and Wellington, which face each other across the valley, contrasts the grandeur of the rugged and wild edges with the formality of Chatsworth Estate.

## ROUTE DESCRIPTION (Maps 48, 49)

Turn R out of the car-park where there is a prominent guidestone which marked the junction of several old packhorse routes, and in a few yards turn L at a stile by the sign 'Boundary of Open Country'. Notice also the important admonition nailed to the tree 'No manure removal', so be sure to clean your boots! Either follow the wide track which leads to the Eagle Stone, or the edge of the escarpment where the view is better. Passing the Eagle Stone *(1)*, reach the edge and turn L to arrive at Wellington's Monument *(2)*.

Walk east from Wellington's Monument along the broad footpath on the edge of the moor, which is fringed with silver birch and rowan. Shortly before the main road there is another guidestone on the R which is inscribed 'CHESTE RFEILD ROADE' ('Road to Chesterfield'). Unusually it is marked on one face only. On reaching the road at a gate, turn R downhill to the crossroads. Crossing over the A621, take the ladder stile at the boundary to open country. Bear almost immediately L off the major track and follow the track heading directly for Birchen Edge. The ground to the left of this track is out of bounds. After scattered birch trees and some boggy ground, a short steep climb on a narrow path to the L leads to the top of the edge close to the OS trig point.

The crag reaches its highest point at Nelson's Monument *(3)*, a less imposing memorial than Wellington's and often treated with scant respect by climbers who use it as a belay. Follow the path along the edge and, at the Water Board manhole covers, the path turns R and descends the edge. Upon reaching the

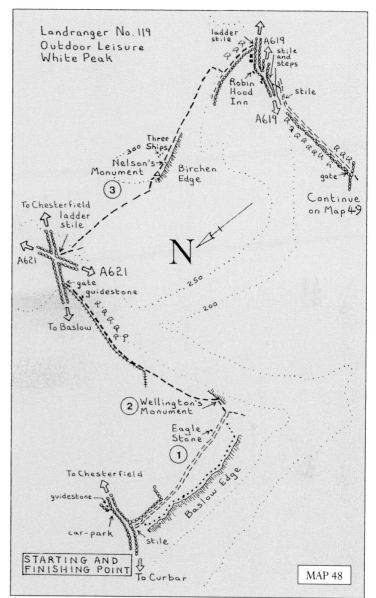

*Curbar from Baslow Edge*

broad path at its foot, turn L with a golf course on your R. At the main road climb a ladder stile over the wall and turn R down the road to join the A619 at the Robin Hood Inn.

Shortly after the Eric Byne campsite entrance, cross the A619 and take the path at the wooden sign 'Concessionary Footpath to Baslow'. A steep flight of steps leads down to a stout wooden bridge. Joining a broad track, turn R and follow the yellow waymarks of the concessionary footpath over a stile and along the lane for ½ mile (800 m) to a gate into a field. At the next

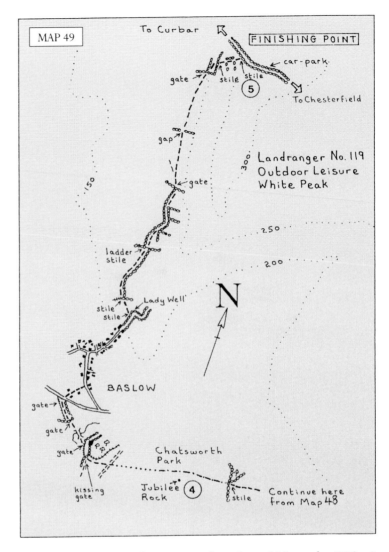

stile Chatsworth Park is entered and in 300 yards (270 m) Jubilee Rock *(4)* will be found a few paces off the track to the L. Follow the indistinct path across the open parkland, marked occasionally with yellow waymarks, to leave Chatsworth Park at 'The Kissing Gate'.

In 50 yards (45 m) turn L through a small kissing gate into the field and then across the hump-backed bridge. Cross the next field to a gate. Go along a path flanked by a stone wall and fence to a flight of steps which will bring you into Baslow at a gate just before the road. Cross the road and go up the narrow path opposite, just to the R of 'Ashton Fields' house. Turn L onto the next road. At Barr road turn R and, where the metalled surface deteriorates to a track just before Lady Well, turn L through a stile.

Follow a rising grassy path to a stile and through the fields to

*Climbers on Curbar Edge*

the L of a wall to a ladder stile. Joining a more major track, follow this between gritstone walls to emerge again onto open country at a gate below Baslow Edge. At the Y-fork take the R branch and continue at the same level on a sandy path through the bracken. At the open country sign, go through a gate onto a wide, green lane which rises to meet the road near Curbar Gap. Turn R at the National Trust sign and through a squeezer stile to avoid the road walking. Emerging onto the road at a stile, a gritstone slab on the R is inscribed with a Biblical text *(5)*. The car-park is a few yards up the road.

*1 Eagle Stone*

Many years ago the young men of Baslow were required to demonstrate their fitness for the responsibilities of marriage by ascending this rock. Nowadays it is the rocks of the edge itself which attract climbers, and anyway, as the climber Morley Wood once said of the climb 'Bachelor's Buttress' at the Roaches, 'Married men are more used to taking risks than bachelors'. These crags are sometimes used by the mountain rescue teams for practising lowering stretchers down the rockface. The quarry on the edge at this point was in use as late as the 1930s.

2 *Wellington's Monument*

The monument is inscribed 'Wellington Born 1769 Died 1852. Erected 1866 by E.M. Wrench late 34th Reg'mt'. From here there is a good view across the valley to Gardom's Edge and also to Nelson's Monument.

3 *Nelson's Monument*

This monument was erected in 1810 by John Brightman, a Baslow man, predating Wellington's Monument by some fifty years. The date 1865 inscribed on the obelisk appears to point to graffiti not being a modern phenomenon. There are three rocks nearby commemorating the ships of Nelson's fleet, *Victory*, *Defiant* and *Royal Soverin*.

4 *Jubilee Rock*

Chatsworth Park was the creation of the fourth Duke of Devonshire, 1720–1764, who employed the landscape architect Lancelot (Capability) Brown. The shape of the woods which follow the contour of the hills is typical of Brown's work. Situated in the park, the Jubilee Rock, carved to commemorate Queen Victoria's golden jubilee, reads:

1837

|  |  |  |
|---|---|---|
| SEND HER | V | HAPPY |
| VICTORIOUS | I | AND GLORIOUS |
|  | T Ⓒ R |  |
| LONG TO | I | GOD |
| REIGN OVER US | A | SAVE THE QUEEN |

1887

5 *Biblical Text*

This slab is inscribed 'Hebrews 7 25' and is one of several such slabs in the vicinity which were carved by Edwin Gregory, a mole-catcher and local preacher.

# 2.32

# ABNEY MOOR AND BRETTON CLOUGH

**STARTING AND FINISHING POINT**
Great Hucklow to Eyam road (119-190781).
**LENGTH**
8½ miles (13.5 km)
**ASCENT**
800 ft (240 m)

Abney Moor, an isolated piece of moorland cut off from the larger and wilder northern moors by Hope Valley, is a quiet and peaceful place where the gliders from Great Hucklow soar in the sky above. The beauties of Bretton Clough will also be appreciated by connoisseurs of the Peak District, with its pleasant tree-lined streams in little steep-sided valleys.

Eyam Edge, the starting point, is an excellent viewpoint. Northwards is Stanage Edge, and through a gap in the intervening hills Win Hill and Derwent Edge can be seen.

## ROUTE DESCRIPTION (Maps 50–52)

Cross the stile and descend the very steep field beside the wall. On the R is an interesting series of hummocks and hills which are the result of landslips. Bretton Brook ('Bretton' meaning 'farm of the Britons') at the foot of the slope is crossed by a footbridge and the track followed uphill to a stile on the L. Continue straight ahead, keeping near the wall, to the next stile on the R; and then head L of the farm to cross a stile onto the farm track. Turn L towards the road and then R to a stile (PFS 'Bradwell') which gives access to Abney Moor.

Follow the clear path across Abney Moor for 1 mile (1.6 km). On many days gliders from the Great Hucklow Gliding Club (1) circle high in the sky above the moor. Leave the moor over a stile onto the old packhorse way from Bradwell to Eyam. Turn R and follow it for about ¾ mile (1.2 km), past the end of the road down to Abney (PBS) until the wall turns R . Turn L (PBS), and in 100 yards (90 m) go through gateposts on to the walled Shatton Lane. Straight ahead, the Great Ridge of Mam Tor to Lose Hill can be seen across the valley. Follow the old lane for 1 mile (1.6 km) with Shatton Edge on the R, first through a gate and then past a tall TV repeater mast, until the lane turns L just after another gate. A ladder stile at the corner leads back to the moor and in a few yards a wall comes in from the L. Follow this wall

*Abney Moor*

191

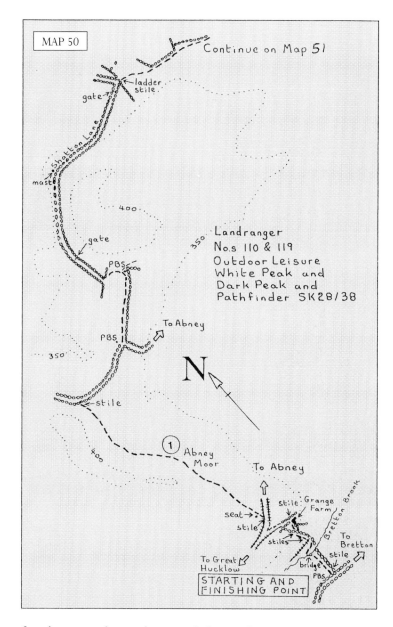

MAP 50

Continue on Map 51

ladder stile

gate

Shatton Lane

mast

400

350

Landranger
No.s 110 & 119
Outdoor Leisure
White Peak and
Dark Peak and
Pathfinder SK28/38

gate

PBS

PBS

To Abney

350

**N**

stile

① Abney
Moor

To Abney

400

seat→

stile

stile

stiles→

To Great
Hucklow

stile Grange
Farm

Bretton Brook

To
Bretton

stile

bridge

PBS

STARTING AND
FINISHING POINT

for about a mile (1.6 km) until the road is met near Offerton Hall at a stile. Turn R onto this and walk uphill. In ¼ mile (400 m) a stile on the L leads to an attractive footpath which is followed down to a stile just before Callow Farm. At the farm, turn L and through a small gate. Go downhill, crossing a broken wall, and enter the wood at another small gate below the farm.

Go through the wood and out into a field at a stile. Cross the field and turn R out of the gate onto the lane, which after about ¼ mile (400 m) passes the entrance to a house and leads up to the road. Go straight across the road, over a stile and half L up the field to another stile on the top of the ridge. Now go R and downhill where a line of signposts leads to the farm road. The bridge immediately below and the stile on its far side lead to a field whose L-hand wall should be followed up to a gate and lane. At the top of the lane turn R and go down towards Tor Farm, passing through a gate on the L just before the farm. Beside the wall a path leads through three field gateways and then a gate into woodland. After passing over a stile in the wood and a stream, the track climbs steadily up the hill through oak and silver birch onto the moorland. In ½ mile (800 m), and having crossed a small clough, Stoke Ford is reached, which is the meeting of several old tracks and has a bridge across the main stream.

Turn L at Stoke Ford (not across the bridge) and climb uphill. In a few yards the track forks. Take the R fork which follows Bretton Brook. In ¼ mile (400 m) you come to a stile and then a little, steep-sided clough. Climbing out of the clough past a ruined barn, go through four ruined walls and into woodland where on meeting a fence turn L to follow it down to a stile and stream. Zig-zag up the hillside and over a stile into fields. Follow the R-hand wall to another stile onto a farm lane. In ¼ mile (400 m) the lane comes out at the Barrel Inn. Turn R and ¾ mile (1.2 km) down the road is the starting point.

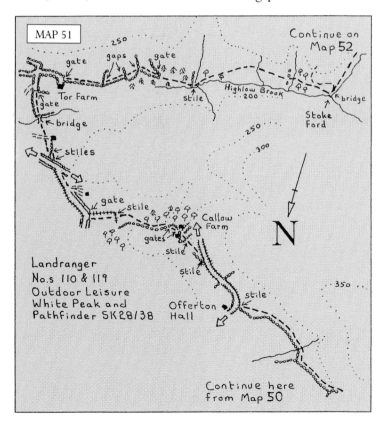

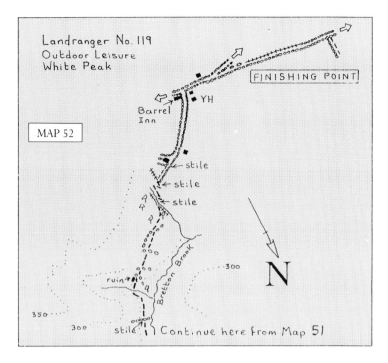

*1  Great Hucklow Gliding Club*

The club, officially known as the Derbyshire and Lancashire
Gliding Club, was formed in 1935 by a group of local flyers,
who leased Camp Hill, and the Manchester Aeronautical
Society, who flew from the Barrel Inn in 1934. The remains
of an Ancient Briton fort on the south and south-west edge of
Camp Hill also cut across the field to the inconvenience of the
club. The field itself is private property.

There was a break in flying during World War II when the
club was banned from using the airfield and obstructions
were placed on the field, but now it has 165 flying members
and on a busy day there can be as many as thirty gliders in the
air at once. The gliders are towed by winch to a height of
1000–1100 ft (305–335 m) before being released. A winch is
used because powered aircraft are not allowed by the Peak
District Park Authorities, and also the conditions are very
windy and are not really suitable for them. The club owns
three single-seater and three dual-seater planes. Many of the
members have their own aircraft and often these are
syndicated, each owner having a quarter share. Members
come mostly from Sheffield, Nottingham and South Manchester, although one comes all the way from Glasgow.

The club height record is 23 000 ft (7 000 m), and the
distance record stands at 317 miles (510 km).

*Eyam Woodlands*

# KINDER SCOUT FROM HAYFIELD

**STARTING AND FINISHING POINT**
Car-park on Kinder Road, Hayfield (110-049869).
**LENGTH**
8 miles (13 km)
**ASCENT**
1400 ft (430 m)

This is one of the most popular walks from Hayfield. The navigation is relatively easy as the walk sticks mainly to the edge of the Kinder plateau, but it gives the flavour of the wild moorland summit. The highlight of the walk is Kinder Downfall. In hard winters this can freeze to a magnificent wall of ice; while if there is much water in the river and a westerly wind is blowing, the water fails to fall at all and instead is ·blown upwards, arching back over the edge.

## ROUTE DESCRIPTION (Maps 53, 54)

Turn L out of the quarry car-park, where there is a plaque to the Kinder Trespass *(1)*, and walk up Kinder Road for nearly ½ mile (400 m) to the gates of the Water Treatment Works. Turn R over the bridge, follow the farm road for about 50 yards (45 m), then go L (PFS 'KINDER 1') and through a small gate to follow the stream up to the next bridge. Cross this, past the mountain rescue post sign, and go through the small gate opposite. Go up the steep path and follow the wall beside Kinder Reservoir to William Clough.

The path up William Clough *(2)* crosses and recrosses the stream innumerable times. Climb up until you reach the watershed at the top. In front is the start of Ashop Clough which descends to the Snake Road. The three-fingered signpost (PWS) points all ways except the one you should go, which is R and up the steep slopes onto the Kinder Scout plateau. At the top of the steep ascent, turn half R and follow the edge of the plateau. In just under a mile (1.6 km), where the rocks form a cliff, there is a white-painted cross on the rocks nearest the edge, embellished with symbols and the initials G K. This is the sacred spot of the Etherios Society whose leader is George King. Continue along the edge for ½ mile (800 m) to reach Kinder Downfall. If it is in spate you may have to make quite a detour to avoid getting a soaking from the blown back spray.

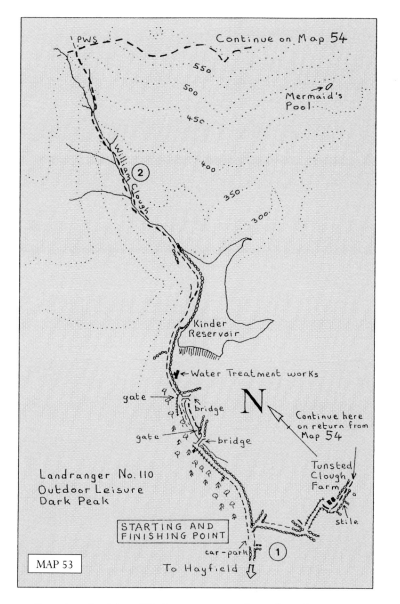

PWS

Continue on Map 54

550

500

Mermaid's
Pool

450

William Clough

②

400

350

300

Kinder
Reservoir

←Water Treatment works

gate →

bridge

N

Continue here
on return from
Map 54

gate →

←bridge

Tunsted
Clough
Farm

Landranger No. 110
Outdoor Leisure
Dark Peak

stile

STARTING AND
FINISHING POINT

MAP 53

car-park ①

To Hayfield

Crossing the River Kinder, continue along the edge now in a
southerly direction, meandering through the peat and strangely-
eroded boulders, to cross the head of Red Brook in ½ mile
(800 m). A similar distance will bring you to the vicinity of
Kinder Low. By keeping high up you should see the OS trig
point and avoid being diverted down the slopes below
Kinderlow End. The OS trig point is only a short way off the
path, but can be tricky to find in mist. From Kinderlow there is
a good view of Pym Chair on the skyline to the east. Now head
just west of south for 300 yards (270 m) to Edale Rocks.
Continue past Edale Rocks to drop down to the path which
contours round Swine's Back. Ignoring the main eroded path

down the hillside, which leads to Brown Knoll, continue contouring round above the wall to meet a ruined sheepfold and then descend by the ruined wall to Edale Cross *(3)*.

Turn R onto the packhorse track and, after following it beside the wall for nearly ½ mile (800 m), turn R over a stile in the wall (PFS 'Hayfield via Tunstead Clough'). The conical-shaped hill to the south is South Head. Follow the path which contours round below Kinderlow End and ignore the L branch which seeks to divert you downhill. In ½ mile (800 m) a gate is reached. Don't go through the gate, but double back to cross a stile on the R. The gate immediately on the L leads to the first of

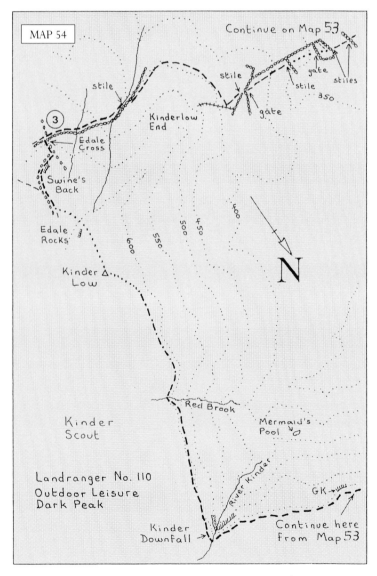

*Path on the northern side of Kinder Reservoir*

*Kinder Reservoir*

three fields, which are crossed at stiles and a gate to a main track. Follow the track down to a stile at Tunstead Clough Farm. Go straight ahead on the footpath, not through the farm, and join the farm road. In 250 yards (225 m) turn R onto the road, and walk back down this to Kinder Road and the car-park.

*1 Kinder Trespass*

For many years Kinder was barred to walkers, being preserved as a grouse moor for the privileged few. On Sunday 24 April 1932 the pent up emotions of the ramblers were released in the celebrated Kinder Scout Mass Trespass. Their intentions had been well advertised in the *Manchester Evening Chronicle* and some 400 people, avoiding the police who were waiting at the planned meeting point in Hayfield, assembled instead in the quarry to hear an address by Benny Rothman, the Mancunian leader of the Trespass. The police who had planned to arrest Benny at the railway station were thwarted when he arrived on his bike.

The Manchester Ramblers Federation opposed the idea of a mass trespass fearing that antagonizing the landowners would hinder rather than promote the cause of access. The walkers, however, set off along the road and up William Clough with the police in close attendance. As they climbed towards the Kinder Scout plateau, gamekeepers appeared and threatened them, but were unable to stop the advance. At the top they were met by more ramblers who had come over from Sheffield and Manchester by other routes, and a victory meeting was held before returning to Hayfield. At Hayfield, Benny and four others were arrested and taken to New Mills, where the next day they were charged with unlawful assembly and breach of the peace. Committed to the Derby Assizes on 21/22 July, they were found guilty of riotous assembly and Benny Rothman was sentenced to four months in prison.

The publicity, however, had made the public aware of the situation and restrictions were gradually lessened until in 1951 the formation of the Peak District National Park opened up the area with the negotiation of Access Agreements with the landowners. Now over 80 square miles (20,737 hectares) of moorland are open to the public all year round, except for a few days each year kept for grouse shooting.

2  *William Clough*

The stream which tumbles down little waterfalls makes this a very pleasant approach to Kinder Scout (from the Saxon 'Kyndwr Scut' meaning 'water over the edge'). The stream, usually small but which after heavy rain becomes a torrent, has cut down through the peat exposing the layers of underlying shale and gritstone. The harder gritstone resists erosion and so causes the stream to flow in these pretty falls. Towards the top of the clough there is a thick deposit of clay covering the underlying rocks. This was formed in very cold conditions towards the end of the Ice Age. The runnels and scars are the work of water erosion.

3  *Edale Cross*

Recently protected and almost enclosed by a stone wall, this stone pillar in the shape of a cross is also called Champion Cross from 'Champayne' which was the name for the southern part of Peak Forest in the Middle Ages. The forest wards of Longdendale, Ashop, Edale and Champayne met near here, and such points were usually marked by a stone. This was an old medieval road and later a packhorse way. The initials J. G. and the date 1810 inscribed on the cross are much later and refer to restoration work.

# SHUTLINGSLOE AND MACCLESFIELD FOREST

**STARTING AND FINISHING POINT**
Car-park at Trentabank Reservoir near Macclesfield (118-961711).
**LENGTH**
8 miles (13 km)
**ASCENT**
1700 ft (520 m)

This very attractive walk on the edge of the Peak District starts from a heronry, visits Shutlingsloe (the 'Cheshire Matterhorn'), and climbs through the charming Cumberland Clough to visit one of the highest inns in England.

## ROUTE DESCRIPTION (Maps 55, 56)

Go over the stile opposite the lay-by just beyond the car-park and the climb starts immediately among the cool shade of the pines. Water Board signs discourage deviation from the path which is followed to a stile at the forest edge and then out onto the moor. Topping the rise ahead, the summit cone of Shutlingsloe (once known as Scyttel's Hill) is seen. Around 2,700 walkers visit the top each year and in 1992, with the aid of a helicopter, the boggy footpath was repaired using massive slabs of gritstone. Turn R over the stile and follow the wall to the ladder stile below the summit. A short, but steep ascent brings you to the OS trig point and an expensive view of the moors ahead beyond Wildboarclough *(1)*.

The path down over the rocks from the summit is waymarked to lead round Shutlingsloe Farm over two stiles to the farm road. Go down this a short way and turn L on the lower path which, passing Banktop, follows the edge of the wood and over two stiles to join the road at a very high ladder stile. Cross this and the narrow bridge opposite, and go through a gate by the barn into the farmyard. Go straight across the road to a gate and follow Cumberland Brook, first on the R bank, and then over a bridge and up the L bank through another gate. A few pine trees line the brook until the path forks at the top gate. Follow the L branch, passing a waterfall, and out onto the open moor. The path continues on the L side of the clough, only crossing to the R near the top. Turn L at the PFS to reach the Cat and Fiddle Inn *(2)* in under a mile (1.6 km).

Turn L on the A537, and at the L bend take the track known

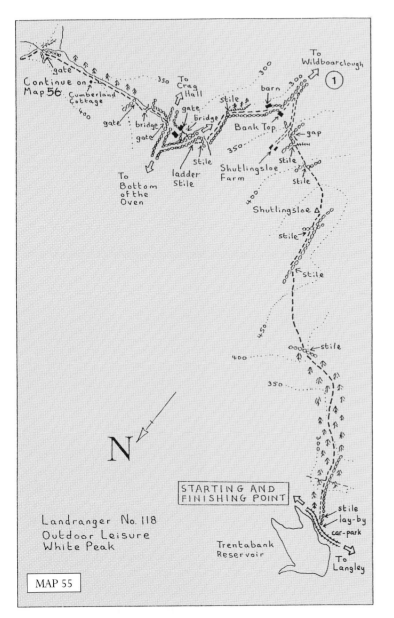

To Wildboarclough

① 1

barn

stile

Bank Top

gap

Shutlingsloe Farm

stile

stile

stile

Shutlingsloe △

stile

stile

stile

450

400

350

N

STARTING AND FINISHING POINT

stile
lay-by
car-park

To Langley

Trentabank Reservoir

Landranger No. 118
Outdoor Leisure
White Peak

MAP 55

gate

Continue on Map 56

Cumberland Cottage

To Crag Hall

350

400

gate

bridge

gate

gate

bridge

gate

ladder stile

stile

To Bottom of the Oven

300

300

300

as Stoneyway *(3)* across the moor and down to the Shining Tor Restaurant. Cross the main road and follow the minor road to reach the Stanley Arms in a mile (1.6 km). Turn L and then R at the fork in 200 yards (180 m). A narrow packway (Oven Lane) between walls on the R leads up to Forest Chapel *(4)*. Go straight ahead down the road to the forest edge (PFS) and turn L over the stile. The path leads downhill through the trees to a small pool. Turn R, and a path avoiding the road brings you back to Trentabank Reservoir.

*Macclesfield Forest*

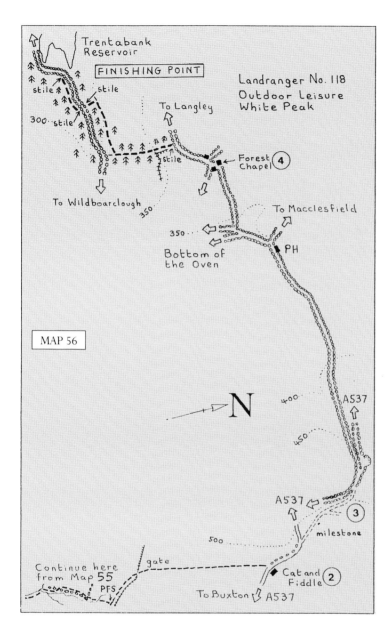

## 1 Wildboarclough

Until recently no less than three mills stood by this little cluster of houses. The first, built in the mid-eighteenth century, employed a contractor to manufacture the machinery, and he had one James Brindley working for him. One Sunday, Brindley walked to Manchester to study the mill on which the Wildboarclough Mill was to be based. Being illiterate, he memorized the details of its construction before returning to complete the installation. Brindley, of course,

*Hills between Forest Chapel and Shining Tor*

went on to become the foremost engineer of his generation. A further two mills were built, employing a total of 600 workers; and these were used as silk mills, then later for carpets. In 1958 the mills were demolished leaving only one building remaining, which, until recently, was used as what must have been the biggest sub-post office in the country. The imposing Crag Hall at the top of the village belongs to Lord Derby.

The area has been a royal hunting forest from medieval times, but if indeed as local history claims the last wild boar in England was killed here, then it must have had more lives than a cat, as it has been exterminated in several other places as well.

2  *Cat and Fiddle Inn*
Built early in the eighteenth century, this is the second highest inn in England (the highest is Tan Hill in Yorkshire). The origin of the name is rather obscure and is variously attributed to Catherine le Fidele, the wife of Czar Peter the Great; or to a Duke of Devonshire who is reputed to have stopped here to play his fiddle; or, rather more probably, to the game of 'Cat', the fiddle being for dancing. There is a carving of a cat and fiddle on the front of the inn. During the winter when the road is often blocked by snow, the inn sometimes becomes an involuntary overnight halt for travellers.

3  *Stoneyway*
This is an early turnpike of 1759, 30 ft (9 m) wide and surfaced with small stones retained between banks. A little way along it is an old milestone showing 'LONDON 164 MACCLESFIELD 6'. The turnpike passed behind the site of the inn and descended to Goyt's Clough. A new turnpike on the route of the present road, which passes in front of the inn, was made in 1821.

4  *Forest Chapel*
This little church of St Stephen continues the ancient tradition of rush bearing and the ceremony is held in mid-August. Rushes taken from the moor are strewn on the floor of the decorated church, as they were when this was the only form of floor covering. The church, with its tower, built in 1673 and rebuilt in 1834, was used as a set in the filming of the TV series 'The Jewel in the Crown'. In the church porch is a list of thirty-seven different varieties of plant which can be found in the churchyard, and an addendum lists another thirty-two to be found nearby.

# 3.35

# DOVEDALE, THE TISSINGTON TRAIL AND ILAM

**STARTING AND FINISHING POINT**
Car-park at the south end of Dovedale (119-146509).
**LENGTH**
17 miles (27 km) or 8 miles (13 km) variant
**ASCENT**
1200 ft (370 m)

*Pickering Tor*

Dovedale has been a favourite from the times of Izaak Walton (author of the seventeenth-century fishing classic, *The Compleat Angler*) to the present day. Limestone cliffs and pinnacles thrust up through the trees in a delightful wooded gorge where the path follows the meandering River Dove accompanied by the sound of rippling waterfalls. The Tissington Trail returns the walker to Milldale; and Ilam, beside the River Manifold, marks the end of this long walk.

As the walk is in the form of a figure of eight, with the intersection at Milldale, if you want a shorter walk in Dovedale, turn back to Ilam after Viator's Bridge.

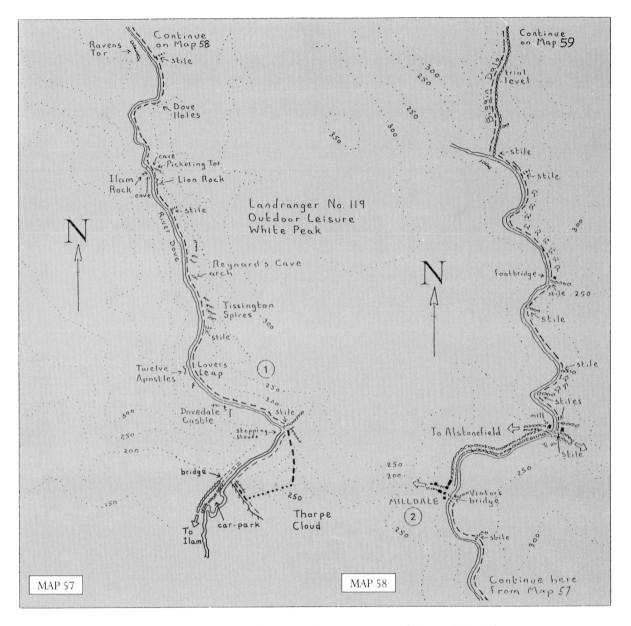

MAP 57

MAP 58

## ROUTE DESCRIPTION (Maps 57–61)

Follow the path upstream for 100 yards (90 m) and turn R over the footbridge. Straight ahead is the uncompromisingly steep ascent of Thorpe Cloud, a coral reef knoll. The 500 ft (150 m) ascent can be omitted by following the river upstream to the stepping stones where the route rejoins the river. From the summit rocks, polished like marble from the passage of thousands of feet, there is an excellent bird's eye view of Dovedale *(1)* far below.

Descending directly to the stepping stones, go through the

stile and follow the river round the bend. The broad path leads to steps which bring you to Lover's Leap, with the pinnacles of the Twelve Apostles opposite. The path descends to pass Tissington Spires and then, high on the R, a huge natural arch, Reynard's Cave. In ½ mile (800 m), Lion Rock (which in profile resembles a lion) is passed and on turning the corner Ilam Rock appears on the L, towering above a footbridge. The top of the stupendously overhanging face is 10 ft (3 m) further out than its base. Dove Holes, ¼ mile (400 m) further, doesn't live up to its imposing entrance as the caves are very shallow.

The hamlet of Milldale (2) (café and toilets) is reached in about a mile (1.6 km) at the delightful Viator's Bridge. Stay by the river following the road for ½ mile (800 m); then cross the bridge by Lode Mill, an old corn mill, to gain the river's R bank. Follow the river for 1½ miles (2.4 km) and turn R up Biggin Dale, which is the second dale on the R. In 1 mile (1.6 km) the dale forks. Take the R branch (PFS) and in ½ mile (800 m) the road is reached. Turn L and then, in a few yards, R along a narrow path beside a house and over a stile. Cross the field to a stile in the far L-hand corner, and then half L and out over a stile onto the road. Turn R and continue straight on at the road bend to follow the track between walls and over a stile. At the next gate on the L, go over the stile beside it and follow the wall immediately on the R. Go through the gap ahead and across the field to a camouflaged stile in the far wall. Turn half R, heading for the bridge, and cross the gate and stile on the R beyond to climb up the embankment and onto the old railway.

Turn R on the Tissington Trail (3) to Coldeaton Cutting. This gives way to an embankment with sweeping views on either side, and in all the railway gives 2½ miles (4 km) of easy walking. Continue until the bridge (which is almost a tunnel) is reached. Just beyond, turn R into a car-park and go through this to the main road.

Go half L and through a stile into the field. Follow the L wall to the stile at the next road. Turn R and after 150 yards (135 m) take the stile on the L. The path goes half R up to the wall and then follows it round high above Dovedale. After two stiles, the wall is followed down to Viator's Bridge. Go across the bridge, again into Milldale, and turn L at the road junction by the café. After 100 yards (90 m) turn L onto a path climbing up the hill-side to the first of five fields, which are crossed to emerge onto a lane. Turn R and then, in 50 yards (45 m) L over a stile. Go half R across the field to a stile and down into a shallow valley. Turn L in the valley bottom, cross the stile ahead and immediately go R over another stile. After a very steep, but short, ascent continue beside the wall and in ⅓ mile (530 m) above Hall Dale there is a good view of Dovedale. Now go R up the green lane to a stile and a barn, and continue to a stile at the road.

Go L for ¼ mile (400 m) to a stile on the R just before a house. Straight across to the wall and a stile, then follow the L wall of the field beyond to a stile, and cross the next field to a stile in the middle of the wall. Half R now and down to the gate in the corner by Castern Hall, which dates from the sixteenth century, and follow the main drive down to the road. Turn L to the lodge and go through the garden gate on its L. A fee of 1p per person is payable for the privilege of this route. The often

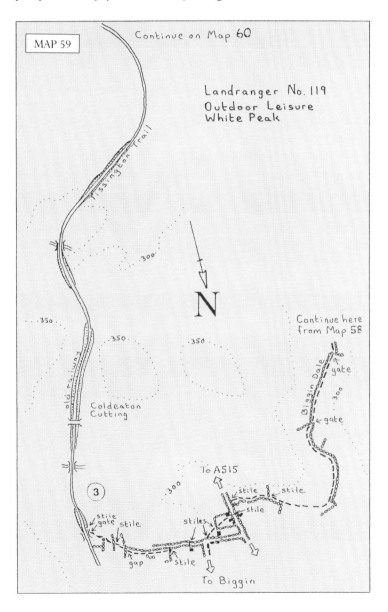

*The River Dove near Dove Holes*

*Viator's Bridge at Milldale*

dry river bed on the R is that of the Manifold. The path goes beside this for the next mile (1.6 km), crossing three stiles to Ilam Hall *(4)*. Go round the front of the hall and down the drive to the village of Ilam. At the cross in the centre of the village turn L, and at the bend go through the small gate on the L. Joining a track, go R and through a gate to a small gate beyond. The path follows the hedge towards the Izaak Walton Hotel, then behind it over two stiles. Downhill now and two final stiles bring you to the road opposite the car-park.

*1 Dovedale*

This is the most famous of all the Peak District dales with the

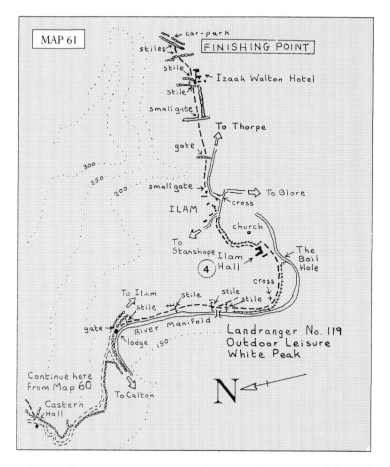

River Dove twisting its way between limestone cliffs and spires in a steep-sided valley. The harder rocks have resisted the erosion process which carved the valley out of the limestone plateau, forming and linking caves into this almost unique environment. Reynard's Cave, distinguished by the remarkable natural arch at its entrance, and Dove Holes, with its large twin entrances, are two of several interesting caves in Dovedale, none of which are very deep. The ash woodland is comparatively recent, most of the trees being less than 150 years old. However, the rocks, each carefully named as the Victorians were wont to do, had begun to disappear beneath the encroaching trees and vegetation until the National Trust, with considerable courage, tackled the problem head on. Many a nature lover must have stood aghast seeing JCBs in Dovedale, but the result is that the famous rocks can now be seen clearly again and the minor disruption can be forgiven. The wide path is a less happy intrusion which hopefully time will heal.

*2 Milldale*

For the fifth edition of *The Compleat Angler* by Izaak Walton, originally published in 1653, an addendum was contributed by his friend, Charles Cotton of Beresford Hall. In this, Viator (the traveller) demurs at crossing this narrow bridge, saying 'Do you travel by wheelbarrows in this country? – tis not two fingers broad'. Since then the parapets have been added. Close by are the remains of an ochre mill which produced the dye from the iron ore mined near Wetton. A millstone lies on the ground by the leat.

3 *Tissington Trail*

Converted to a grassy track in 1971 from the disused Buxton to Ashbourne railway line, this was one of the first ventures of its kind. The railway was opened in 1899 and although constructed to take a double track, in fact only a single line was laid. Although it carried passengers, its principal use was to convey limestone to the works at Buxton. The line closed in 1967 and the following year the Peak Park Board bought 11½ miles (19 km) of track. The rails and sleepers were removed, five stations demolished and grass seed sown. It now provides a pleasant way for walkers, cyclists and horse riders. One of the features of the trail is Coldeaton Cutting, ¾ mile (1.2 km) long and 60 ft (18 m) deep. The grand bridge high above is only for a farm track. The brickwork of the bridge under the A515 is set in beautiful curves as the bridge is built at an angle to the line to take the road above.

4 *Ilam Hall*

After a subterranean journey of 6 miles (9.5 km) from Wetton Mill, the River Manifold reappears at the 'Boil Hole' in the grounds of Ilam Hall. The small cave nearby is reputed to have been the home of the hermit, St Bertram. Paradise Walk, the Happy Valley of George Eliot's *Adam Bede*, leads beside the river to a Saxon 'Battle Cross' discovered in the foundations of a cottage during the construction of the model village of Ilam.

Ilam Hall, which probably dates from the sixteenth century, was rebuilt in 1840 in extravagant pseudo-Gothic style by a London businessman, Jesse Watts-Russell, who also reconstructed the village and built the cross in the village centre as a memorial to his wife. In the early 1930s most of the house was demolished and the remaining part, now a Youth Hostel, was saved at the last moment by Sir Robert McDougall who presented it to the National Trust. The church nearby dates from the thirteenth century.

# WALKS IN
# THE PEMBROKESHIRE COAST
# NATIONAL PARK

*Trwyncastell headland*

# 1.36

# Dinas Island

STARTING AND FINISHING
POINT
Car-park at Cwm-yr-eglwys
(Pathfinder Sheet SN 04-14/015401)
LENGTH
3¼ miles (5 km)

This wonderful little walk will take you right around Dinas Island (an island in name only: it was cut off from the mainland 8000 years ago but is now linked to it by a low-lying valley). Walkers are rewarded with expansive views eastwards and westwards along the Pembrokeshire coast, and a glimpse of teeming bird life. The walk is suitable for all the family, as long as extra-special care is taken with younger children on certain sections of the route where the path passes close to abrupt drops to the sea.

## ROUTE DESCRIPTION (Map 62)

From the car-park near the church *(1)* follow the metalled road up the hill. Within 150 yards (140 m) turn R at the footbridge, following the sign for the coast path, and climb up the side of the thickly wooded and bracken-covered hillside above Cwm-yr-eglwys. Within about 250 yards (225 m) go over a stile into open countryside, where you will enjoy magnificent coastal views eastwards to Cemaes Head and the start of the Pembrokeshire Coast National Park.

On the approach to Needle Rock *(2)*, the path narrows as the grassy hillside becomes steeper. Continue past the rock and climb up a series of steep steps to a stile. For the next ¼ mile (400 m) or so, the narrow path hugs the cliff-tops, often close to the edge—so great care should be taken.

Pwll-glas, a huge, black, sea-washed rock, comes into view and the hillside becomes a little less precipitous. (The latter is carpeted in a splendid display of bluebells in late spring.) Follow the path up the flank of the hill to Dinas Island's 463-ft (141 m) summit of Pen-y-Fan, which stands directly above Dinas Head. From the OS obelisk, there are more superb views, this time westwards along the coast right into Fishguard Bay, where the ferry boats from Ireland dock, and farther west again to St David's.

Follow the path downwards along the exposed, west-facing coast of Dinas Island, for ¾ mile (1.2 km). On the approach to

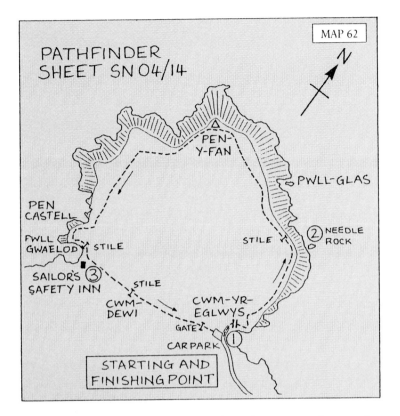

Pwll Gwaelod, the path descends abruptly, passing close to the cliff-edge above the shingle cove of Pen Castell before joining the metalled road above the pretty sandy beach at Pwll Gwaelod.

At the stile, turn half R and walk down this metalled road towards the Sailors' Safety Inn *(3)*. Just before the inn, turn L at the PFS and follow the path along the little valley of Cwm-Dewi (a glacial melt-water channel), past marshy ground to the R. Within ¼ mile (400 m) go straight on over a stile. On the approach to Cwm-yr-eglwys, go through the gate and follow the path along the side of a small caravan park next to the car-park, the starting-point of the walk.

*1 Cwm-yr-eglwys*

The Welsh name of this pretty little village means 'the valley of the church'. Unfortunately, the church, which overlooks the sea, is in poor shape. Only the belfry and part of the west wall remain of this twelfth-century Celtic-style church. It was wrecked by a huge storm in October 1859 which also claimed over 100 ships off the Welsh coast. A religious site may well have been founded here as early as the sixth century, for the church is dedicated to St Brynach, an early Christian missionary from Ireland.

2 *Needle Rock*

The path overlooking this angular sea stack is a perfect vantage point for bird-watchers. The rock, a thriving bird colony, is at its busiest between April and July. Herring gulls, razorbills, great black-backed gulls, shags, feral pigeons and guillemots nest on the rock, while fulmars, rock pipits and jackdaws nest on the cliffs just below the path.

3 *Sailors' Safety Inn*

This unusually named inn, which dates back to the late sixteenth century, has always displayed a light at night to help guide ships across Fishguard Bay. It is also one of the few pubs located on the coast path—so make the most of it.

*Pwll-glas (in the foreground) and Needle Rock, Dinas Island*

# 1.37

# Trevine to Abereiddy

---

STARTING POINT
Small parking area off coast road just west of Trevine (Pathfinder Sheet SM 83-93/834324)
FINISHING POINT
Car-park beside Abereiddy beach (Pathfinder Sheet SM 62-72/798314)
LENGTH
3¾ miles (6 km)

On this walk, you will come across some of the strangest places along the Pembrokeshire coast. Abandoned industrial sites and quarries (one of which is submerged) appear unexpectedly along an otherwise unspoilt coastline; not that these abandoned sites altogether mar their settings, for in themselves they possess an unorthodox beauty.

## Route Description (Map 63)

Park the car at the bottom of the hill. First visit Trevine's old corn mill *(1)* by following the path opposite the row of cottages down to the mill ruins, 50 yards (45 m) off the coast road. Then retrace your steps back onto the road and walk up the hill. At the farm on the R near the top of the hill, follow the signpost for the coast path and turn R, through the gate and past the farm. Within 200 yards (180 m), you leave the farm behind as you go through a gate onto a grassy headland above a line of cliffs.

For the next mile (1.6 km), the well-defined coast path crosses a number of stiles as it runs beside the boundary of cliff-top fields. At the stile near the approach to Ynys-fach, keep to the R of the field boundary. After the next stile (within about 250 yards/225 m) the path skirts the top of eroded cliffs, giving fine views of grass-topped Ynys-fach just offshore.

At the next stile (again within about 250 yards/225 m of the previous stile) turn half R and follow the path around Trwynelen headland, which commands panoramic views along the coast. As you approach Porthgain, two strange objects come into view—a pair of tall, inverted cones. These are the towers which mark the narrow, rock-bound entrance to Porthgain harbour *(2)*.

The path descends via the eastern marker tower (or you can take a well-defined short-cut) to the quayside. At the western end of the quay turn back half L up a series of steep stone steps to the headland. Follow the path in the direction of red-bricked ruins across terrain which shows plentiful evidence of past industrial activity. On the approach to the ruins, the path runs

*Overleaf:* Porthgain harbour

beside the line of an old tramway (on the R) leading to a quarry.

Beyond the quarry, Pembrokeshire's natural beauty reasserts itself. From the path there is a fine view of the arch on the narrow-necked Penclegyr promontory above Porth Dwfn. Continue on the path above Porth Egr, then follow the line of the fence to a stile above the bay, where there is access to the attractive sandy beach of Traeth Llyfn. Follow the path west across steep cliffs and on the approach to Abereiddy *(3)* another navigation tower comes into view. Skirt the base of the Trwyncastell promontory, past the viewpoint for the 'Blue Lagoon', and follow the path down to the car-park by the black sands of Abereiddy beach.

*1  Melin Trevine Mill*

Although abandoned and quiet now, this mill was once a busy place. The cottages opposite were the homes of quarrymen and fishermen, and trading boats made their calls. For 500 years, the mill was vital to the life of Trevine. Wheat was milled here into flour for bread, and barley was ground to provide winter feed for cattle and pigs. But by the early twentieth century, the advent of cheap grain from overseas, larger, more efficient mills located in the towns, and improved communications between urban and country areas dealt a death blow to local village mills such as this. In 1918, the mill closed.

*2  Porthgain*

If it were possible to remove the remains left by the quarrying industry—the great stone shell of the crushing plant and the ruined hoppers along the quayside—Porthgain would look like the perfect smugglers' cove. The narrow entrance to this sheltered little harbour makes it the ideal hideaway on North Pembrokeshire's rock-bound coast. Yet in the nineteenth and early twentieth centuries, this quayside was a hive of activity as ships queued for their cargoes.

Porthgain's industrial past is based on slate and granite quarrying, brick making and the production of stone and chippings for the roads of Britain. Slate, granite and bricks were much in demand in Britain's rapidly growing nineteenth-century urban and industrial centres (many public buildings in London and Liverpool are of Porthgain granite). As this trade declined in the early twentieth century, another grew to replace it. With the advent of the motor car came the need for properly surfaced roads, for which Porthgain's crushed granite was ideal. The boom was big, but comparatively short-lived. By 1931, the trade was over.

This odd place has a beauty all of its own, and the various

*Trwyncastell headland*

remains tell a fascinating tale. Evidence of industrial activity is not confined just to Porthgain. The headland above the harbour is gouged by quarries, and the trackway of the 3-mile-long (5 km) railway that once connected Porthgain to Abereiddy can still be traced.

Be sure to call in at Porthgain's Sloop Inn, a typical harbourside pub dating from 1743, where there is a display of old photographs depicting the quayside in its heyday.

### 3 Abereiddy

Abereiddy's industrial prosperity was based exclusively on slate. Scant ruins, the remnants of workers' cottages, stand above the beach, which has an unusual dark sand produced by the erosion of the area's black, shaly rocks. A striking reminder of the slate industry can be seen on the eastern headland, where a deep quarry has been flooded by the sea to form a spectacular feature known as the 'Blue Lagoon'.

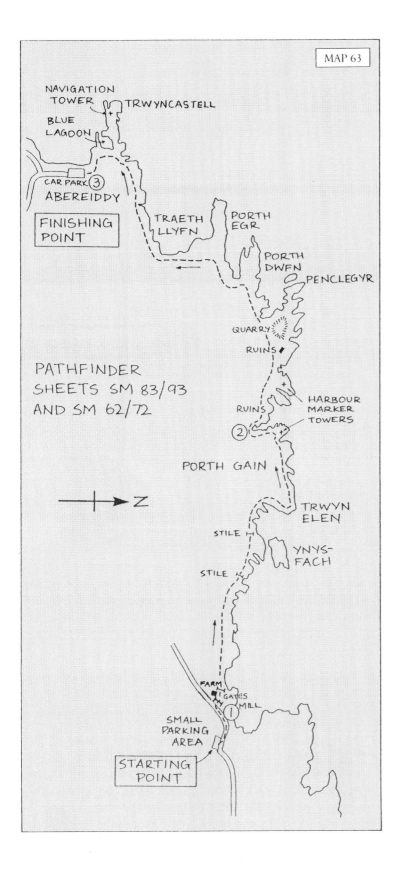

MAP 63

NAVIGATION TOWER

TRWYNCASTELL

BLUE LAGOON

CAR PARK ③
ABEREIDDY

**FINISHING POINT**

TRAETH LLYFN

PORTH EGR

PORTH DWFN

PENCLEGYR

QUARRY

RUINS

PATHFINDER SHEETS SM 83/93 AND SM 62/72

RUINS

HARBOUR MARKER TOWERS

②

PORTH GAIN

Z

TRWYN ELEN

STILE

YNYS-FACH

STILE

FARM
GATES
MILL
①

SMALL PARKING AREA

**STARTING POINT**

# 1.38

# STACK ROCKS TO BROAD HAVEN

STARTING POINT
Car-park at Stack Rocks on the Royal
Armoured Corps Castlemartin Firing
Range (Pathfinder Sheet
SR 89-99/925946)
FINISHING POINT
National Trust car-park above Broad
Haven beach (Pathfinder Sheet SR
89-99/976938)
LENGTH
5 miles (8 km)

This windy, exposed walk will take you across grassy headlands, flat for much of the way. There is nothing tame, though, about this route. Those headlands sit on top of southern Pembrokeshire's spectacular curtain of limestone cliffs, coastal scenery at its most awesome. Two of the most impressive sights can be seen right at the start of the walk—the famous sea-arch known as the Green Bridge of Wales and the neighbouring pinnacles of Stack Rocks.

Access to this walk is dependent on military activity—or rather the absence of it—on the Royal Armoured Corps Castlemartin Firing Range. When the range is in use, the road off the B4319 to the car-park at Stack Rocks is closed, as is the coast path from Stack Rocks to St Govan's Chapel (a distance of 3½ miles/5.5 km). When firing is taking place, there are warnings by red flags by day and lights by night, on flagpoles and control towers.

In strict terms, this 5-mile (8 km) walk appears out of order in the book. It comes before the 3-mile (5 km) Broad Haven to Stackpole Quay walk (see Route 1.39, page 230) since the two can be joined together to create a continuous 8-mile (13 km) walk. The split comes at Broad Haven for a very good reason: just above the beach are the Bosherston Lakes, freshwater ponds famous for their waterlilies and wildlife, which are accessible by a detour off the coast path. (The detour is described at the start of the next walk.)

## ROUTE DESCRIPTION (Maps 64, 65)

From the car-park, turn half R and walk across the cliff-top turf for 300 yards (275 m) to the viewing platform for the magnificent Green Bridge of Wales (1). From here walk east along the cliffs to Stack Rocks, also known as Elegug Stacks (2), where you pick up the coast path proper at the gate into the firing range (3). (The area immediately west of the Green Bridge

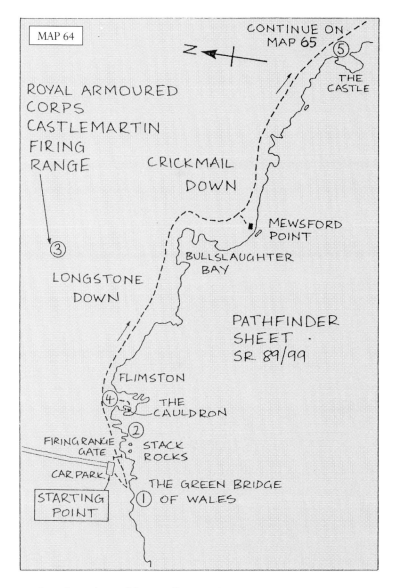

CONTINUE ON MAP 65

is closed to the public at all times.)

Take note of the warning signs. Children are warned not to touch anything lying on the ground which could be dangerous (shells or bullets, for example). Follow the line of white markers, which determine the path right the way through the range. Do not let this necessarily overt evidence of military activity put you off, for everything is eclipsed by stunning coastal scenery as cliffs plunge vertically into the sea in a great, jagged curtain of limestone.

From Stack Rocks, there is easy, airy walking on the flat path across well-cropped turf. To the L is the bleak, open expanse of Longstone Down and, in the distance the tall chimneys of Milford Haven's petrochemical plants.

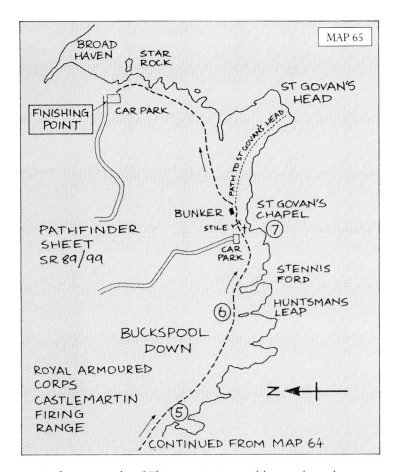

At the peninsula of Flimston, it is possible to take a detour R off the path beside the pronounced, well-preserved defences of an Iron Age fort *(4)* to the spectacular Cauldron at the end of the rugged little promontory. Continue eastwards along the wide, well-defined pathway, past Bullslaughter Bay, in the direction of the coastguard lookout station at Mewsford Point for a superb, though precipitous, cliff-edge view back along the coast.

Then rejoin the path (a short detour will have been necessary to reach the view-point) and walk along Crickmail Down and Buckspool Down past The Castle promontory, with its ingenious Iron Age fort *(5)* and evidence of modern military activities in the form of a radar station on its south-eastern approach.

After The Castle, continue on open grassland away from the cliffs and sea-views for ½ mile (800 m) to the spectacular chasm known as Huntsman's Leap *(6)* and, next to it, a second, wider ravine, called Stennis Ford. Within ¼ mile (400 m) turn R opposite the car-park and go down the steps cut into the cliff for St Govan's Chapel *(7)*.

Return to the cliff-top and follow the metalled path leading east from the car-park. Very soon, cross over a stile signposted coast path. Within 200 yards (180 m), bear half L—the turning is unsignposted and slightly hard to spot—off the metalled path at a low, bunker-like building. Go past the bunker on your L and across gorse-covered heathland, following the white markers. (If you stay on the metalled path, you end up at St Govan's Head.)

Continue along the path for another mile (1.6 km) to the car-park on the headland above Star Rock and Broad Haven beach.

1 *The Green Bridge of Wales*
This famous example of marine erosion has an arch around 80 ft (25 m) tall. The 'bridge' has been produced by a pounding sea which has joined two caves originally on opposite sides of an old headland.

2 *Stack Rocks*
The next stage on from the Green Bridge in the cycle of marine erosion can be seen at the neighbouring Stack Rocks. These massive limestone pillars were once connected to the mainland by arches which have now collapsed, leaving a pair of towers marooned offshore. The flat-topped Elegug Tower, 150 ft (45 m) high, is the tallest; the Elegug Spire, with its pointed summit, stands 130 ft (40 m) high. Both rocks are a mecca for birds and a magnet for bird-watchers. Stack Rocks' sea-bird colonies are the largest in Pembrokeshire that can be viewed from the path. The inhabitants include guillemots, kittiwakes, auks, fulmars and razorbills. The rocks are at their most densely populated in the nesting times of spring and early summer.

3 *Royal Armoured Corps Castlemartin Firing Range*
This large tank gunnery range of 5884 acres (2380 hectares) is one of Western Europe's most important NATO training areas. It extends down to the finest stretch of limestone-cliff coastline in Pembrokeshire, preventing public access to the coast path when military exercises, including tank and weapon training, are taking place (the coastline west of the Green Bridge up to Freshwater Bay is permanently closed). From the path, you can see the detritus of military activity—mangled tanks, bunkers and targets—scattered across the flat, rough grasslands.

4 *Flimston Iron Age Fort*
This rugged promontory is defended by a series of banks with a well-defined entrance at the centre and traces of hut circles. Just below the fort is the Cauldron, an aptly named blowhole 150 ft (45 m) deep. Take special care on the rocks here.

*Near St Gordon's Head*

5 *Buckspool Down Iron Age Fort*

This encampment makes even better use of natural features as an aid to defence. The cliff-bound promontory is protected not only by the usual earthen barrier; a blowhole has been cleverly incorporated into the defences. (Blowholes, through which the sea gushes and spouts during gales, are a feature of this stretch of coastline.)

6 *Huntsman's Leap*

The legend surrounding this deep, narrow sea-fissure is almost believable. A horseman, after jumping this chasm, looked back and died of shock! This fault in the rocks is indeed a remarkable natural phenomenon. Its sheer cliffs—a popular rock-climbing venue—drop away to a gloomy, sea-filled ravine 130 ft (40 m) below.

7 *St Govan's Chapel*

A steep flight of worn steps, cut into the limestone, leads down to this tiny chapel built into the base of the cliffs just above the sea. Originally a hermit's cell of the sixth century, the chapel as it now stands dates largely from the thirteenth century. It is probably dedicated to an Irish abbot and contemporary of St David known as Gobhan, who died here in AD 586. St Govan's holy well was said to have miraculous healing powers, with the ability to cure eye troubles and crippled limbs. It was a place of pilgrimage until the mid-nineteeth century, but is now dry.

# 1.39

# BROAD HAVEN TO STACKPOLE QUAY

STARTING POINT
National Trust car-park above Broad
Haven beach (Pathfinder Sheet
SR 89-99/976938)
FINISHING POINT
National Trust car-park at Stackpole
Quay (Pathfinder Sheet
SR 89-99/992958)
LENGTH
3 miles (5 km)

This walk combines spectacle and scenic variety. Stackpole Head is undoubtedly the most impressive feature along the route. The walk also takes in two exceptionally attractive, sandy beaches—Broad Haven and Barafundle—and, on a slight detour, the unusual freshwater lily ponds at Bosherston. The route is easy, but there is the usual proviso concerning the steep Pembrokeshire cliff-top paths and sudden drops to the sea. By combining this walk with the preceding Route 1.38, you can create a continuous route of 8 miles/13 km (see the note in the introduction to Route 1.38 on page 224).

## ROUTE DESCRIPTION (Maps 66, 67)

From the National Trust building at the car-park, pass Stackpole National Nature Reserve information board and follow the path down to Broad Haven beach. Walk along the edge of this attractive, sheltered beach, following the line of the sand dunes. At the northern end of the dunes, bear L along the narrowing stretch of sand leading to the neck of the beach. Then continue along the remainder of the beach, crossing a few boulders on the approach to the narrow strip of land, a barrier between salt-and freshwater, that separates the beach from Bosherston Lakes *(1)*.

At the lakeside signpost here, bear R toward Stackpole Head. (This signpost is also the point of departure from the coast path for those wishing to take a circular walk around the banks of Bosherston Lakes.) Continue on the path and within 100 yards (90 m) ascend a log staircase laid across the fragile dunes, climbing to a grassy headland with good views of the lakes.

Follow the path to Saddle Point, where the angular, towering sea-cliffs of Stackpole Head come into view. Go past a spectacular blowhole on the R (one of the many along South Pembrokeshire's limestone coast), its sea-filled basin sunk deep into the headland. Continue on for ¼ mile (400 m) to the stile

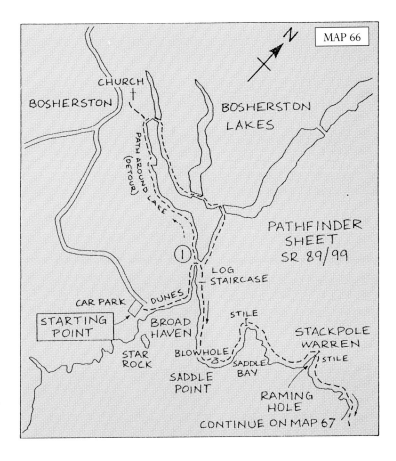

MAP 66

BOSHERSTON

CHURCH

BOSHERSTON
LAKES

PATH AROUND LAKE
(DETOUR)

PATHFINDER
SHEET
SR 89/99

①

LOG
STAIRCASE

CAR PARK

DUNES

STARTING
POINT

BROAD
HAVEN

STILE

STACKPOLE
WARREN

STAR
ROCK

BLOWHOLE

SADDLE
BAY

STILE

SADDLE
POINT

RAMING
HOLE

CONTINUE ON MAP 67

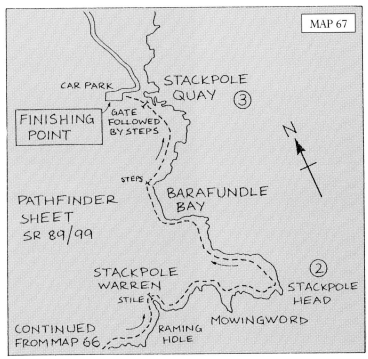

MAP 67

CAR PARK

STACKPOLE
QUAY

③

FINISHING
POINT

GATE
FOLLOWED
BY STEPS

N

STEPS

BARAFUNDLE
BAY

PATHFINDER
SHEET
SR 89/99

STACKPOLE
WARREN

STILE

②

STACKPOLE
HEAD

CONTINUED
FROM MAP 66

RAMING
HOLE

MOWINGWORD

231

above Saddle Bay, a small, sandy, cliff-bound bay with very steep, difficult access.

From the stile, follow the yellow waymarked posts across Stackpole Warren headland (the grassland here is peppered with rabbit holes). These posts come to an end at the stile beside the narrow sea-fissure known as Raming Hole. Turn R here along the path beside the cliffs for Stackpole Head. The path first passes the lesser promontory known as Mowingword before running around the wild, windy and truly spectacular Stackpole Head *(2)*. Take special care on this exposed, precipitous headland, particularly on a gusty day.

Continue on the path for ½ mile (800 m) to the fine view-point (with benches) which overlooks Barafundle Bay, one of Pembrokeshire's prettiest beaches. Go down through the woods to the sands, walk across the beach and ascend a series of steps at its north corner. Beyond the gate and arch at the top of the steps the path crosses a grassy headland on the approach to Stackpole Quay *(3)*. Go through the gate above the quay, turn L at the bottom of the steps and follow the path beside a wall to the car-park.

*1  Bosherston Lakes*

These lakes are part of the Stackpole National Nature Reserve. They wind their way like three long, thin fingers through the undulating greenery close to Broad Haven beach. It comes as a surprise to discover that the lakes are man-made—the valley was dammed in the late eighteenth century—for they blend in harmoniously with their surroundings. The lakes cover 80 acres (32 hectares), the largest expanse of open water in the National Park. They are surrounded by peaceful woodlands, creating a sheltered haven for a wide variety of birds, including swans, mallard, kingfishers and herons. Most of all, though, these lakes are famous for their splendid waterlilies which are at their best in June (the underlying rock is limestone, creating the non-acidic waters ideal for this attractive aquatic plant).

A lakeside path encircles the western lake (a distance of just over 2 miles/3 km), with access to Bosherston, a pretty little village ranged around its Norman cruciform church.

*2  Stackpole Head*

This is one of the most spectacular promontories in Pembrokeshire. Stackpole Head juts out into the sea in a south-easterly direction. At its extremity, it narrows into a small platform of land, with shuddering drops into the waters

*Mowingword headland, on the approach to Stackpole Head*

far below. Take care here, especially on a windy day. The limestone cliffs around and about are breeding grounds for razorbills, kittiwakes and guillemots.

3 *Stackpole Quay*

With its solid but small stone jetty, Stackpole Quay is a harbour in miniature, reputedly the smallest in Britain. Limestone was quarried locally—the quay is located almost on the geological dividing line between old red sandstone to the east and carboniferous limestone to the west—and shipped out from the harbour.

The quay is part of a large National Trust holding, based on the old Stackpole Estate, for many centuries the home of the earls of Cawdor. The trust's Stackpole acquisitions include the coastline from the quay to Broad Haven and the Bosherston Lakes. Old farm buildings near the quay have been tastefully renovated by the Trust and now serve as self-catering holiday cottages. The Trust's car-park occupies the site of the former limestone quarry.

*Sheltered, south-facing Broad Haven*

# PORTHSTINIAN TO CAERFAI BAY

STARTING POINT
Car-park above St Justinian's Lifeboat
Station (Pathfinder Sheet SM 62-72/
724252)
FINISHING POINT
Car-park above Caerfai Bay
(Pathfinder Sheet 62-72/759244)
LENGTH
6½ miles (10 km)

St David's Peninsula is a magical part of Pembrokeshire. Its storm-tossed, deeply indented coast is dotted with ancient religious sites associated with the early Christian missionaries. The best known among them is, of course, St David, patron saint of Wales. His story is central to our appreciation of this savagely beautiful coastline. David founded a religious community a mile inland at a site on which St David's Cathedral now stands. This purple-stoned cathedral was one of the great historic shrines of Christendom, attracting many pilgrims to this remote south-western corner of Wales, and bestowing the improbable status of a city on a settlement that is no bigger than a village. As with some of the other Pembrokeshire walks, there is a surfeit of stiles on this route. Mention has been made only of those that serve as useful reference points along the way.

## ROUTE DESCRIPTION (Maps 68, 69)

From the car-park, follow the road to a point directly above St Justinian's Lifeboat Station *(1)* and turn L onto the Pembrokeshire Coast Path. The path hugs cliff-tops which, at certain times of the year, are alive with bluebells, foxgloves, thrift and gorse. Within ¼ mile (400 m), pass the little headland and natural arch of Ogof Mary. Cross the stile into the National Trust property of Lower Treginnis.

Follow the path south through a gate and within 200 yards (180 m) the route runs beside an attractive stretch of stone wall infilled with earth and topped with turf. Go through the gate directly above the tiny, rocky Carn-ar-wig Bay (note the rusty winch and old landing stage·on the cliffs north of the bay). The path rounds the headland and drops down to a flat, grassy platform of land, the remains of an old copper mine, with superb views across Ramsey Sound and The Bitches to Ramsey Island *(2)*.

Proceed south and south-east along the path across exposed

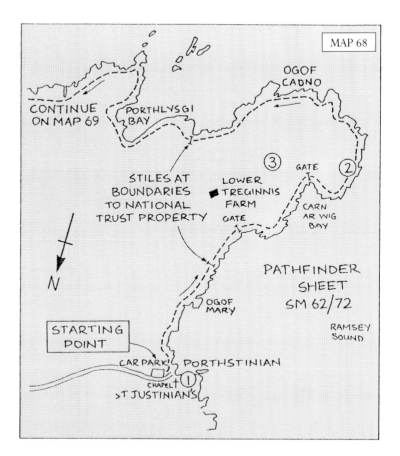

headlands with magnificent views—at Ogof Cadno, for example—across St Bride's Bay and past Newgale Sands toward Marloes and the southern Pembrokeshire coast. Half a mile (800 m) after Ogof Cadno, cross the stile at the eastern boundary of the National Trust's Lower Treginnis property *(3)*.

On the approach to the pebbly Porthlysgi beach, the coast path runs beside green farmlands. Here, the path drops almost to sea level as it rounds Porthlysgi. Continue north-eastwards along more rugged headlands to a precarious-looking natural arch angled into the sea. (Take care, for the path travels close to the cliff-edge at this point.)

Within a few hundred yards, the path passes above bands of razor-sharp rocks on the approach to Porth-clais *(4)*. The inlet of Porth-clais itself is marked by smooth, near-vertical slabs of rock at its mouth. Cross the stile above the breakwater and follow the path down to the quayside. Turn R at the head of the inlet over the bridge and back out along the opposite bank. Turn L at the lime kilns, following the coast-path signpost along the eastern shore of the inlet. At Trwyncynddeiriog ('Furious Point'), ½ mile (800 m) from the harbour, there is another spectacular, exposed headland view-point.

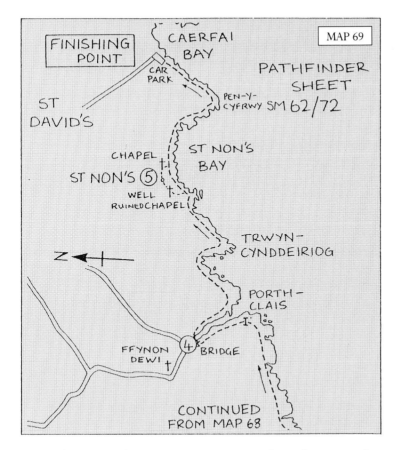

On the approach to St Non's Bay, turn L through a gap in the hedge to take a short deviation off the coast path for St Non's Chapel (ruined), and the Holy Well and Chapel of Our Lady and St Non *(5)*. Go across the field for the ruined chapel, then visit the ancient well which is close to the gate at the top of the field. From here, follow the concrete path a short distance before turning L through a gate for the second chapel. After visiting the chapel, rejoin the concrete path, which after a little way meets up with the coast path.

Follow the path along Pen-y-cyfrwy headland and within ¼ mile (1.2 km) of St Non's you will arrive at the car-park above Caerfai Bay *(6)*.

### 1  St Justinian's

Justinian (Stinian) was a sixth-century hermit, born in Brittany, and reputedly a colleague of St David. Legend has it that this strict disciplinarian retreated to Ramsey Island to devote himself to God. His followers eventually rebelled against his severe rule, cutting off his head, whereupon the saintly Justinian walked across the waters of Ramsey Sound carrying his head in his arms. He was buried at St Justinian's

Chapel (rebuilt in the early sixteenth century) which stands in the private grounds of the coastguard station, but can be seen from the road. His remains were later taken to St David's Cathedral.

The chapel gave the name to Porthstinian (also known locally as St Justinian's), a confined little harbour bounded by jagged rocks and steep cliffs overlooking the dangerous waters of Ramsey Sound. A spectacularly located lifeboat station just manages to squeeze itself in among the rocks. This is the home of the St David's lifeboat, built in 1911–12 for £3000. Porthstinian is also the harbour for day-trips in the tourist season to Ramsey Island.

2 *Ramsey Island*

Ramsey is the Norse name for this lovely, cliff-backed island. Known otherwise as Ynys Dewi—St David's Island—it is about 2 miles (3 km) long and covers some 600 acres (243 hectares). The island, which is a nature reserve, has large sea-bird populations (more than thirty species of bird breed here) and huge numbers—too many—of rabbits. The rocks, coves and inlets around the island are popular with seals, which are particularly conspicuous during September and October, when the Atlantic grey seal hauls itself ashore to breed.

The island is separated from the mainland by the Ramsey Sound (at its narrowest point ½ mile/800 m across), a treacherous stretch of water with a tide-race of up to 8 knots. It is made doubly dangerous by the existence of The Bitches, a ridge of rocks lying close to the surface of the water which claimed the St David's lifeboat *Gem* and three of its crew in October 1910.

3 *Lower Treginnis*

This is one of the many National Trust landholdings in Pembrokeshire. Lower Treginnis incorporates the farmlands and coastline of the little peninsula which juts out south-westwards between St Justinian's and Porthlysgi. This mixed habitat supports a wide variety of wildlife. The cliff-tops are carpeted by colourful maritime grass, pockets of heath cover part of the land, and the rocky coast is a nesting place for yet more sea-birds. The farmer at Lower Treginnis was one of the fifteen survivors when *Gem* went down.

4 *Porth-clais*

This narrow inlet is the perfect sheltered haven for shipping along the stormy western shores of Pembrokeshire. Geologically, it is a valley deepened by glacial melt-water and subsequently drowned by rising sea levels. Historically, it was the harbour for St David's for the many centuries when sea routes served as the main lanes of communication between

Pembrokeshire and the rest of the world. The early Christian missionaries travelling between St David's and Cornwall, Ireland and Brittany must have arrived and departed from here. We know that boats were using Porth-clais in 1385 to off-load cargoes for the cathedral. Between 1585 and 1620 timber was shipped in from Ireland, together with corn, malt and wool from, respectively, mid-Wales, Bristol and Barnstaple. There were also exports: wheat, barley, corn and rye to the West Country. Well into the twentieth century, coal was brought into Porth-clais, then transported by cart to St David's, a mile (1.6 km) away. The kilns along the harbour were used to produce lime (by burning limestone and coal) which was spread on the farmlands to sweeten the acid soil.

A little way along the road leading north-westwards from Porth-clais is Ffynnon Dewi (David's Well), where St David was baptized by Elvis, Bishop of Munster.

5  *St Non*

St Non, or Nonnita, was the mother of St David. Legend has it that David was born on the grassy slopes above St Non's Bay during a great storm around AD 500. The spot is marked by the ruins of a chapel of obscure origin, traditionally associated with St Non, which may date from before the Norman Conquest. The chapel was probably abandoned in the middle of the sixteenth century.

A small, white statue of St Non stands nearby, close to the holy well dedicated to her. This famous well, the waters of which were said to have miraculous powers for healing eye diseases, was much visited by pilgrims to St David's.

The Chapel of Our Lady and St Non, although built in the style of Pembrokeshire chapels of 500 years ago, dates from the 1930s. This little chapel with its sturdy, buttressed walls is associated with the larger building standing on the hillside above. This is St Non's Retreat, a centre for spiritual renewal, which was completed in 1929.

6  *Caerfai Bay*

This beautiful, sheltered bay of firm sands is the closest beach to St David's. Stones from the quarries in the cliffs (below the site now occupied by the car-park) were used to build St David's Cathedral.

Previous page: *The lifeboat station, St Justinian's*

Limekilns at Porth-clais

240

# WALKS IN
# THE SNOWDONIA
# NATIONAL PARK

*Landscape near Dwygyfylchi*

# THE PRECIPICE WALK

Car-park at Saith groesffordd (124-746212). Leave Dolgellau on the A494 to Bala, branching L $\frac{1}{4}$ mile (400 m) after the bridge. Follow minor road for $2\frac{1}{2}$ miles (4 km) through three junctions to reach car-park.
LENGTH
$3\frac{1}{2}$ miles (5.5 km)
ASCENT
125 ft (40 m)

A short and easy walk with little climbing around the two summits of Foel Cynwch and Foel Faner and the lovely Llyn Cynwch. For much of the route, the way is a narrow path running across the steep hillside high above the Afon Mawddach with superb views over the valley and the great forest of Coed y Brenin beyond.

This path is not a public right of way, but access has been granted by the Nannau Estate since 1890. The National Park Authority has provided stiles, waste bins and information boards around the walk. This should not be confused with the New Precipice Walk which is further to the west near Borthwnog.

## ROUTE DESCRIPTION (Map 70)

Leave the car-park and turn L along the road past an Information Board. After a short distance turn L through a gate (sign 'Precipice Walk') and walk along a path between conifers.

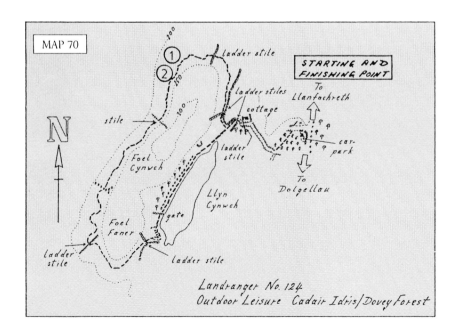

MAP 70

STARTING AND FINISHING POINT

ladder stile

ladder stiles

cottage

To Llanfachreth

car-park

stile

ladder stile

Foel Cynwch

ladder stile

To Dolgellau

Llyn Cynwch

gate

Foel Faner

ladder stile

ladder stile

N

Landranger No. 124
Outdoor Leisure Cadair Idris/Dovey Forest

242

The path soon bends R and continues between fences to a cottage. Turn L before the cottage, up to a ladder stile. The path turns R after the stile and then bends to the L to reach a second ladder stile. Cross and shortly afterwards take the R fork at a path junction. The path climbs to a wall and bends R with it; continue with this wall keeping it to your R, crossing a further ladder stile.

The path from there is clear and follows the 800 ft (245 m) contour around Foel Cynwch and then further along around Foel Faner. Magnificent views open up as you progress along this walk, over the Mawddach Valley *(1)* and beyond to the Coed y Brenin Forest *(2)*. For a short distance the slope below the path is particularly steep, hence Precipice Walk.

Eventually the path bends away from the main valley crossing a ladder stile, and runs along the hillside to the L of a small dry valley. Cross another ladder stile and continue to the lake Llyn Cynwch, there cross a low wall and turn L. Walk along the L side of the lake to rejoin the original path at a junction. Return to the car-park.

*1 The Gold Mines of the Mawddach*

The gold belt of North Wales extended in an arc, about one mile wide along the valley of the Afon Mawddach from its estuary at Barmouth to its upper reaches within the Coed y Brenin Forest. Although some gold may have been extracted in this region prior to the nineteenth century, the industry really began in 1844 with the discovery of gold at the Cwmheisian Mines, which were being worked at that time for lead, and ended to all intents and purposes during World War I. A total of nearly 130,000 oz of gold was extracted during that period, of which the vast bulk came from two mines: the Clogau, between Barmouth and Dolgellau near the village of Bontddu, and Gwynfynydd, at the northern extremity of the field. Both mines were in continuous production from around 1890 to their closures in 1911 and 1916 respectively.

The gold occurs as very fine yellow particles embedded in veins of quartz, called lodes. The distribution of gold is by no means uniform, which accounts for the violent fluctuations in the output from the mines (and hence their profitability). A tunnel or level was driven along the lode until a gold-rich area was discovered, this would then be dug out, the extracted ore being taken up to the surface in small waggons. The ore was crushed to free the metallic particles, which were then separated from the waste by amalgamation with mercury. The amount of waste was enormous; in the case of the Clogau, for instance, between 1900 and 1910 inclusive, its most successful years, no less than 108,329 tons of quartz had to be crushed to produce 54,970 oz of gold, a ratio of 52,972:1.

The wedding rings of Queen Elizabeth the Queen Mother (1923), The Queen (1947), The Princess Margaret (1960), The Princess Anne (1973) and The Princess of Wales (1981) were made from the same nugget of Welsh gold, which came from the Clogau. In 1981 the Royal British Legion presented the Queen with a sample of Welsh gold weighing 36g and it was from this that the wedding ring of the Duchess of York was made in 1986.

2 *Coed y Brenin Forest (The Forest of the King)*
Coed y Brenin Forest, owned by the Forest Authority and Forest Enterprise, covers an area of over 23,200 acres (9400 ha) round the valleys of the Afon Mawddach and its tributaries. Most of the land for the forest was purchased from the Vaughan family, owners of the local estate of Nannau — hence its original name of Vaughan Forest — and planting commenced in 1922. The name was changed to its present form in 1935 to commemorate the Silver Jubilee of George V. There are over 100 miles (160 km) of forest roads and paths open to walkers, of which approximately half have been waymarked, a nature trail, a mountain bothy, a small arboretum at Glasdir and a Visitor Centre near Maesgwm, 8 miles (13 km) north of Dolgellau on the A470.

*View towards The Precipice Walk*

# 1.42

# THE ROMAN STEPS

## STARTING AND FINISHING POINT

Cwm Bychan (124-646314). On the A496 from Barmouth to Harlech turn R at Llanbedr (signs to Cwm Bychan) and follow the very narrow and winding road to its end at the far side of the lake.
## LENGTH
3 miles (5 km)
## ASCENT
925 ft (280 m)

An easy and clear path climbs slowly up from the lovely valley of Cwm Bychan, through a deciduous wood, to the famous Roman Steps, an ancient causeway of stone flags leading up the Bwlch Tyddiad. It is worth going on to the top of the col for the view to the east before returning by the same route. The route enters the Rhinog National Nature Reserve for a short distance.

## ROUTE DESCRIPTION (Map 71)

Leave the car-park at Cwm Bychan and turn R along the road. Opposite a barn (on the L), turn R through a gate (signs 'Roman Steps' and 'Public Footpath'). The path crosses a stone causeway

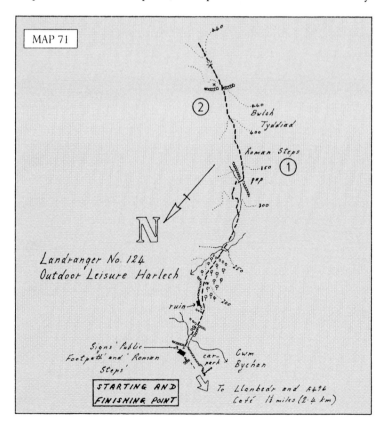

*The Roman Steps, Bwlch Tyddiad*

over a small stream and then continues, with a wall to the R, through a gap. Continue along this clear path, which slowly rises to pass to the R of a small ruin and through a deciduous wood. Beyond the wood the paths head towards a ravine, later swinging to the R to pass through a gap in a wall. Immediately after the gap the path turns L along a particularly fine section of the Roman Steps *(1)*.

Follow the Roman Steps, slowly climbing on the R-hand side of the ravine to eventually enter the Rhinog National Nature Reserve *(2)*. Continue in the same direction on the path as far as the large cairn at the top of the pass, from which there is a magnificent view.

Return by the same route back to Cwm Bychan.

1 *The Roman Steps*

The paved path running from Cwm Bychan to the Bwlch Tyddiad is traditionally known as the Roman Steps, but its actual origin is obscure. Various theories place the path in the period of the Roman occupation, in Medieval times for the transport of wool from Bala to the sea at Llanbedr and

Harlech, and as late as the seventeenth century as a local path for the occupiers of the farmstead at Cwm Bychan. This section of the path is in a fine state of preservation but other sections have been identified which are now neglected.

2 *Rhinog National Nature Reserve*
An area of 991 acres (401 ha) around the Bwlch Drws Ardudwy (The Pass of the Door of Ardudwy), which includes the summit of Rhinog Fawr. A difficult area for walking with thick heather and rock, and also one of the loneliest regions in the Park.

# Cwm Idwal and the Devil's Kitchen

STARTING AND FINISHING POINT
Ogwen (115-649603), on the A5 from Capel Curig to Bethesda.
LENGTH
3 miles (5 km)
ASCENT
1200 ft (370 m)

Cymoedd — great hollows carved out of the mountains by glaciers during the Ice Age — are a characteristic feature of North Wales. Of these, Cwm Idwal is one of the most spectacular; and fortunately also one of the most accessible, reached easily from the road at Ogwen. The route includes a steep climb up to the Devil's Kitchen and a steep, rough descent over boulders afterwards (both of which can be avoided), but otherwise the path is clear and the walking easy. The scenery throughout is superb.

## ROUTE DESCRIPTION (Map 72)

Start in the car-park (Warden Centre, refreshment kiosk and toilets), beside the Youth Hostel in the minor road at Ogwen and take the path leaving from the far corner. This climbs, crossing a fence and a footbridge. Continue ahead along the footpath, which soon bends R and rises to a gate. This is the entrance to the Cwm Idwal National Nature Reserve (1). Take the L-hand path around the L-hand shore of the lake. This path passes to the R of the Idwal Slabs (2), then bends round to the R and climbs steeply up to the foot of the Devil's Kitchen (3), which is the prominent cleft in the cliff ahead with huge boulders on the slope below.

For the return, descend down the steep slope below the Kitchen to the L of the stream, gradually leaving it towards the L. The path descends to the L shore of the lake (4) and follows it round back to the entrance gate of the Reserve. From the gate, follow the path down and back to your starting point at Ogwen (5).

While at Ogwen, walk a few yards along the minor road to a magnificent viewpoint over the Nant Ffrancon (6) and the falls (7).

*1 Cwm Idwal*

This magnificent cwm is part of the Ysbyty Estate of the National Trust, but has been leased to the Countryside

ALTERNATIVE: The climb up to the Devil's Kitchen, which is the hardest part, can be avoided by traversing the slopes around the head of the lake from just past the Idwal Slabs, to meet the return path on the far side.

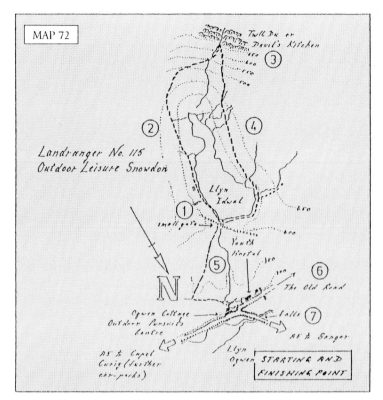

MAP 72

Twll Du or
Devil's Kitchen

③

②

④

Landranger No. 115
Outdoor Leisure Snowdon

Llyn
Idwal

①
small gate

Youth
Hostel

⑤

⑥
The Old Road

N

Ogwen Cottage
Outdoor Pursuits
Centre

falls ⑦
A5 to Bangor

A5 to Capel
Curig (further
car-parks)

Llyn
Ogwen

STARTING AND
FINISHING POINT

Council for Wales. It was established as a National Nature Reserve in 1954, of considerable interest both to geologists and to botanists. Although free access is allowed, care should be taken not to disturb any rocks or plants. The small enclosures in the cwm are part of an experiment on the effects of sheep grazing and should not be entered.

*Cwm Idwal National Nature Reserve Nature Trail*, Countryside Council for Wales.

2 *The Idwal Slabs*

The slabs lying at an easy angle of about 50° to the horizontal to the south-east of Llyn Idwal are the famous Idwal Slabs. First climbed in 1897 by Rose and Moss, they give mainly longish climbs with small holds, but of relatively low standard because of their easy angle. They are therefore regarded primarily as a training ground for beginners. All the main rock faces hereabouts have been given names: the East and West Walls lie L and R of the slabs themselves, whilst above are Holly Tree Wall and Continuation Wall.

3 *The Devil's Kitchen*

This is the most popular name, but the Welsh name is Twll Du or the Black Hole. It is a huge chasm, deep and dark, fed by a stream coming down from a small lake on the col above.

Walkers can follow the stream down as far as a small grass

Opposite *Looking towards Foel-goch from the top of Ogwen Falls*

platform where it is possible to look down into the cleft and to Llyn Idwal below. It is also possible to scramble up the bed of the stream from below as far as the large boulder which blocks the gully. The full ascent of the Kitchen was first completed by J. M. Archer Thomson and Harold Hughes in 1895 who, using a coal hatchet borrowed from Ogwen Cottage, cut hand- and foot-holds into the frozen waterfall. The first ascent on rock was by Reade and McCulloch in 1898. The route is about 100 ft (30 m) long, of Very Strenuous standard and should *not* be attempted by non-climbers.

4 *Llyn Idwal*

The low hills by the lake on the return leg are moraines left there by the glacier during the Ice Age. The lake itself has a certain sinister reputation, for legend has it that a young Prince Idwal was deliberately drowned there. For that reason, it is said, no bird will fly over the water.

5 *Llyn Ogwen*

Formed long ago on the bottom of a valley gouged out by glaciers, it is the shallowest lake of any size within the Park, being no more than about 10 ft (3 m) deep. As with all lakes in the Park, Llyn Ogwen is becoming shallower and will eventually fill up altogether due to material coming into it from the hillsides. This has already happened to the lake that once occupied the Nant Ffrancon on the opposite side of the falls.

6 *The Nant Ffrancon Pass*

The best view of the Nant Ffrancon can be obtained from the Old Road just beyond the Youth Hostel. On the left are the hanging valleys of Cwm Bual, Cwm Perfedd, Cwm Graianog and Cwm Ceunant, ahead is the Nant Ffrancon with its flat floor of green fields over which the Afon Ogwen meanders and to the right is the steep face of Penyrole-wen and of the western Carneddau. The old Penrhyn road can be seen running along the left-hand side of the valley and on the right-hand side is the present A5 which also marks the old line of Telford's Turnpike.

Among the most spectacular in Snowdonia. View either from above or from the Old Road.

*Nant Ffrancon*

# CONWY MOUNTAIN AND THE SYCHNANT PASS

STARTING POINT
Conwy Castle (115-784775)
FINISHING POINT
On the road from Conwy to the
Sychnant Pass near Brynrhedyn
(115-770775), about 1 mile (1.6 km)
from Conwy.
LENGTH
6½ miles (10.5 km)
ASCENT
1475 ft (450 m)

The northern tip of the Snowdonia National Park contains two scenic gems: Conwy Mountain (Mynydd y Dref), which gives magnificent views over Conwy and the north coast of Wales, and the Sychnant Pass, which carried the old road over the high ground to the west of Conwy. This walk from Conwy links them both with a pleasant stretch up the wooded valley of the Afon Gyrach.

## ROUTE DESCRIPTION (Maps 73, 74)

From Castle Square in Conwy *(1) (2)*, walk down Rose Hill Street, soon bending R with it to pass through Lancaster Square and the gateway in the town wall directly ahead. Continue along the Bangor Road (A55) from the gateway, taking the second road to the L (sign 'Conwy Mountain and Sychnant Pass'). Immediately after crossing the railway bridge, turn R and walk along Cadnant Park Road following it past the cul-de-sac of Cadnant Park. After the cul-de-sac and a L bend, take the first road to the R (Mountain Road). At the end of the road at a junction, bend L (sign 'To Mountain Road') and follow the rough road up to a fork in front of some cottages (Machno Cottages). Take the R fork and pass in front of the cottages to continue along a narrow path through bushes. The path climbs steadily to the R through bracken up towards the ridge top. There are many paths around the mountain: follow the one that keeps on or close to the ridge top for magnificent views on three sides. Eventually reach the cairns on top of Conwy Mountain *(3)*.

Continue over the top to pick up a broad track; this bends down on the R of the ridge and then goes over the ridge to the L to descend to a wall. Turn R and follow the wall to its end (i.e. where it bends L) near a small pool and the junction of three paths. Take the path to the L to a fence and a cross-path. Continue along the track across heading in the same direction and descending to a farm road, there turn R and go around the

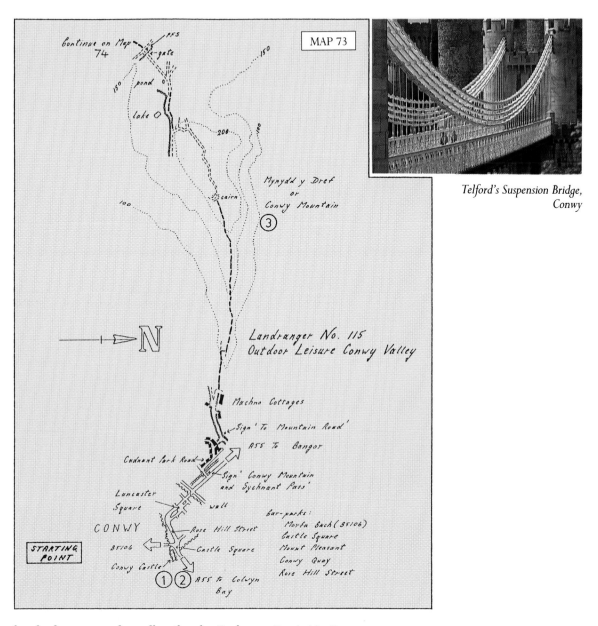

*Telford's Suspension Bridge,*
*Conwy*

head of a spectacular valley (by the Sychnant Pass) *(4)*. Do not continue as far as the road ahead, but drop down some steps at the head of the valley to the R and follow a path through the valley to reach a road by some cottages. Turn L and then R at a road junction to descend to Capelulo (café and hotels).

Turn L up the minor road immediately after the Fairy Glen Hotel and follow it as far as a bridge over a stream to the L. Cross and follow the drive to a house, here turn back half L along a path which then bends R and climbs the hillside (look back as you climb for lovely views over Capelulo towards the sea). At the top, go to the L of a wall and follow it past a

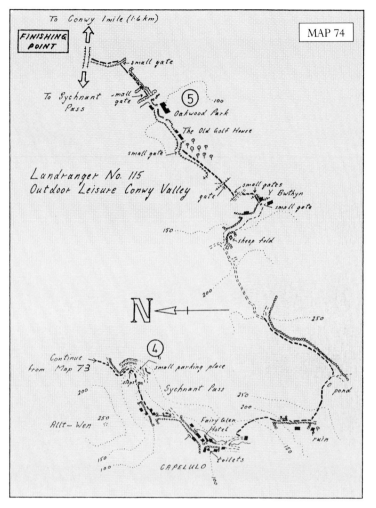

farmhouse. Go over the top into a small valley; just before a small group of trees and a ruin (over the wall to the R) turn L down a shallow valley to reach a crossing wall. Turn L and follow the wall until it bends R; just beyond the bend, go L at a path junction and to the L of a prominent hill to a T-junction by some sheepfolds. Here turn R and follow the path to a road. Turn R in the road and then L through a small gate just before the next house (Y Bwthyn).

Go past the house garage to a second small gate and then, with a fence on your R, to a third small gate. Here, go half L across a field to still another small gate and on again through a large gate; later reach a lane at the L edge of a wood by a cottage. Turn R and follow the lane to pass an exceptionally large house on the R *(5)* and then on to meet a minor road. Turn

*Sychnant Pass and Conwy Mountain*

R and then almost immediately L through a gate. Follow the hedge on your R to its end (i.e. where it swings R), then keep in the same direction to a small gate. Immediately after the gate turn L and go to road (PFS). Turn R and follow the road for about 1 mile (1.6 km) back to Conwy.

1 *Conwy Castle*
A Cistercian monastery holding the Charter of Llewelyn the Great and built on the site of the present parish church marked the beginning of the modern town of Conwy. But much more significant was the construction in the remarkably short time of four years between 1283 and 1287 of a great castle and fortified town on the orders of Edward I, to safeguard his recent victories over the Welsh. Since then the castle has played a part in other struggles: the rising of Owain Glyndŵr, the Wars of the Roses and the Civil War. During the summer arrange your return to Conwy after dusk, when the walls are floodlit to produce a superb spectacle.

2 *Telford's Suspension Bridge and Stephenson's Tubular Bridge*
Two famous bridges span the Conwy: the Suspension Bridge built by Thomas Telford in 1822 to carry a road and the Tubular Bridge constructed by George Stephenson in 1846–48 for the railway track. The latter is still in use, but the former was superseded by a modern bridge and is now owned by the National Trust.

3 *Castell Caer Lleion*
The summit of Conwy Mountain was the site of the Celtic hill-fort of Castell Caer Lleion probably built in the early Iron Age. The site was well chosen on a promontory with hillsides falling away steeply on all sides and high cliffs to the north, its isolated position giving it a magnificent view over the surrounding countryside. The fort occupied about 10 acres (4 ha) and was further strengthened by the building of ramparts, which are still visible.

4 *The Sychnant Pass*
The Sychnant Pass (the name means 'Dry Gorge') carried the old road from Conwy to the west thus avoiding the difficulty of forcing a road past the headland of Penmaen-bach. The road was used for this purpose until 1826.

5 *Oakwood Park*
The very large and unusual house with square tower and spire passed on the walk was originally a private house, but in its time has also served as a hotel, war-time school and hospital for mentally handicapped children.

*Landscape near Dwygyfylchi*

# The Ascent of Moel Siabod

STARTING AND FINISHING
POINT
Plas y Brenin, near Capel Curig
(115-716578). Plas y Brenin is the
very large building on the L about
550 yd (500 m) from Capel Curig
along the road (A4086) to Llanberis
and Beddgelert.
LENGTH
6½ miles (10.5 km)
ASCENT
2225 ft (680 m)

From Plas y Brenin, forest roads and paths run through beautiful woods by the Afon Llugwy to reach the old bridge of Pont Cyfyng. From there, a long gradual climb leads up the eastern flank of Moel Siabod to reach the ridge of Daiar Ddu above Llyn y Foel. The Daiar Ddu gives a long but easy scramble, finishing at the summit cairn. The summit ridge is traversed, followed by a descent over grassy slopes to the coniferous forests above Plas y Brenin. The view from the footbridge at Plas y Brenin towards the Snowdon Horseshoe is considered one of the finest in Snowdonia.

## Route Description (Maps 75, 76)

Go through a small gate (PFS) to the R of the main building of Plas y Brenin *(1)* and descend to a footbridge. Immediately after the footbridge, turn L along a forest road which runs along the R-hand side of a small lake. Keep along this forest road passing a house on the L and another forest road coming in from the R. Take a second forest road to the R just afterwards and follow it to its end at some steps, where a path continues in the same direction. Follow this path to a footbridge. Do not cross, but instead turn R and keep along the R bank of the river passing over a ladder stile and then through a gate. Beyond go to the L of a small barn, then head slightly R for a gap in a fence at the front of a farmhouse. Go through the gap, over a small stream and up to the house wall, there turn L. Rise to a gate which leads into a minor road and turn R.

Follow the road, turning R at a junction after 100 yards (90 m), until it ends at the farm of Rhôs; there continue on the rough road beyond to a ladder stile by an old house and then on again to a second ladder stile in a fence *(2)*. Higher still, take the L fork at a junction and, crossing a third ladder stile, continue to a lake. Follow the clear path to the R of the lake and then up to some slate quarries ahead *(3)*. Go past the spoil heaps and

*Opposite* The Snowdon Horseshoe from the Llynnau Mymbyr

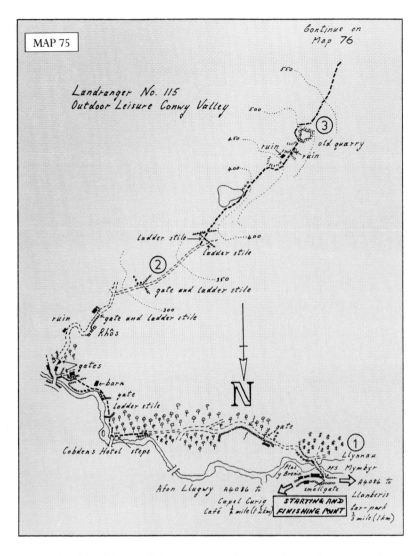

Continue on Map 76

MAP 75

Landranger No. 115
Outdoor Leisure Conwy Valley

ruined buildings of the quarry and on to the L of a deep sinister pit filled with black water into which the water cascades on the far side. The path continues beyond the pit up the valley to reach the top of a ridge from which a second lake can be seen. Keep on the path to pass this lake also on its R side and continue on to a further ridge ahead (there is a splendid view from here of the Lledr Valley) *(4)*. Turn R and climb up the ridge following a path and cairns to the OS obelisk on the summit of Moel Siabod.

For the return, turn R from your approach route along the rocky summit ridge to the far end and drop down to the start of the grassy slopes of the mountain, here turn half L leading downhill (aim for the R-hand end of the lake in the valley). There is no path at first, but later you should be able to pick up a path marked with cairns; follow it down to a ladder stile in a

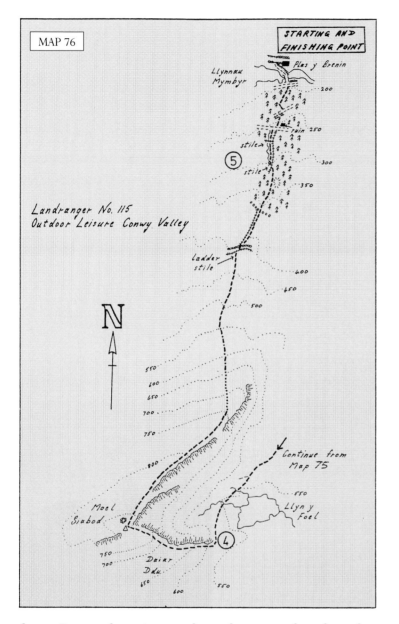

fence. Cross and continue to descend on a rough path, with a fence on the L, to a forest (5). Continue to follow the path down through the forest to a stile in a fence and then later to meet a forest road. Cross half R to go on a path to the L of a small ruined hut, and then down a particularly delightful stretch of path under trees. At a crossing track turn R, then immediately L and down again to reach the bridge by Plas y Brenin.

*1 Plas y Brenin (The King's House)*

The Old Road up the Nant Ffrancon Pass was constructed by Richard Pennant – owner of the great quarry at Bethesda – to connect his lands at Bethesda and near Bangor with those at Capel Curig. At the latter place he built an inn, the Capel Curig Inn, in 1800–1801 to serve the tourist trade. In later years, 1808–1848, it also served the Royal Mail Coach which carried the Irish Mail up the new turnpike between Shrewsbury and Holyhead. George Borrow, author of *Wild Wales*, visited the inn in 1854 on a day's walk from Cerrig-y-Drudion to Bangor and found it '... a very magnificent edifice ... from whose garden Snowdon may be seen towering in majesty at the distance of about six miles'. Other visitors over the years included Queen Victoria, Edward VIII, Sir Walter Scott, Queen Mary, George V and Lord Byron. In 1870–71 – no doubt as a result of this heavy visitation by royalty – the name of the inn was changed to the Royal Hotel.

During World War II, the inn was taken over as a training centre for mountain warfare, but returned to its former use afterwards. In 1954, however, it was purchased by the Central Council for Physical Recreation and opened in 1955 as The Snowdonia National Recreation Centre. In a reorganization during the early 1970s the CCPR was replaced by the Sports Council, who became responsible for the management of the Centre. It is now called Plas y Brenin, The National Centre for Mountain Activities.

*2 Bryn-y-Gefeiliau*

The conquest of the Ordovices in Snowdonia in AD 78 by the Roman Army under Agricola marked the end of active campaigning in Wales; their control over a vanquished foe was then assured by a series of forts placed at strategic points and joined together by roads, along which supplies and reinforcements could be speedily passed. One such fort was built about 1½ miles (2.4 km) from Capel Curig towards Betws-y-Coed, where the great Roman road of Sarn Helen from Carmarthen to the Conwy Valley crossed the River Llugwy. It was built early in the second century and formed a permanent base for an auxiliary unit of perhaps 500 or 1000 men. The site can be seen from about the second ladder stile on the climb up to Moel Siabod, it is to the R of the camp site (brightly coloured tents) in the valley behind you.

*3 The Capel Curig Slate Quarry Company*

The deep and awesome pit, by the path to Moel Siabod was worked by the Capel Curig Slate Quarry Company from the nineteenth century. The company was amalgamated with

*View from the footbridge behind Plas y Brenin*

several others in 1918 to form the Caernarvonshire Crown Slate Quarries Company but, like most other slate quarries in the area, closed down later.

4 *Dolwyddelan Castle*

From the bottom of the ridge beyond Llyn y Foel and before the final climb to the summit of Moel Siabod there is a splendid view of the Lledr valley ahead and half left. The prominent castle, perched on the edge of a rocky crag which falls steeply into the valley below, is Dolwyddelan. Built by a Prince of Gwynedd in the thirteenth century, it was reconstructed later in the same century by Edward I as part of his massive programme of castle building. The present remains consist of the rectangular keep to the east, the smaller West Tower, ditches and part of the curtain-wall.

5 *The Gwydyr Forest*

The forest behind Plas y Brenin is part of the Gwydyr Forest acquired by the Forestry Commission in 1920. The plantings have been of conifers, but there is a belt of natural oak to the north of the forest towards Capel Curig.

# 3.46

# Carnedd Llewelyn
# from Ogwen

STARTING AND FINISHING
POINT
Ogwen (115-649603) on the A5 from
Capel Curig to Bethesda.
LENGTH
11 miles (17.5 km)
ASCENT
3200 ft (975 m)

A magnificent walk over the southern section of the Carneddau Ridge. The walk is long but straightforward except for two sections: the steep rise up to Pen y waun-wen and the longer, steeper and more arduous descent of Penyrole-wen at the end of the day. Undoubtedly one of the finest walks in Snowdonia, which includes three of the 3000 ft (914 m) peaks. Most of this land is owned by the National Trust and is part of the Carneddau Estate.

## Route Description (Maps 77–80)

*(1)* From Ogwen walk along the A5 towards Bethesda; immediately after the bridge go through a stile on the R. The path goes on the L bank of the lake as far as a stile over a wall; from the wall the path rises up the hillside to the L. After the rise, the path contours along the hillside crossing several small streams and heading towards a farmhouse, Tal-y-llyn-Ogwen. Just before the farmhouse rise L to a stile in a wall, turn R and drop down hill to a farm road (white arrows). Turn L and follow the farm road to the A5, at the end passing by a wooden hut and conifers. Cross the road half R and go through a small gate.

Follow the farm road beyond (The Old Road) *(2) (3)* to the first of two farms, Gwern Gof Uchaf. Pass it to the R over stiles. Continue along to the second farm, Gwern-gof Isaf; pass this to the L across a field. Just beyond the farmhouse, the path leads over a small stream, through a gateway and ahead to the R of a wall. In the middle of a small belt of conifers turn L through a white metal gate and follow a lane to the A5. The cottage to the R is Helyg *(4)*.

Turn L along the A5 *(5)* for 400 yards (365 m) and then R through a gate and up a road. Continue along the road *(6)*, rising slowly through further gates with magnificent views — particularly of Tryfan — to the L. Immediately before a sheep-fold, about 400 yards (365 m) from the last gate, where the road

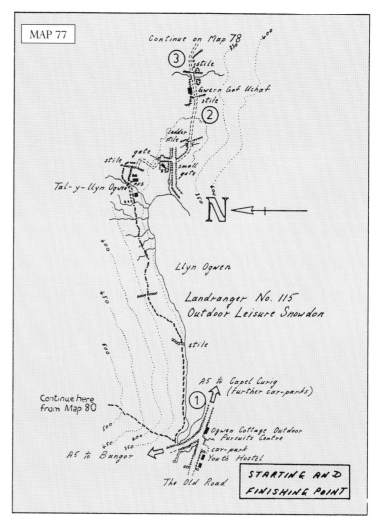

swings L, take the path leaving to the R. This continues in approximately the same direction along the R shore of Ffynnon Llugwy Reservoir; beyond the reservoir rise up a steep slope to reach the top of a ridge at a cairn *(7)*.

Turn L and follow the distinct path along the crest of the narrow ridge, rising eventually to the summit of Carnedd Llewelyn *(8)*. The ridge is narrow at first with a little scrambling but broadens further along beyond the great cliffs of Craig yr Ysfa. From the summit turn L and descend on a faint path to the R of a ruined wall. The path drops to a small col and then continues along the ridge in the same general direction to the summit of Penyrole-wen ($2\frac{3}{4}$ miles, 4.5 km from Carnedd Llewelyn).

To reach the summit of Penyrole-wen, bend L with the path up the final rise keeping to the L side of the ridge, to a cairn which marks the summit. From there it is important to find the best

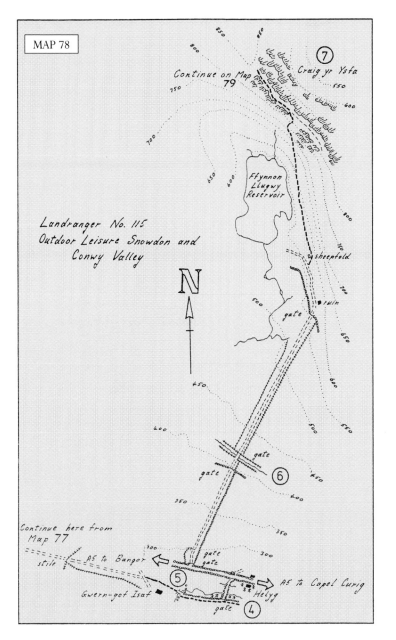

MAP 78

Continue on Map 79

⑦ Craig yr Ysfa

Ffynnon Llugwy Reservoir

Landranger No. 115
Outdoor Leisure Snowdon and
Conwy Valley

N

sheepfold

ruin

gate

⑥ gate

gate

Continue here from
Map 77

A5 to Bangor ←

stile

gate
gate

⑤

A5 to Capel Curig →

Gwern-gof Isaf

Helyg

gate ④

descent point as the summit top is ringed on three sides by very steep slopes and cliffs. Leave the summit to the R from your approach and cross the top, descending slightly to reach a very prominent cairn with stone shelters on the opposite side. From there continue ahead bending slightly L (210° magnetic). After a few yards, you should pick up a very faint path which grows more distinct as you descend, keeping to the L of a cliff edge.

The descent of Penyrole-wen is very long and very steep, particularly in its middle section. The rigours of the descent are matched only by those of the long climb in the opposite

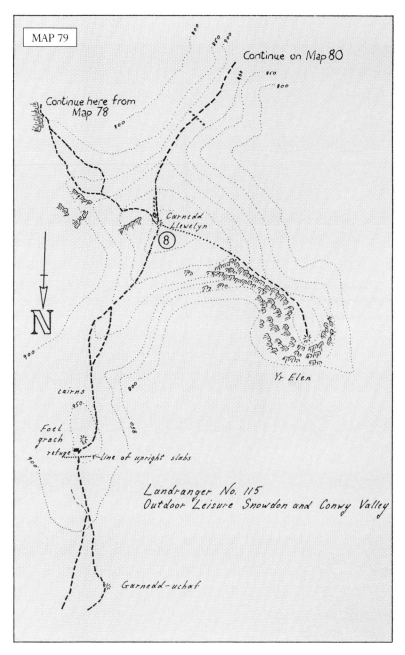

direction, which is generally acknowledged to be one of the most arduous in all Snowdonia.

Eventually, much later, arrive — probably in a considerably weakened condition — at Ogwen where you started earlier.

*1 Aircraft in Snowdonia*

Military aircraft are a prominent feature of the Park, particularly around Ogwen and the Nant Ffrancon Valley. These may be UK or NATO aircraft from any of the airfields

*Opposite Llyn Ogwen*

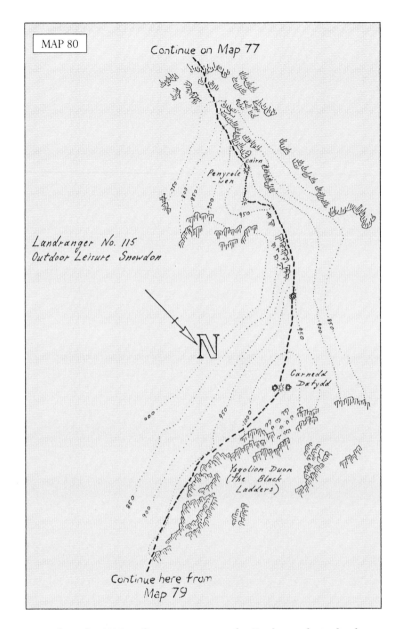

MAP 80

Continue on Map 77

cairn

Penyrole
-wen

770
950
900
950

Landranger No. 115
Outdoor Leisure Snowdon

N

Carnedd
Dafydd

850

000
900
1000

900
850

Ysgolion Duon
(the Black
Ladders)

850
900

Continue here from
Map 79

within the UK as flying time into the Park is relatively short. Many come from the Advanced Fast Jet Training School at Royal Air Force Valley, a few miles from Holyhead on Anglesey.

This station was first opened in February 1941 as a base for day and night flights. Today, it is the home of a number of units including 'C' Flight of No. 22 Squadron an operational search and rescue flight, the Search and Rescue Training Unit (SARTU) which trains helicopter pilots, navigators and winchmen to carry out search and rescue duties, and the No. 4 Flying Training School for fast jet pilots. The latter unit has operated the British Aerospace Hawk T1 since 1976, and these red and white training aircraft may be frequently seen around the Park.

## 2  The Old Road

The main obstacle to road construction through the Nant Ffrancon Valley lies at the western end of Llyn Ogwen where the Afon Ogwen plunges over a rock cliff over 200 ft (60 m) high. The first road through the valley to surmount this step was built in 1791 by Lord Penrhyn, owner of the Penrhyn Quarry at Bethesda, to reach his lands at Capel Curig with the intention of developing them for the tourist trade. The Penrhyn road was soon supplanted by a turnpike built in 1805 and later by a second and much superior turnpike built by Thomas Telford. The Old Road runs roughly parallel with the present A5 but on the opposite side of the valley and of the Afon Ogwen, remaining reasonably level at around the 725 ft (220 m) contour, to a short distance beyond Pentre where it begins to climb. Its route coincides with that of the A5 around Llyn Ogwen, but from there it again takes a more southerly route on the opposite side of the stream as far as Capel Curig, which it enters over a single span stone bridge over the Afon Llugwy.

## 3  Telford's Turnpike

The A5, running from Bethesda to Capel Curig through the valley of the Nant Ffrancon and surmounting the steep rise by the Rhaeadr Ogwen at an easy gradient of 1 in 22, stands as a memorial to the genius of one man, Thomas Telford, probably the greatest builder of canals, roads and bridges during the years of the Industrial Revolution.

Telford was born in 1757, the only son of a humble shepherd of the border region of Eskdale in eastern Dumfries and Galloway; when he died in 1834 he was laid to rest among the famous in the nave of Westminster Abbey. The Birmingham and Liverpool Junction Canal, the Caledonian Canal, the Holyhead Road and the bridges at Conwy and over the Menai Straits were but the greatest of his many achievements.

In addition to the road built by Lord Penrhyn up the Nant Ffrancon, a turnpike had been constructed by 1805 to reach the harbour at Holyhead, which serviced the cross-channel boats to Ireland. Although initially successful, shortage of money, both in the building and in the maintenance, soon produced such a deterioration in the state of the road that passage became extremely difficult and at times impossible, and an attempt to run the mail coach along it proved a failure.

Largely as a result of the influence of two Irish Members of Parliament, John Foster, Chancellor of the Irish Exchequer, and later Henry Parnell, member for Queen's County, Telford was commissioned to survey the route. A preliminary report was completed in 1811 and a detailed one in 1817. The work itself lasted for fifteen years, although a through route was established by 1826 with the opening of the bridge over the Menai Straits.

4 *Helyg*

The cottage of Helyg below the cliffs of Gallt yr Ogof about $2\frac{1}{2}$ miles (4 km) out of Capel Curig on the Bangor Road was visited in 1854 by George Borrow who stopped there for a drink of water on a long walk of 34 miles (55 km) from Cerrig-y-Drudion to Bangor, which he covered in a single day. In his book, *Wild Wales, Its People, Language and Scenery*, published in 1862, which has become a classic and still sells well today, he described it as 'a wretched hovel'.

It was derelict and unoccupied when acquired by the Climbers' Club in 1925, opening as a club hut on 30 October. Under the pressure of increasing use it was rebuilt and extended in 1933.

5 *Tryfan from Helyg*

A magnificent view of the east face of Tryfan is obtained from the road by Helyg Cottage. The two objects close together on the summit are often mistaken for climbers, but are in fact two stone blocks about 6 ft (2 m) high, called Adam and Eve. The Heather Terrace lower down the East Face is used by climbers to reach the base of some rock climbs, whilst the usual walkers' route traverses the peak more or less along the skyline of the mountain.

6 *The Leat*

The watercourse crossed about $\frac{1}{2}$ mile (0.8 km) from the road is a man-made leat that diverts water from the high ground above into Llyn Cowlyd. From Llyn Cowlyd the water is taken by pipeline to the power station at Dolgarrog.

7 *Craig yr Ysfa*

A great crag in the Carneddau on the eastern slopes of Carnedd Llewelyn. The crag was late in being explored by rock climbers due to its remote situation, but now has numerous routes. The first climbing hut in Britain was established below the crag in Cwm Eigiau by the Rucksack Club in 1912.

8 *Carnedd Llewelyn and Carnedd Dafydd*

These are the two highest peaks in the range of mountains

*View SE from the rise to Ffynnon Llugwy Reservoir*

between the Nant Ffrancon and the sea, which give the name to the entire range. The peaks are named after Llewelyn the Last who was recognized as Prince of all Wales by the Treaty of Montgomery in 1267 and his brother Dafydd (or David) who attempted to assume that title after his brother's death. Llewelyn was the last native Prince of Wales.

# WALKS IN
# THE YORKSHIRE DALES
# NATIONAL PARK

*The Swale*

# 1.47

# AROUND SEMER WATER

STARTING AND FINISHING
POINT
On the foreshore at the north-east
side of Semer Water, by the road
from Countersett to Stalling Busk,
where cars may be parked for a small
fee (pay at Low Blean Farm on the
walk if no one is in attendance)
(98-921876)
LENGTH
3¾ miles (6 km)
ASCENT
150 feet (45 m)

Unlike some other National Parks such as Snowdonia or the
Lake District, there are few lakes, natural or otherwise, within
the area of the Yorkshire Dales. But, of the few, Malham Tarn
and Semer Water are outstanding. This walk follows pleasant
field paths and farm lanes around Semer Water as far as Marsett;
a length of quiet road has to be walked on the return leg.

## ROUTE DESCRIPTION (Map 81)

Turn R in the road and walk along it as far as a farm (Low Blean)

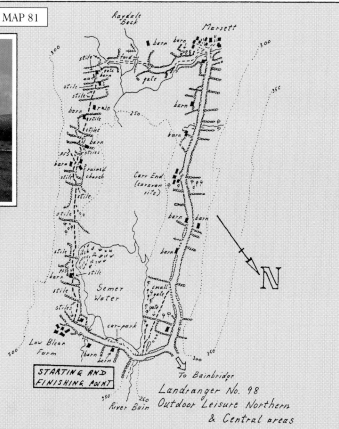

Opposite *Near Low Blean Farm, Semer
Water*

*Semer Water*

on the L, keeping the lake on your R (pay any parking fee at the farm). Immediately after the farm, where the road starts to climb, go R through a stile (PFS). Follow a clear footpath across three fields to a stile to the R of a barn. Beyond, continue on this path in the same direction leaving Semer Water behind to eventually pass to the L of a ruined church and churchyard.

From the church continue with the wall on your R; at a path junction taking the R-hand one (PFS 'Marsett') to a stile in a wall corner. The path then continues in the same general direction over nine fields to reach a farm lane to the L of a barn. Turn R and follow the lane to the village of Marsett.

At the road in Marsett turn R over the bridge and follow the road for about 1 mile (1.6 km). Where the road starts to descend steeply into a valley (Semer Water will be down to your R) go through a small gate to the R (PFS) a short distance down the hill. Take a path which goes down half L to a gate in a wall corner. Beyond the gate continue in the same direction across a pasture to reach a clear path, follow this to the road. Turn R for the parking place.

# 1.48

# THE WATERFALLS WALK

STARTING AND FINISHING
POINT
Ingleton (98-695733)
LENGTH
4 miles (6.5 km)
ASCENT
550 feet (170 m)

The adjacent valleys of the Twiss and Doe to the north of Ingleton narrow in places to impressive gorges and hold high and magnificent waterfalls. The Waterfalls Walk (sometimes called the Ingleton Glens Walk) follows a circular route in the best of the two valleys. It is one of the most popular walks in the Dales, rightly regarded as a local classic. The walk follows the Twiss upstream to above Thornton Force, then crosses over to the Doe which is then followed downstream and back to Ingleton. The paths in the two valleys have been extensively re-surfaced giving them a somewhat artificial character. In no way does this detract from the route however, for it is superb throughout and few others — if any — can match it for sustained interest. At some points the path is unfenced and runs above considerable drops; care is therefore essential, particularly with children. A small charge is made for admission.

## ROUTE DESCRIPTION (Map 82)

From the church in Ingleton take the road which drops down steeply to a bridge. Continue along the road soon crossing a second bridge. (The two rivers crossed by the bridges are the Doe and Twiss respectively which meet a short distance to the south-west.) Immediately after the second bridge, where the road bends L, go R through a gate. Pass the café to a small hut, just before the old railway embankment *(1)*.

Continue ahead through the gap in the embankment and cross the car-park to the far end. From there, follow the clear path which leads through small gates along the gorge of Swilla Glen and through lovely woods, keeping to the L of the river throughout. After about ¾ mile (1.2 km) cross the stream over a footbridge (Manor Bridge) and continue along the opposite bank of the stream, to re-cross after a bend by a second footbridge (Pecca Bridge). Just ahead of this footbridge are the first waterfalls (Pecca Falls) set in spectacular rock-scenery. The path

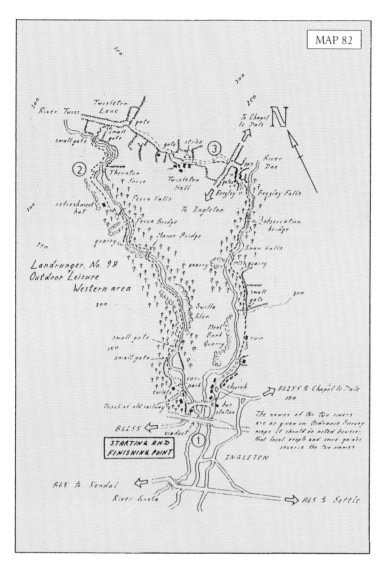

MAP 82

continues on the L bank up steep steps past Pecca Falls and a refreshment hut to a further waterfall, Thornton Force *(2)*. This is by far the largest and most interesting of the waterfalls along the route. Continue past the Force to a third footbridge (Ravenray Bridge).

Cross and climb the steps ahead up the hill to a small gate in the top R-hand corner of the field. In the walled lane beyond (Twisleton Lane) turn R and follow it to a farm (Twisleton Hall). Go past barns and through the stile by a gate to the L of the house. Follow the farm road through a further stile and down to a road *(3)*. Take the lane opposite, soon turning R in front of a

*Thornton Force*

farmhouse (Beezley Farm — refreshments). Go past the farm-house to a gate and along the farm road to a second gate. Immediately after the second gate turn down L to reach a river (the Doe) by a waterfall (Beezley Falls).

Follow downstream on the very obvious path keeping to the R bank. As a spectacle this is easily the most impressive part of the route, for the path follows a deep ravine past white falls, brown watershoots and dark, sinister pools of deep water. In one place an observation bridge has been erected across the gorge to give a breathtaking and unforgettable view of the ravine at its most savage point.

Much lower down, cross over a second footbridge to the opposite bank and follow the path as it leaves the stream to the L. Continue along the obvious path past a quarry and through woods to a small gate, then beyond over more open ground to a road. Follow this back to Ingleton.

1  *Railways at Ingleton*
The large viaduct crossing the Greta to the south-west of the village centre carried the now disused railway line over the river, the old railway station being at the south-eastern end. The embankment immediately after the small hut at the entrance to the Waterfalls Walk carried a branch line from the main track to Mealbank Quarry which is passed towards the end of the walk.

2  *Thornton Force*
The Pecca Falls are a series of magnificent cascades, Thornton Force by comparison is a mad torrent of white water falling in one tremendous leap into a plunge pool below. Its open situation, directly opposite the footpath as it curves to the right above the small refreshment hut, is ideal, for the Force is both a spectacle and one of the most interesting and well-known geological features in Britain. It is also a place to stir the imagination. The upper part of the rock-face of the fall is of grey, horizontal limestone, the lowest part of vertical and greenish Ingleton slates. Separating the two is a thin conglomerate of smoothly rounded pebbles cemented together. It is the site of an ancient pebble beach over which the sea washed some time between 350 and 500 million years ago. Later the beach was covered by shallow seas and deposited organic remains formed the overlying limestone layer. The junction of the limestone and slate is called an unconformity — the rocks above were not laid down in succession to those below, but instead there is a gap in the time scale of origin caused by the erosion of intervening layers of rock.

3 *Skirwith Quarry*

The large quarry, seen across the Doe Valley as you descend towards it, is Skirwith Quarry worked for gritstone by Amey Roadstone Company, a member of the Gold Fields Group. The rock, which is very hard and abrasion resistant, is used as a road surface aggregate and railway ballast.

*The Twiss below Manor Bridge*

# 1.49

# TO HARDRAW FORCE

STARTING AND FINISHING
POINT
The National Park Centre and
car-park at Hawes (98-876899)
LENGTH
$4\frac{3}{4}$ miles (7.5 km)
ASCENT
350 feet (110 m)

Hardraw Force is the highest unbroken fall in Britain; much less well-known or visited are the upper falls set in sylvan woods. This walk is unique in that it includes a compulsory traverse of The Green Dragon public house. Not surprisingly, it is one of the most popular walks within the Park.

## ROUTE DESCRIPTION (Map 83)

Go on to the old platform *(1)* behind the National Park Centre and cross the track at the bridge end. Turn R along the far platform and then L up to the road. There turn R. About 100 yards (90 m) from the bridge go L through a small gate and

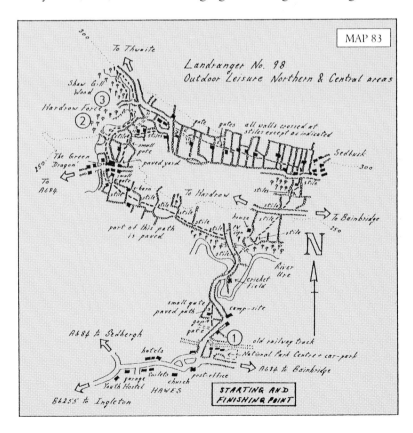

follow a paved path through two fields to rejoin the road further along. Turn L over a bridge and past a small cricket field. When the road starts to climb, immediately after a belt of trees, go L up some steps and through a stile (PW sign). Follow the path by the wall along the bottom edge of the field. Little or no difficulty should now be found in following the clear path (much of it paved) which goes in an almost straight line through a series of stiles to Hardraw. Reach the road opposite the church and The Green Dragon.

Hardraw Force *(2)* can only be reached through The Green Dragon on payment of a small fee. From the rear of the public house go along a path to the R of the river. After viewing, return to the front of the public house.

Leave Hardraw down the R-hand side of the public house through the small paved yard of a cottage. Climb up the field beyond to a small gate and up the next field to a stile L of a house (West House). In front of the house turn L and follow the farm road as far as a road, there turn L. Where the road bends R go straight ahead down a walled path to a footbridge *(3)*. Cross and follow the stream on its L bank past several small falls to a further footbridge. Cross and return on the opposite side back to West House.

*Old Bridge near the Ure. Hawes can be seen in the distance.*

Back at the house turn L between the house and a barn and follow a path to a stile to the R of a further barn. Cross the next field to enter a lane. Turn R to road, there turn L. After 25 yards (23 m) turn R over a stile. Go half L to a farm road and gate and beyond by a large barn leave the farm road half L again to a further stile. The path goes in a straight line over a number of stiles and gates (on my count thirteen!) towards Sedbusk.

In the last but one field before the village, turn R immediately after the stile along a path to a stile in the far corner. This leads into a road. Cross the road half R to another stile and descend the field beyond past a barn to a lower stile. Continue in the same general direction over two further fields to reach a lower road. Again, cross to a stile opposite and descend past a house to the bottom R-hand corner of the field. Continue to descend over an old bridge and into a road. Turn L and retrace your steps back to Hawes.

*1 The Wensleydale Railway*

The station at Hawes was built as a joint station between the Midland Railway Company's branch line from Garsdale (then called Hawes Junction) and that of the North Eastern Railway Company's line from Leyburn, the linkage being completed in 1878. It remained open until 1964 when the entire line between Garsdale and Redmire was closed. The state of the station buildings, platforms and trackway rapidly deteriorated, and it was fortunate that they were taken over by the National Park Authority. The main station building is now used as a National Park Centre, the goods warehouse and office have become the Upper Dales Folk Museum and the station yard is a car-park, whilst the waiting room on the far platform is a warden's workshop. The house to the left of the car-park entrance was the Station Master's residence.

*2 Hardraw Force*

The slopes of Wensleydale are characterized by near-horizontal banks of relatively hard-wearing limestone of the Yoredale Series which produce superb waterfalls where side streams flow over them. The Force at Hardraw was produced in this way by the water of a beck flowing over a limestone scar resting upon softer shales. The light-grey horizontal bands of limestone are obvious as are the much darker shales at their base. In the course of time the stream has eroded back considerably into the hillside to produce the ravine, and

*Hardraw Force*

the greater erosion of the shales has formed a bank under the overhangs of limestone.

The thunder of the Force can be heard long before you reach it, but a sight of the fall is delayed until the final yards. Even so, the great drop of brownish water nearly 100 feet (30 m) high set in its amphitheatre of high cliffs is extremely impressive; the cloak of trees removing from the scene that bareness and austerity that is characteristic of Gordale.

The gorge was the scene during the nineteenth century and again in the 1920s for brass band contests and the old bandstand can be seen on the left just after the footbridge; on the hillside opposite are the tiers cut for spectators. These contests were revived recently, but have now been discontinued once more.

3  *Shaw Gill Wood*

Above the Force, this is largely neglected compared with the Force itself, but it is a delight not to be missed if a few extra minutes can be found for a diversion away from the main route. Neither of the two main waterfalls approaches the Force as a spectacle, but their setting is much superior.

In the Yorkshire Dales National Park, as elsewhere, teams of public-spirited people — mainly young people — have given up much of their free time so that the countryside should be the pleasanter for others. Duke of Edinburgh Award Scheme Volunteers assisted in the restoration of the paths at Shaw Gill in August, 1980 and the top footbridge was built by the Army Apprentices College, Chepstow, in October, 1979.

# 2.50

# The Ascent of Pen-y-ghent

STARTING AND FINISHING
POINT
Horton in Ribblesdale car-park
(98-808726)
LENGTH
6½ miles (10.5 km)
ASCENT
1550 feet (470 m)

After Ingleborough, Pen-y-ghent is the most popular mountain in the Dales. Some of this popularity is probably due to its fine name which has a challenging sound about it much in keeping with the mountain itself. Its finest aspect undoubtedly is from the south around Churn Milk Hole, where its bold shape is said to resemble a crouching lion, but it is an imposing sight from any direction. The ascent from Horton in Ribblesdale via Brackenbottom and the subsequent descent via Hunt and Hull Pots is a magnificent walk, although a great deal of work has had to be done on it in order to combat the effect of erosion caused by the number of walkers.

## Route Description (Map 84)

Walk from the car-park into the road and turn R. Continue along the road for 700 yards (640 m) to turn L by the village church and cross a bridge. Immediately after the bridge turn L along a minor road; continue along this road to the small hamlet of Brackenbottom.

Immediately before the first building on the L (a barn) go through a gate (PFS 'Pen-y-ghent') and on to a second gate (i.e. the centre one of three gates). After this second gate turn L and go up the hill with a wall on the L. The path follows near to the wall in a long and steady climb up the western flank of the south ridge of Pen-y-ghent, crossing three walls at stiles, to eventually reach the ridge crest at a ladder stile. Cross and turn L to commence the final steep climb. Some scrambling can be enjoyed here, but the path avoids the worst of the rocks by detouring to the R. Above the rocks follow the path to the R of the wall across to the summit *(1)*.

At the summit, cross the ladder stile and descend half R on a broad path to reach the edge of a steep section (cairns). Here the path bends R to descend slowly along the edge. Lower down, below the start of a cliff on the R, the path bends back L

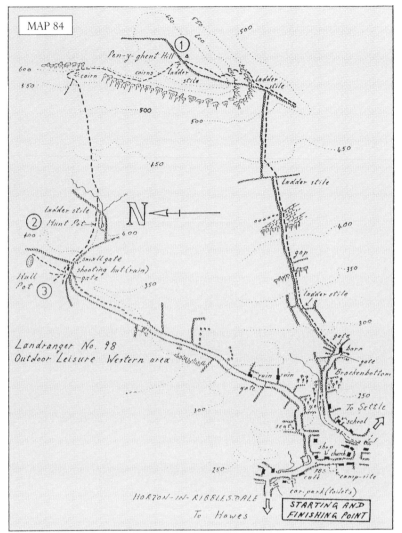

MAP 84

Pen-y-ghent Hill

cairns

ladder stile

ladder stile

ladder stile

ladder stile

600

550

500

500

450

400

400

350

ladder stile

Hunt Pot

small gate

shooting hut (rain)

gate

Hull Pot

350

Landranger No. 98
Outdoor Leisure Western area

gap

350

ladder stile

300

gate

barn

gate

Brackenbottom

250

To Settle

school

ruin   ruin

gate

300

seat

shop   church

250

PBS.
café   camp-site

car-park (toilets)

HORTON-IN-RIBBLESDALE

To Hawes

**STARTING AND FINISHING POINT**

by a large cairn. Go through the bend and then take the prominent path to the L descending the moor. Later cross a ladder stile, pass a pot-hole (Hunt Pot) *(2)*, and through a small gate to the end of a lane. (It is well worthwhile making a short detour here to see another famous pot-hole, Hull Pot *(3)*. At the lane end turn R and follow a path through a shallow valley for 350 yards (320 m). The pot-hole is very obvious. Afterwards return by the same route back to the lane end.) Go through the gate to enter the lane and follow this for 1⅔ miles (2.5 km) back to Horton in Ribblesdale. In the village turn R for the car-park (and the Pen-y-ghent café).

*Pen-y-ghent from near Hull Pot*

*1 Pen-y-ghent*

The meaning of the name is still somewhat obscure, although it is Celtic in origin. Among the possibilities suggested are 'hill of the plain or open country' and 'hill of the winds'. The rock foundations are similar to those of Ingleborough: the flat top of the hill is formed by a cap, about 50 feet (15 m) thick, of Millstone Grit, underneath which are the Yoredale Series with Great Scar Limestone beginning at around 1300 feet (395 m). The characteristic 'stepped' appearance of Pen-y-ghent is due to the Millstone Grit and the beds of the Yoredale Series which have worn at different rates, so that the more resistant rocks now stand proud of the hillside. Pot-holes, caves and scars are characteristic features of the plateau formed by the limestone belt. Both Ingleborough and Pen-y-ghent are the remnants of a great rock plateau which originally covered the whole area around Ribblesdale. Rock climbing takes place on the gritstone edges of the mountain.

*2 Hunt Pot*

The sinister slit of Hunt Pot leads directly to a sheer drop of about 90 feet (27 m) followed by a second drop of about 70 feet (21 m). It was first descended in 1898.

*3 Hull Pot*

The opening of Hull Pot is enormous, about 185 feet × 45 feet (56 × 14 m). A stream bed reaches the lip of the pot on the north side, but water only flows over this in wet weather; more usually the stream sinks underground a short distance away to emerge as a waterfall from an opening below the old bed. The water then sinks immediately into the bed of the pot to re-appear at Brants Gill Head north of Horton. In extremely wet conditions, when the outlet passages cannot cope with the excess flow, the floor of the pot becomes covered with water.

*Pen-y-ghent from near Churn Milk Hole*

# 2.51

# UPPER SWALEDALE

**STARTING AND FINISHING POINT**
Thwaite (98-892982). Leave cars outside the village at some suitable point.
**LENGTH**
8 miles (13 km)
**ASCENT**
900 feet (270 m)

Considered by many to be the finest of all the Yorkshire Dales, Swaledale is remote and rugged with quiet villages of great charm. Appropriately, the Pennine Way follows it for several miles and another long-distance footpath, The Coast to Coast Walk, crosses it at Keld. This very popular route links the villages of Thwaite, Keld and Muker. The first section follows the Pennine Way over the flanks of Kisdon to the west of the Swale and is well waymarked. The return journey is southwards along the opposite bank of the river and then westwards from Muker.

## ROUTE DESCRIPTION (Maps 85–87)

Start at the centre of the village facing the Kearton Guest House and the shop *(1) (2)*. Turn R going down a side lane as far as a R-bend; there, go through a stile in the wall to the L by a PW sign. Turn R between a wall and a barn and go through two further stiles. Immediately after the last stile turn L and cross a field to a gap and then to a small bridge. On the opposite bank turn R and follow a path by the stream; at the wall ahead the path bends L and climbs up the hillside by the wall to a stile at the top. After the stile turn R and follow the clear path which slowly climbs up the hillside. (As you climb, glorious views begin to open up over the dale to the R.)

At the top, meet a wall and follow it to a barn, here the path goes half L to a stile (PW signs). Follow the wall on the L round to a gate; beyond the gate follow the wall on the R as it bends R and along to a farmhouse *(3)*. Go through the gate at the far end of the house and then L through a second gate into a lane between walls (PW sign). At the end, bend R with the wall and then after 45 yards (40 m) turn back half L at a PW sign. Go up the hill to a gap at a wall corner. Continue with a wall on the R. The path now goes ahead across the hillside with wonderful views down to the R into Swaledale. A succession of walls are crossed at stiles, gates or gaps, but the path is clear and yellow waymarks will be found throughout. After $1\frac{1}{2}$ miles (2.5 km)

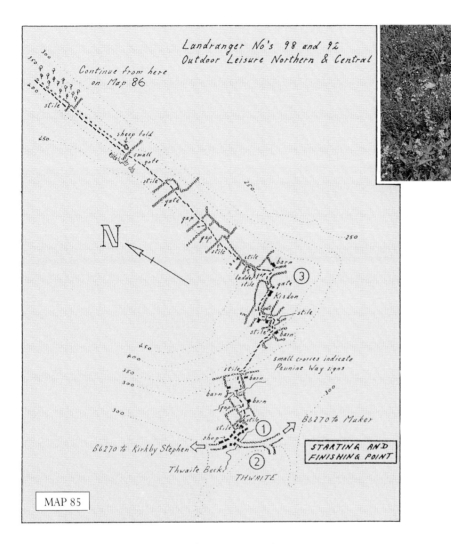

Landranger No's 98 and 92
Outdoor Leisure Northern & Central

Continue from here
on Map 86

stile

sheep fold

small
gate

stile

gate

gap
gap
stile

stile    barn

ladder
stile    gate

Kisdon

stile

stile    barn

small crosses indicate
Pennine Way signs

stile

stile    barn

barn    barn

gap

stile

③

N

small crosses indicate
Pennine Way signs

shop    ①

B6270 to Muker

B6270 to Kirkby Stephen

②

STARTING AND
FINISHING POINT

Thwaite Beck

THWAITE

MAP 85

(PW sign), towards the end of a long wood on your R, go R
through a stile (PW sign) and descend to the R of a small scar.
Meet a path lower down and turn L along it, soon to enter Keld
(toilets and shop, but no pub) by the church.

Leave by the same path. After 250 yards (230 m) turn down L
to a footbridge *(4)*. Cross and go up the path to the L to meet a
farm road, there turn R along it soon crossing a bridge. Follow
the farm road beyond for $2\frac{1}{2}$ miles (4 km) keeping on or near to
the R-bank of the Swale to a footbridge crossing it to the R.
Cross and on the opposite side turn R to a stile and then on 45
yards (40 m) to a second stile. Follow the path which now goes
half L across seven fields to the small village of Muker. At the
village go through a gate and across a yard for a short distance to
reach a road. Turn R and walk along the road between houses,
at the end turning R to a stile and a gate by a house. (The church
*(5)* to the L is well worth a short detour.)

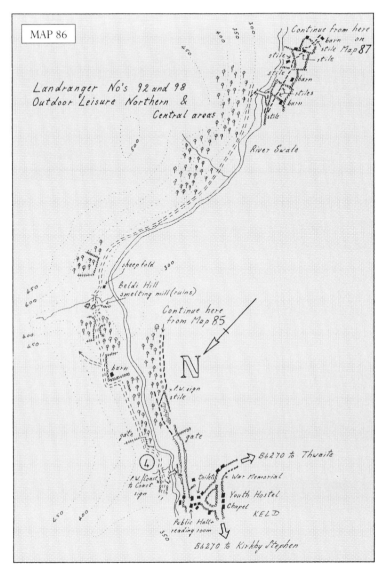

MAP 86

Landranger No's 92 and 98
Outdoor Leisure Northern &
Central areas

Continue from here
barn on
stile Map 87

stile

stile

barn

stiles

barn

stile

River Swale

sheep fold

Beldi Hill
smelting mill (ruins)

Continue here
from Map 85

N

barn

P.W. sign
stile

gate

gate

B6270 to Thwaite

P.W./Coast
to Coast
sign

toilets

War Memorial

Youth Hostel

Chapel

KELD

Public Hall +
reading room

B6270 to Kirkby Stephen

Go along a paved footpath with a wall on the L. This continues across six fields. In the seventh field the path bends to the L past a large barn to a stile to the R of a further barn; after the stile turn L down a drive to the road. In the road turn R and walk along to a bridge. Do not cross, but instead go through a stile on the R and along the R-bank between the stream and a wall. Cross a stile and then continue on this path over three fields; at the end turn L over a small bridge and immediately R to a stile. The path gradually leaves the stream to the L over three small fields to reach a further stream. Continue on the R-bank of

*Thwaite*

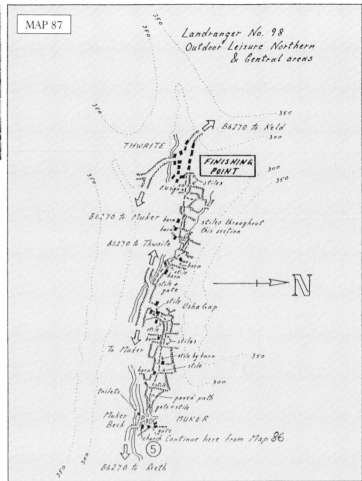

MAP 87

Landranger No. 98
Outdoor Leisure Northern
& Central areas

B6270 to Keld

THWAITE

FINISHING POINT

stiles

B6270 to Muker — barn

B6270 to Thwaite

barn

stiles throughout
this section

barn

stile

barn

stile + gate

stile  Usha Gap

stiles

To Muker

stile by barn

stile

barn

stile

paved path

gate + stile

toilets

Muker Beck

MUKER

gate

church  Continue here from Map 86

⑤

B6270 to Reeth

this stream to a stile and then follow a footpath back to Thwaite.

### 1 Upper Swaledale

To many walkers Upper Swaledale has a special quality, that is not to be found elsewhere in the Yorkshire Dales. Undoubtedly this is partly explained by its more remote situation in the north of the Park, to which high and wild moorlands, crossed by narrow and unfenced roads of impressive steepness, impose a barrier. Partly, it must also be due to the character of its villages: Keld, Muker, Thwaite and Gunnerside; small compact huddles of cottages — stone-walled and flag-roofed — their position carefully chosen to give them some protection against the rigours of the northern winter. 'Timeless' is always the word that comes to mind when you visit them, at their best perhaps on warm summer evenings when grey-blue smoke drifts from old chimneys and swallows

*The Swale*

and martins circle overhead; the music of running water providing a constant background, for each village rests on a stream, either on the Swale itself or on one of its tributaries.

In the eighteenth and nineteenth centuries Swaledale was one of the centres of lead mining, and the mouths of abandoned levels, hushes, spoil heaps and the ruins of old smelt mills are a common feature in most of the northern gills; occasionally, it must be admitted, disfiguring, but seldom less than fascinating. And, finally, the special character of Upper Swaledale lies partly in its place-names which are Scandinavian in origin; for Norsemen came into this area from the west early in the tenth century and, finding it much to their liking, settled there. Thwaite denotes a forest clearing, Muker a narrow field, Keld a spring, whilst Gunnerside was Gunnar's saetr or Gunnar's spring pasture. Common names such as beck, fell, gill and moss are also Old Norse.

### ? *Thwaite*

Thwaite is perhaps best known to most as a watering place on the long trek up the Pennine Way. It was also the birthplace of the Kearton brothers, early pioneers of nature photography. On the wall of the schoolhouse in Muker, where they received their early education, two plaques were placed by public subscription: the first 'In memory of Cherry Kearton. Naturalist, author and explorer. Pioneer of wild life photography. July, 1871–Sept. 1940.' and the second '... in memory of Richard Kearton, FZS. Naturalist, author and lecturer. Born 2nd Jan. 1862, died 8th Feb. 1928.'

*3  The Corpse Way*

In the vicinity of Kisdon the line of an old road is crossed which ran from Keld to Grinton through Muker and Gunnerside. The oldest road in Swaledale, it became known as the Corpse Way, because it was the way along which corpses were carried from the upper dale villages to the nearest consecrated ground at Grinton. In extreme cases this involved a journey of about 15 miles (24 km), the corpses being carried in wicker coffins. Muker church was consecrated in 1580 as a Chapel-of-ease to Grinton, considerably reducing the journey, although the first people were not buried there until some years later.

*4  Kisdon Force*

As is the case with Wensleydale to the south, the base of Swaledale was formed in rocks of the Yoredale Series, although in this case at a higher level. The immediate result of this is a superb series of waterfalls formed over the bands of limestone both on the Swale itself and on its tributaries. Kisdon Force is passed on this route, Catrake and Wain Wath Force are a short distance north of Keld, and a further waterfall in East Grain lies about a mile (1½ km) away.

*5  Muker Church*

Originally built in 1580 as a Chapel-of-ease to Grinton (see above) for the benefit of folk in the upper part of the dale, it was considerably extended in 1761, 1793 and again in 1890. The clock was placed in the tower to commemorate the coronation of George V and Queen Mary on 22 June, 1911.

# 3.52

# The Calf and the Eastern Howgills

**STARTING AND FINISHING POINT**
Sedbergh (97-657921)
**LENGTH**
11 miles (18 km)
**ASCENT**
2300 feet (700 m)

Although a part of the Yorkshire Dales National Park in the extreme north-western corner, the area of the Howgills is tied geologically, politically and socially to Cumbria rather than to North Yorkshire. It is a splendid region of great whale-backed hills — smooth, steep-sided and grassy (for there is little heather or bracken in the Howgills) — crossed only by lovely green tracks, with superb views both over the Dales and into the Lakes. Essentially, at present, an area for connoisseurs of walking, for the hordes who climb Ingleborough and Whernside, and think them marvellous, have yet to discover it. This is one of the best routes in the Howgills, up the long ridge past Winder and Arant Haw to the summit of The Calf and then down White Fell to Castley. Part of the Dales Way is followed back to Sedbergh.

In cloudy conditions proficiency with map and compass is essential in the Howgills.

## Route Description (Maps 88–90)

From the church in Sedbergh take the Kirkby Lonsdale road (A683) past the post office, turning R after 50 yards (45 m) at a junction (sign 'Howgill $2\frac{3}{4}$'). Follow the road up a hill and past some playing fields; 85 yards (80 m) after a telephone box turn R up a lane (PFS 'To the Fell'). Soon reach a farm, go through a gate directly opposite and up a short lane which leads to a further path opening on to the open fell. Turn L and follow the boundary wall for about 200 yards (180 m) then, immediately after a small wood, turn half R up the hillside on a grassy track. Soon reach a crossing track and turn R along it. Follow this grassy track through bracken as it climbs slowly up the flanks of Winder. Eventually, at a cairn, the track swings L and goes up on the L side of Settlebeck Gill to the top of a ridge.

On the ridge meet a crossing track and turn R along it. Follow this very clear and grassy path as it slowly climbs, first on

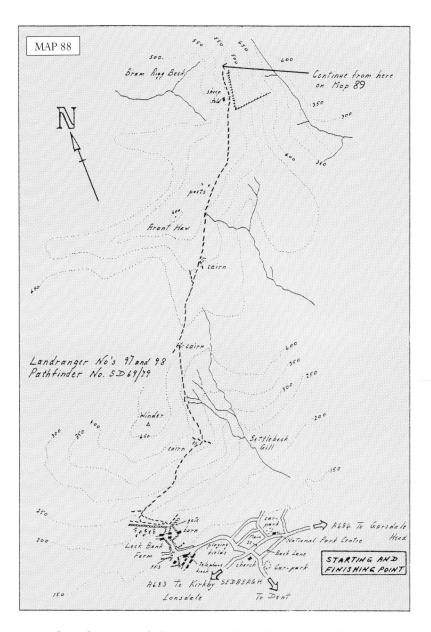

MAP 88

Bram Rigg Beck

Continue from here on Map 89

sheep fold

posts

Brant Haw

cairn

Landranger No's 97 and 98
Pathfinder No. SD 69/79

cairn

Winder
△

cairn

Settlebeck Gill

cairn

car park

National Park Centre

A684 To Garsdale Head

Lock Bank Farm

playing fields

Main St

Beck Lane

Car park

Telephone box

church

A683 To Kirkby
Lonsdale

SEDBERGH

To Dent

STARTING AND
FINISHING POINT

the ridge top and then over to the R; later the path dips into a spectacular col and crosses it to a fence on the opposite side. Climb to the L of the fence, turning sharply to the R with it later. 200 yards (180 m) from the fence corner at a cairn on the hilltop turn L and cross the open moor (no path) away from the fence to pick up a clear path. Follow this path to the OS obelisk at the summit of The Calf.

Continue beyond the obelisk in the same direction picking up a path after a few yards; follow this to a crossing track and turn L along it. This path goes alongside a ridge and then later descends steeply on its L side. Eventually after a long descent

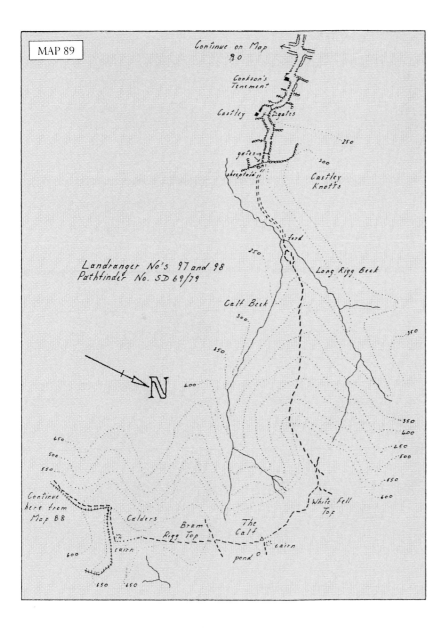

MAP 89

reach a stream junction. Cross the R-hand tributary at a ford and go downstream on a farm road. At a gate cross into a green lane and follow this, later metalled, for $\frac{2}{3}$ mile (1.2 km) to a cross roads. Turn L.

Walk along the road for about $\frac{1}{2}$ mile (0.8 km) to a bridge. Immediately after the bridge turn R through a gate and walk along a minor road past a small church, at a house continuing up the road half L. At the top the road bends L to reach two gates at a junction, turn R and follow a farm road down to a farm (Thwaite). Do not enter the farm, but instead turn L and then R between two farm buildings to a gate, here immediately turn L

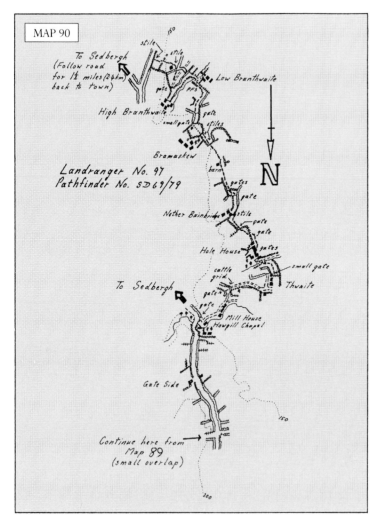

MAP 90

To Sedbergh
(Follow road
for 1½ miles (2½km)
back to town)

stile · a stile
↳ Low Branthwaite
gate  PFS

High Branthwaite
small gate  stiles
gate

Bramaskew

Landranger No. 97
Pathfinder No. SD 69/79

barn
gates
pate
N
Nether Bainbridge  stile
gate
gate
Hole House  gates

cattle
grid  small gate
Thwaite
To Sedbergh  gate
gate
Mill House
Howgill Chapel

Gate Side

150

Continue here from →
Map 89
(small overlap)

200

through a small gate and go along the hillside to the R of a hedge. Where the hedge bends L drop down to a footbridge. Go L up the lane beyond, through a small gate and between a house and a barn into a farmyard (Hole House). At the end of the farmyard go between the last two barns on the R (two gates), then turn L and climb to the R of a hedge to a gate. Cross to the wall opposite and turn L, soon turning R through the first of two gates. Follow a wall to a farm (Nether Bainbridge), going through a stile to the R of a large barn and R again down the lane beyond.

At the end of the lane go through a gate and then half L through double gates, continuing to a small barn. At the barn go half L up a hill to a stile and then on to a further stile to the R of another farm (Bramaskew). Continue across the next field

*The Lakeland fells in the distance seen from Arant Haw, Howgills*

*Sedbergh*

beyond the farm to a gate to the R of a small hut, this leads into a lane which goes to the next farm of Low Branthwaite. Go through the gate to the L of this farm (PFS) and over a bridge into a lane, follow this to the last farm (High Branthwaite). Do not enter the farm, but turn back half R at a junction just before. Follow the farm road for a few yards beyond a gate then go half L across the field to a stile. Turn L after the stile up another field to reach a road at the top. Turn L in the road to a T-junction, and then R for 1$\frac{1}{2}$ miles (2.4 km) back to Sedbergh.

# Appendices

# *Access for the Walker*

It is important to realize that the designation of large areas of country as National Parks did not in itself change the ownership of the land in those areas in any way. The vast bulk of the land within our National Parks is still held by private individuals or organizations just as it was before designation. Furthermore, the laws of access and trespass apply just as much to areas of private land within a National Park as to those outside it.

Nevertheless, the public has the right to walk along many miles of path and to roam over large areas of open country within the National Parks just as they have elsewhere. The Yorkshire Dales National Park, for example, has a network of 1100 miles (1770 km) of footpaths and bridleways over which the public has a legal right to walk; Exmoor and Dartmoor together have a total of about 1000 miles (1609 km). That right to access is enshrined in legislation. Furthermore, in practice the position is even better as other paths and areas of open country have been opened to the public in other ways. The purchase of land by local authorities, the opening of permissive paths, access agreements between landowners and local authorities, and the policy of some large organizations in allowing controlled access have all played a part. Finally, there is a long tradition of de facto access over large areas of some Parks.

## PUBLIC RIGHTS OF WAY

The National Parks and Access to the Countryside Act of 1949 required County Councils in England and Wales to prepare maps which showed all paths over which the public had a right to walk. The final form of the map is referred to as a definitive map and copies are held at the offices of the County Council and District or Borough Council and sometimes by the Parish Council concerned. These definitive maps may be inspected by the public. Public paths can only be diverted or deleted from a definitive map by the raising of a Diversion Order or an Extinguishment Order respectively. The paths are classified as either footpaths (for walkers only) or bridleways (for walkers, horseriders and cyclists). These public paths were included on the now withdrawn one inch to one mile (1:63 360) Seventh Series, most 1:25 000 second Series (i.e. Pathfinder maps), 1:50 000 First and Second Series (i.e. Landranger maps) and Outdoor Leisure maps.

A 'road used as a public path' is a highway, other than a public path, used by the public mainly for the purpose for which footpaths or bridleways are used. They may still be shown as such on Ordnance Survey maps, although they are being reclassified on definitive maps as either footpaths, bridleways or byways open to all traffic. In any event a public right of way exists. Furthermore many unmetalled roads (fenced and unfenced) which give excellent walking are open to the public, although the Ordnance Survey map does not specifically show them as having public rights of way.

## ACCESS AGREEMENTS

Under the National Parks and Access to the Countryside Act of 1949, National Park Authorities have the power to negotiate Access Agreements with landowners whereby access is given in return for compensation in some form. This access may be subject to conditions as appropriate to the area; for example, the right to close the path on certain days each year. This has been particularly successful in the Peak District where access to 76 square miles (19 760 hectares) of moorland has been negotiated, but other Authorities have opened up important areas.

## PERMISSIVE PATHS

A permissive path is one which is used by the public with the expressed permission of the landowner, but on the understanding that it does not become a right of way. This understanding may be achieved, for example, by the erection of notices on the path or by the act of closing it on one day each year. In some cases landowners do ask for a small payment to be made for the use of the path. A few permissive paths are marked on Ordnance Survey maps; others are shown on notice boards erected in the local area or described in guides by the National Park Authorities. One disadvantage of permissive paths is that permission may be withdrawn if, for example, there is a change of ownership.

## PUBLIC OWNERSHIP

In some cases the National Park Authorities have purchased areas of land which have particular importance, over which there is now public access. An example is the Eastern Moors Estate in the Peak District, covering Froggatt, Curbar and neighbouring edges, which is owned by the Peak Park Joint Planning Board.

## FORESTRY COMMISSION FORESTS

The Forestry Commission have opened up large areas of their forests to public access so that walkers may use paths or forest roads within them, provided that they do so in a safe and sensible manner and do not obstruct essential forestry work. In addition, they have provided numerous facilities for public enjoyment, such as car-parks, picnic sites, visitor centres and way-marked forest trails. A notable example of this is the Border Forest Park, made up of nine forests around the Scotland–England border, which offers a wide range of superb walks.

## COMMONS

The public has a right of access to borough and urban commons, but not to commons generally. However, in some cases special provision has been made. Under the Dartmoor Commons Act 1985, for example, the public now has a legal right of access (subject to certain byelaws) to all registered common land on Dartmoor, a total of some 90,000 acres (36 423 hectares).

## NATIONAL TRUST PROPERTIES

The Trust policy is to give free access at all times to its open spaces; however there cannot be unrestricted access to tenanted farms, young plantations and woods, or certain nature reserves where the preservation of rare fauna and flora is paramount. For example, in the Snowdonia National Park a large area of wild country in the Carneddau range from near Aber to the Nant Ffrancon Pass and beyond is owned by the Trust. Access is permitted throughout the area except for parts of the Nant Ffrancon and Ogwen valleys where public footpaths must be used.

## TRADITION

Walkers have for very many years walked freely in some of the hill and mountain areas of the Parks with the tacit agreement of the landowners concerned, even though they may have had no legal right to do so. The tolerance shown will vary from landowner to landowner and, in any case, depends for its continuation upon the sensible behaviour of the walkers themselves. Litter, broken glass, ruined walls, unruly dogs, noisy behaviour, etc. are likely to make it more difficult for the next people to go that way.

# Safety

The routes described in this guide vary considerably in both length and difficulty. With reasonable care some at least of the easy walks should be safe at any time of the year and under almost any weather conditions. The more difficult walks, on the other hand, cross some of the wildest and roughest country in Great Britain and should only be attempted by fit walkers who are properly clothed and equipped and have command of the techniques involved in walking, scrambling and route finding.

It cannot be too strongly emphasized that weather and conditions can change very rapidly in mountain and moorland areas; during a day, from one part of a mountain or moor to another or as you climb to higher ground. This must be borne in mind when selecting clothing and equipment before a walk; as a general rule select clothing and equipment for the worst conditions that you may reasonably expect to encounter. The severity of a walk will also generally be much greater in the winter when snow and ice are lying. Some routes, which should be within the reach of any reasonably fit and competent group in summer, can in the depth of winter become a difficult undertaking even for experienced mountaineers. Even hot summer days can have their hazards; for example, sunburn and heat exhaustion.

The golden rules for safety in mountain and moorland areas are:

## DO

Plan a route which is within your competence (and that of every member of your party).

Carry appropriate footwear, clothing and equipment, all of which should be in a sound condition.

Carry a map and compass and be able to use them competently.

Ensure that you are carrying sufficient nourishing food for the day, plus an emergency supply (which should be kept for the emergency!).

Leave a note of your intended route with a responsible person (and keep to it, unless circumstances make it advisable to do otherwise). Report your return to that person as soon as possible.

Keep warm, but not over-hot, at all times.

Eat nourishing foots and rest at regular intervals.

Avoid becoming exhausted.

Know First Aid and the correct procedure in case of accidents or illness.

Obtain a weather forecast before you start.

Keep an eye on the weather throughout your walk and be prepared to alter your plans if the weather deteriorates.

Watch other members of the party to ensure that they are not in difficulties and they are not falling behind.

Take particular care of any children in the party who can wander away very easily and get themselves into dangerous situations.

Keep well away from cliff edges in very windy conditions.

## DO NOT

Go out on your own unless you are very experienced: three is a good minimum number.

Leave any member of the party behind on a mountain or in a remote moorland area, unless help has to be summoned.

Explore old mine workings, potholes, quarries or caves, or attempt to climb cliffs (except scrambling ridges if these are within your competence).

Walking along a coastline also requires care if accidents are to be avoided. Keep well clear of cliff edges which may overhang and be unsafe (dry grass, for example, can be very slippery); do not attempt to climb cliffs at any time, even soft ones which may collapse and bury you; take great care if you walk along a beach, particularly under cliffs, to ensure that you are not cut off by the tide; and, finally, do not touch any strange objects as hazardous items are sometimes washed ashore.

The Ministry of Defence has control, either as owner or the holder of a lease or licence, of over 33,000 acres (13 000 hectares) of the Dartmoor National Park. This area contains three firing ranges (Okehampton, Merrivale and Willsworthy), the boundaries of which are marked on the ground by a series of red and white posts, and by noticeboards on the main approaches. All three ranges are on north Dartmoor and, when wishing to walk there, firing times will need to be checked. One walk in this book which enters the Ranges is No. 9, Cox Tor—White Tor—Staple Tors (Merrivale). When firing is in progress warning signals are displayed (red flags by day and red lights by night) on tor and hill summits in or abutting the ranges. Entry into the range(s) during such times is forbidden and, of course, unsafe. Red and white striped warning posts indicate the limit of safe approach to a range area. Care must be taken when walking is permitted on the ranges— do not pick up any metal objects in, or even near, a firing range.

No firing takes place on Dartmoor on public holidays, nor during the month of August. Firing at other times is advertised in local newspapers every Friday and notices are displayed in neigh-bouring police stations, some post offices, some public houses and National Park Information Centres (open Easter to end of October), or you can use the telephone answering service on the following numbers: Torquay (0803) 294592, Exeter (0392) 70164, Plymouth (0752) 701924, Okehampton (0837) 52939.

Similarly the Ministry of Defence owns 58,000 acres (23 500 hectares) of the Northumberland National Park which comprise the Otterburn Training Area. Firing within the range is indicated by red flags and lamps and the closure of barriers; at such times access is not permitted. At present, firing takes place on some 300 days each year. However, the Ministry has accepted a recommendation to open up some 8000 acres (3250 hectares) of former impact area north of the River Coquet to wider public access. All public footpaths and bridleways in this area have now been cleared and opened to the public. Route No. 22, Windy Gyle and the Border Ridge, uses a path in this latter area, the boundaries of which are indicated by large red notices. Access to this path is open at all times, but for the sake of safety it is important to keep to the path and not touch any objects within or near to it.

Access to Walk No. 38, Stack Rocks to Broad Haven, is dependent on military activity on the Royal Armoured Corps Castlemartin Firing Range. When the range is in use the road to the starting point is closed, as is the coast path as far as St Govan's Chapel. When firing is taking place, there are warnings by red flags by day and lights by night, on flagpoles and control towers.

# Giving a Grid Reference

Giving a grid reference is an excellent way of 'pin-pointing' a feature, such as a church or mountain summit, on an Ordnance Survey map.

Grid lines, which are used for this purpose, are shown on the 1:25 000 Outdoor Leisure, 1:25 000 Pathfinder and 1:50 000 Landranger maps produced by the Ordnance Survey; these are the maps most commonly used by walkers. Grid lines are the thin blue lines one kilometre apart going vertically and horizontally across the map producing a network of small squares. Each line, whether vertical or horizontal, is given a number from 00 to 99, with the sequence repeating itself every 100 lines. The 00 lines are slightly thicker than the others thus producing large squares each side representing 100 km and made up of 100 small squares. Each of these large squares is identified by two letters. The entire network of lines covering the British Isles, excluding Ireland, is called the National Grid.

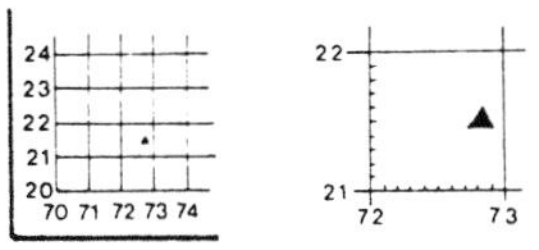

*FIGURE 3 Giving a grid reference*

The left-hand diagram of Figure 3 shows a corner of an Ordnance Survey 1:50 000 Landranger map which contains a Youth Hostel. Using this map, the method of determining a grid reference is as follows:

*Step 1.*
Holding the map in the normal upright position, note the number of the 'vertical' grid line to the left of the hostel. This is 72.

*Step 2.*
Now imagine that the space between the grid line and the adjacent one to the right of the hostel is divided into ten equal divisions (the diagram on the right does this for you). Estimate the number of these 'tenths' that the hostel lies to the right of the left-hand grid line. This is 8. Add this to the number found in Step 1 to make 728.

*Step 3.*
Note the number of the grid line below the hostel and add it on to the number obtained above. This is 21, so that the number becomes 72821.

*Step 4.*
Repeat Step 2 for the space containing the hostel, but now in a vertical direction. The final number to be added is 5, making 728215. This is called a six-figure grid reference. This, coupled with the number or name of the appropriate Landranger or Outdoor Leisure map, will enable the Youth Hostel to be found.

A full grid reference will also include the identification of the appropriate 100 kilometre square of the National Grid; for example, SD 728215. This information is given in the margin of each map.

# Countryside Access Charter

**YOUR RIGHTS OF WAY ARE:**

- public footpaths — on foot only;
- bridleways — on foot, horseback and pedal cycle;
- byways (usually old roads), most 'roads used as public paths' and, of course, public roads — all traffic.

Use maps and signs – Ordnance Survey Pathfinder and Landranger maps show most public rights of way — or look for paths that have coloured waymarking arrows – yellow on footpaths, blue on bridleways, red on tracks that can be legally used by vehicles.

**ON RIGHTS OF WAY YOU CAN:**

- take a pram, pushchair or wheelchair if practicable;
- take a dog (on a lead or under close control);
- take a short route round an illegal obstruction or remove it sufficiently to get past.

**YOU HAVE A RIGHT TO GO FOR RECREATION TO:**

- public parks and open spaces — on foot;
- most commons near older towns and cities — on foot and sometimes on horseback;
- private land where the owner has a formal agreement with the local authority.

**IN ADDITION:**

You can use the following by local or established custom or consent — ask for advice if you're unsure:

- many areas of open country like mountain, moorland, fell and coastal areas, especially those of the National Trust, and most commons;
- some woods and forest, especially those owned by the Forestry Commission;
- country parks and picnic sites;
- most beaches;
- towpaths on canals and rivers;
- some land that is being rested from agriculture, where notices allowing access are displayed;
- some private paths and tracks.

Consent sometimes extends to riding horses and pedal cycles.

**FOR YOUR INFORMATION:**

- county and metropolitan district councils and London boroughs have a duty to protect, maintain and record rights of way, and hold registers of commons and village greens – report problems you find to them;
- obstructions, dangerous animals, harassment and misleading signs on rights of way are illegal;
- if a public path runs along the edge of a field, it must not be ploughed or disturbed;
- a public path across a field can be ploughed or disturbed to cultivate a crop, but the surface must be quickly restored and the line of the path made apparent on the ground;
- crops (other than grass) must not be allowed to inconvenience the use of a right of way, or prevent the line from being apparent on the ground;
- landowners can require you to leave land to which you have no right of access;
- motor vehicles are normally permitted only on roads, byways and some 'roads used as public paths';
- follow any local byelaws.

AND, WHEREVER YOU GO, FOLLOW THE COUNTRY CODE:

- enjoy the countryside and respect its life and work;
- guard against all risk of fire;
- fasten all gates;
- keep your dogs under close control;
- keep to public paths across farmland;
- use gates and stiles to cross fences, hedges and walls;
- leave livestock, crops and machinery alone;
- take your litter home;
- help to keep all water clean;
- protect wildlife, plants and trees;
- take special care on country roads;
- make no unnecessary noise.

This Charter is for practical guidance in England and Wales only. It was prepared by the Countryside Commission.

# Addresses of Useful Organizations

British Trust for Conservation
Volunteers
36 St Mary's Street
Wallingford
Oxfordshire, OX10 0EU
(0491) 839 766

The Camping and Caravanning Club
Greenfields House
Westwood Way
Coventry, CV4 8JH
(0203) 694 995

Council for National Parks
246 Lavender Hill
London, SW11 1LJ
(071) 924 4077

Countryside Commission
John Dower House
Crescent Place
Cheltenham
Gloucestershire, GL50 3RA
(0242) 521 381

Countrywide Holidays Association
Birch Heys
Cromwell Range
Manchester, M14 6HU
(061) 225 1000

English Nature
Northminster House
Northminster Road
Peterborough
Cambridgeshire, PE1 1UA
(0733) 340 345

HF Holidays Ltd
Imperial House
Edgeware Road
Colindale
London, NW9 5AL
(081) 905 9556

The Long Distance Walkers Association
Membership Secretary
117 Higher Lane
Rainford
St Helens
Merseyside, WA11 8BQ
(0744) 882 638

The National Trust
36 Queen Anne's Gate
London, SW1H 9AS
(071) 222 9251

Ramblers' Association
1/5 Wandsworth Road
London, SW8 2XX
(071) 582 6878

Youth Hostels Association
(England and Wales)
Trevelyan House
8 St Stephen's Hill
St Albans
Hertfordshire, AL1 2DY
(0727) 885 215

NATIONAL PARK AUTHORITIES

Brecon Beacons National Park
7 Glamorgan Street
Brecon
Powys, LD3 7DP
(0874) 624 437

The Broads Authority
Thomas Harvey House
18 Coldgate
Norwich, NR3 1BQ
(0603) 610 734

Dartmoor National Park
Parke
Haytor Road
Bovey Tracey
Devon, TQ13 9JQ
(0626) 832 093

Exmoor National Park
Exmoor House
Dulverton
Somerset, TA2 9HL
(0398) 23665

Lake District National Park
Murley Moss
Oxenholme Road
Kendal
Cumbria, LA9 4RH
(0539) 724 555

Northumberland National Park
Eastburn
South Park
Hexham
Northumberland, NE46 1BS
(0434) 605 555

North York Moors National Park
The Old Vicarage
Bondgate
Helmsley
York, YO6 5BP
(0439) 70657

Peak District National Park
Aldern House
Baslow Road
Bakewell
Derbyshire, DE4 1AE
(0629) 814 321

Pembrokeshire Coast National Park
County Offices
St Thomas Green
Haverfordwest
Dyfed, SA61 1QZ
(0437) 764 591

Snowdonia National Park
Penrhyndeudraeth
Gwynedd, LL48 6LS
(0766) 770 274

Yorkshire Dales National Park
Hebden Road
Grassington
Skipton
North Yorkshire, BD23 5LB
(0756) 752 748

# Index

Page numbers in *italics* indicate an illustration away from its text.

317